# ADVENTURES IN MUSIC AND CULTURE

To Oozh,

I hope you enjoy this book!

God bless,

Rob Ball

# ADVENTURES IN MUSIC AND CULTURE
*Travels of an Ethnomusicologist in West Africa*



Printed in the UK

ISBN: 978-1-62020-037-7

AMBASSADOR INTERNATIONAL
Emerald House
427 Wade Hampton Blvd.
Greenville, SC 29609, USA
www.ambassador-international.com

AMBASSADOR BOOKS
The Mount
2 Woodstock Link
Belfast, BT6 8DD, Northern Ireland, UK
www.ambassador-international.com

*The colophon is a trademark of Ambassador*

# Adventures in Music and Culture

*Travels of an Ethnomusicologist in West Africa*

## Rob Baker

## Ambassador International

GREENVILLE, SOUTH CAROLINA & BELFAST, NORTHERN IRELAND

www.ambassador-international.com

# Contents


| | |
|---|---|
| About this Book | 6 |
| Thanks to… | 7 |
| Introduction | 9 |
| Baobabs and Bucket Showers | 13 |
| Millet Beer and Madmen | 41 |
| Watermelons and Woodcutters | 71 |
| Tin Roofs and Trance Drums | 95 |
| Biting Ants and Bowls of Clay | 121 |
| Kick-Drums and Chaos | 143 |
| Deforestation and Drenching | 167 |
| Dedication Songs and Dust | 195 |
| The final journey of *The Beast* | 217 |
| Publications Referred to in this Book | 225 |

# About this Book

This book is based on events which actually happened, and with people who actually existed. However, it is not a historically accurate document in any way, but rather a recollection according to my memory, notes I made at the time, and the photos I took. Therefore (and from a legal point of view), it should be viewed as a work of fiction inspired by real life events and people. I do not in any way guarantee that the people described in this book are exactly as they were or are, or that they said or did what I describe them as doing. With this in mind, I have also changed the names of all characters besides my immediate family.

Geographical locations, town names and language names all remain unchanged – this is, after all, a travel journal of sorts and would be less useful if you could not refer to it for genuine travel information. And, yes, my car was very definitely a grey, 1990, Land Rover Discovery and I really did christen it *"The Beast"*!

# Thanks to…

Eddie Arthur, for seeing the potential in me, even before I even knew what ethnomusicology was!

Julie Taylor, for teaching me what ethnomusicology really is.

Mary Hendershott, for showing me how much fun this job can be!

Paul Neeley, for inspiring and encouraging me.

Tom Ferguson, for teaching me how to run a song-writing workshop.

Ken Hollingsworth, for his list of ten questions for songs.

Lois, for holding the fort back home during all the times away chronicled in this book.

Mark Knight, for his funky Togo-Benin map.

Marianne Harvey for the cover photo and her photo of Gangam musicians (pg. 12).

Clive Rahn for his photo of Cotonou traffic (pg. 70).

Edouardo Lapiz, James Krabill, Joyce Scott, Vida Chenoweth and Brian Schrag for your books and articles, which have all been invaluable sources of knowledge and inspiration to me.

Mike Webb, Megan Larson, Brian Garland, Rebekah Drew, Mary Hendershott, Rachel Harley, Paul Neeley, Cari Friesen, Tom Ferguson, Julie Taylor, Gabrielle Jones, John Trout, Roger Thomassen, Neil Zubot, and Richard Sedding for their invaluable assistance with proof-reading.

All those I met during the travels related in this book, and who inspired the characters in it. It was a joy spending time with so many amazing people!

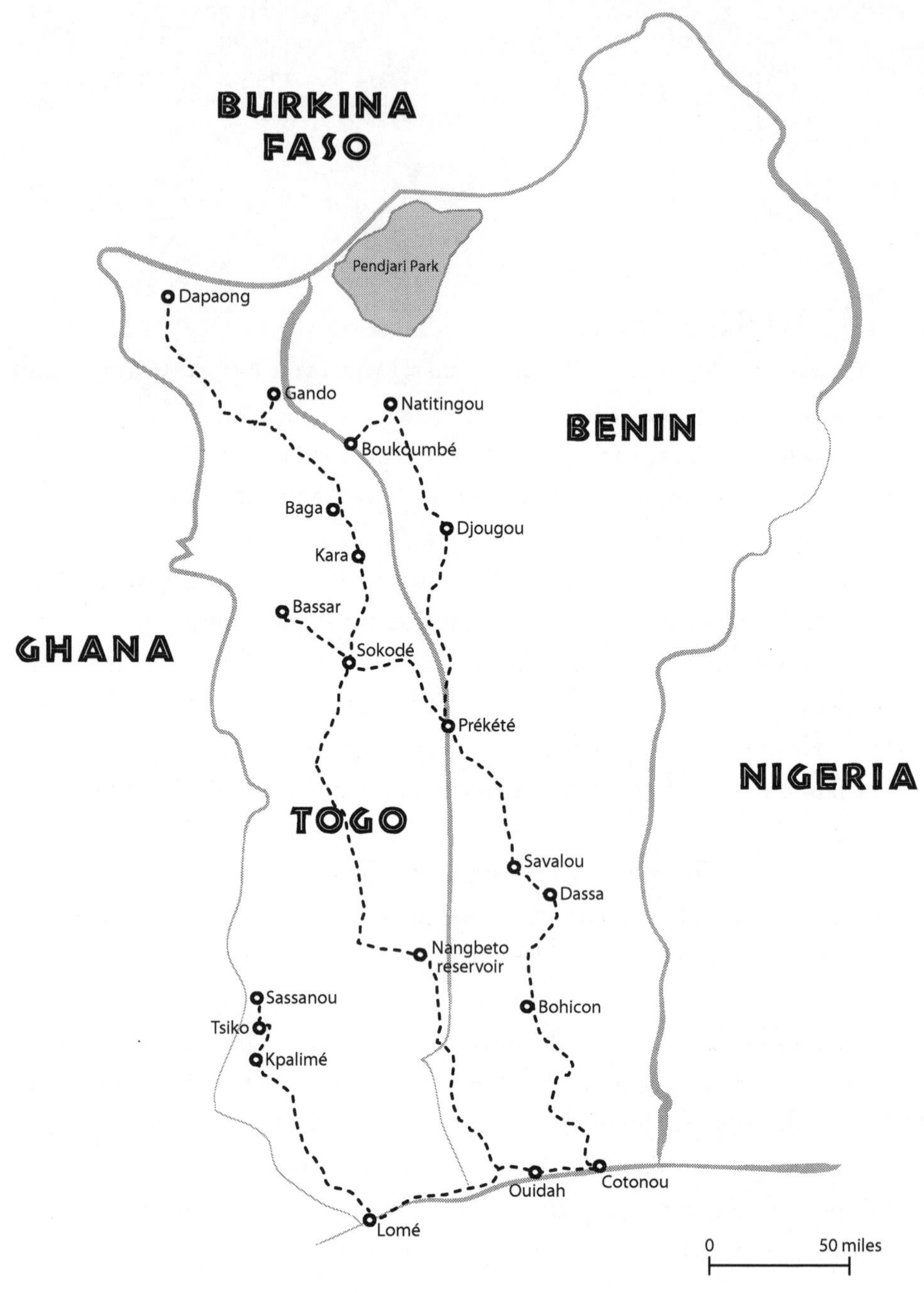


MAP SHOWING THE LOCATIONS VISITED IN THIS BOOK

# Introduction

At last – I have an interesting job!  One to which people respond: "Oh, how fascinating," or: "Tell me more about what you do!"  Although there's not much money in it, it's a job which is exciting, enriching, pioneering and intriguing.  At times it can be frustrating, exhausting – even dangerous, but it is *never* boring, tedious or repetitive, like some jobs I've had.

I used to have a job which I enjoyed, but which nobody else found particularly exciting.  I would almost dread the inevitable party question: "What do *you* do for a living?"

"I'm a French teacher," I would reply, shamefully.

"Oh, right. Where do you teach?"

And that was one of the more interesting responses.  The bravest (or most foolhardy) would reply: "Ah oui!  Un kilo de tomates, s'il vous plaît!"  Others would merely reel out a string of random French words, presumably in an attempt to impress me: "Ooh là là! Gerard Depardieu, Arc de Triomphe, Joe le Taxi, tarte aux pommes…"  However, by far the most common response inflicted upon me on such occasions was the likes of: "I was rubbish at French in school," or "I had a terrible French teacher who wore corduroy, smelt of garlic, and gave me a 'D' grade even when I did my best."  How can the conversation spontaneously evolve following such a statement?  And so my job was the definitive conversation stopper; I may as well have said I watched paint dry for a living (which would, in fact, probably have sparked off more interest).

So, this is why I'm delighted to have a job which is not only interesting to me, but for which other people show a genuine interest.  It's a job they can scarcely pronounce, let alone define or describe: I am an *ethnomusicologist*. "What does one of those do?" you're asking yourself. See, you're doing it too already!

Without going into too much boring detail, there are two main types of ethnomusicologist. The first is the *secular* type, who studies world music for the same reason Sir Edmond Hilary climbed Everest: *because it's there.* Of course, this kind provides much vital information about music in culture and many useful anthropological insights along the way. The second type is the *missionary ethnomusicologist* or *ethnodoxologist*, who does the same kind of research as the first, but then applies this to Christian mission. "So, I've found this fact out about their music, how can I use it to help encourage local Christians and their churches?" The results – as I hope you'll see – are often stunning, as people begin using *their* music, rather than something pertaining to a foreign culture.

My childhood experience of missionaries consisted mainly of sitting in cold church halls on hard wooden chairs and drinking overly-strong tea, whilst some old single lady showed us endless slides of Nepal. They were always small with short hair, spoke with an accent impossible to localize, and dressed in clothes a decade or two out of fashion. Now, there's nothing necessarily wrong with any of the above. However, they mostly failed to inspire me – I was not an old lady and had no desire to become one! Neither was I particularly interested in Nepalese pottery. It seemed to me that these ladies had been out on the field for eons and were somehow 'super-spiritual' beings who endured unimaginable hardships for the sake of the Gospel. I could never attain their level and, besides, I had so little in common with them.

It was only when, in my early twenties, I travelled to the a tropical island in the Indian Ocean, that I met younger, more dynamic missionaries, who were not only doing a great job for God but also having the time of their lives! Like Jean-Pierre, the French youth worker who ran a Christian group at the university. He would drive his Austin Mini like a rally car through the country lanes of the island in second gear, dodging plantations of sugar cane all the way – just for fun!  Or Nancy, who ran the Christian bookshop in town, but also enjoyed picnics, parties and generally 'doing fun social stuff' whenever she could (as well as being excellent at her job).

People often say to me: "Rob, it's such a sacrifice, what you do," and in many ways it is. But that's not to say that missions work isn't also fascinating, enriching and – on many occasions – just great fun!  What you give up back home before coming on the field, God gives back to you in so many different ways – and more.

Now, most people work somewhere sensible like in an office, a shop, a factory or a hospital.  My place of work is far less predictable, and changes with every trip I make. Ask me where I work and I may answer: "Halfway up the hillside in a mouldy, derelict hotel," or: "In a lush, green village with no roads in a deep valley fifty yards from the Ghanaian border." Other possibilities would be: "Under an ant-infested mango tree as the sun is setting and the mosquitoes start to bite," and: "In a tin-roofed church on a dusty plain, with the village madman mumbling nonsense at me all morning." They've all happened: they're all in the book.

Read this book if you love music, culture or travel.  Read this book if you want to know what God is doing in Africa through music and missions. Read this book if you enjoy adventures and their inevitable unpredictability.  Read this book if you want to know what an ethnomusicologist *really* does for a living.

All eight trips take place in Togo or Benin, two small, French-speaking countries in West Africa, wedged between the Anglophone giants of Ghana and Nigeria.  Both fascinating countries, so close to each other geographically, and yet quite contrasting linguistically, politically and topographically. So, what are you waiting for?  Come and join me for a trip of a lifetime filled with interesting people, breathtaking landscapes, unusual customs and amazing music.  Bon voyage!

Gangam percussion ensemble, including baobab shaker

# Chapter One

# Baobabs and Bucket Showers

*The Gangam People of North-Eastern Togo*

What's in a name?  People have names, countries have names – I suppose they'd have to really.  Towns and cities have names too, and the city I'm driving out of this crisp, dry February morning is called *Cotonou*.

Cotonou is the largest city in Benin and, when I first moved here three years ago, I assumed it was so named because of Benin's extensive cotton industry.  I was wrong: Cotonou, I later found out, has an altogether more sinister meaning.

Take a name like Newcastle, Bridgewater or Land's End and you know exactly where you stand – the names speak for themselves.  In West Africa, though, it is never quite that simple for an outsider.  For example, 'Burkina Faso' means 'land of the honest men', 'Bamako' (Mali) means 'river of crocodiles', and 'Timbuktu' – I am reliably informed – is named after a lady with no navel.

Now, Cotonou, spelt *Kútɔnù* in the local language, actually means 'mouth of the river of death'.  And what's more, until 1976 Benin was called 'Dahomey', which means 'in the belly of the snake' (*Danxomɛ*). With Benin's historic backdrop of slavery, voodoo, human sacrifice and witchcraft, it's not hard to see the origin of these names.  Nevertheless, Benin – and even Cotonou itself – has quickly become a place I both love and enjoy. Against the odds, some would say.

In his book 'French Lessons in Africa', Peter Biddlecombe described Cotonou as "a fishing village which has become a town but insists on calling itself a city."[1] Fourteen years on and it has become considerably more city-like, with multi-storey buildings, decent hotels, well-stocked supermarkets and restaurants serving delicious cuisine of at least a dozen nationalities.

There are also hundreds of churches — mostly grey, concrete structures varying only in size and denomination. These days, in fact, the churches are larger and more dominant than the voodoo temples, which still exist in many parts of the city. Thanks to a concentrated mission effort in Benin, both from Westerners and the Beninese themselves, Christianity here has grown rapidly over the past century (with around 40 per cent of the country now Christian). Some of this growth, especially in recent years, has been due to the introduction of local music for worship — music which speaks to the heart of the Beninese people, because it's *theirs*. Rather than singing 'the white man's hymns' they have begun to compose and use their own indigenous songs, based upon local melodies and rhythms. One pastor told me, "When we play traditional music, local people are very interested and they say 'that's our thing,' so this is part of our method for reaching them." Another pastor started a church denomination in 2002, which grew to 400,000 members by 2008 — a phenomenon which he attributed, in part, to the use of local worship styles from the outset. Music is a powerful thing and is an important part of anyone's culture.

So my job as an ethnomusicologist is to harness the richness of local musical heritage and use it as a tool for communication, evangelism or worship. Africa has a rich and dynamic musical tradition, loved the world over. Why, then, would any missionary not want to use this to reach Africans? Would you use Chinese music to speak to the French? Or Mozart to evangelize teenagers? No! Rather we use the music which is the most culturally appropriate, and that's what I'm on my way to do today with the Gangam people of northern Togo.

I have a total journey of around ten hours, spread over two days, before I reach my destination. So I set off bright and early this morning in the Land Rover.

Driving in Benin, and especially in Cotonou, is something of a challenge for the newly-arrived Westerner – for anyone, come to think of it. Then there is the added complication, for an Englishman like myself, of having to drive on the opposite side of the road with a steering wheel on the left. The number one rule to remember on the roads here is as follows: there are no rules. Who has right of way? Answer: whoever has the courage to forge on and fill the gap before the other person gets a chance. Crazy, but kind of fun once you get used to it!

Cotonou is a chaotic mass of unevenly-paved roads, dirt tracks, insane roundabouts and mind-boggling junctions. Motorbikes everywhere you look, clapped-out yellow and green taxis, huge lorries and heavily-laden pedestrians haphazardly attempting to avoid all of the above. Along the roadside are ramshackle stalls of wood and metal with rusty, corrugated roofs selling car parts, groceries, soaps and toiletries, household goods, vehicle parts, tools, clothes – you name it. Large, colourfully painted signs by the roadside indicate: 'God is Good, Snack Bar', 'Mamma Benin Restaurant', or 'Noah's Ark Hardware Store'. Then there are the huge, invasive billboards advertising mobile phone networks, banks, presidential candidates and – of course – those two ubiquitous caffeine sources: *Nescafé* and *Coca Cola*.

I also pass a dozen or so 'dodgy imported petrol stations', which have popped up across the city and now coexist alongside the conventional ones. Most consist of a long, wooden table with a dozen or so large, glass jars on top, today glowing amber in the morning sunlight. These rounded receptacles look more like a home-brew kit from a distance; they actually contain petrol, imported illegally – I am told – from Nigeria next door.

One of the greatest challenges for the driver here is the motorbikes. Literally thousands upon thousands of these hairdryers on wheels – far more than there are cars, far more than you could imagine, swarming around you like ants round a cupcake, filling every conceivable gap in front, behind and on either side of your vehicle. Frequently passing within inches of your front bumper, performing U-turns with no prior warning and happily driving the wrong way down a carriageway, if it suits their needs. At traffic lights it is common to see a glut of them eight bikes wide and six deep; yes, that's almost 50 *motos* in front of you (and no question of attempting to overtake them for a while). As a car driver, a different way of driving is required to survive this bicyclical maelstrom: no sudden movements in *any* direction, as there is probably a *moto* inches from your vehicle on every side. So, no swerves left or right, no abrupt accelerating or braking and use *all* of your mirrors maybe five times more than you would back home. Also, in order to cope with this onslaught, it has become acceptable for motorists here to drive in the *middle* of the road, with a separate lane of *motos* – two or three abreast – passing on either side, one in each direction. Only when another four-wheeled vehicle approaches do you slot yourself back in on the right, amidst a couple of hundred *motos*; a tricky manoeuvre, but the best way of coping with such unconventional driving conditions.

After a few weeks, all of the above gradually becomes both tolerable and achievable, although I can safely say that driving here has never come close to the enjoyable, leisurely experience which an English country road provides.

You'll notice that many of the motorcyclists are wearing yellow shirts; this is to show that they are, in fact, taxi drivers. Yes, not only does one have to contend with this incessant plethora of two-stroke mayhem; you are actually supposed to get *on* them to travel from A to B (or, occasionally, from A to RIP). The taxis are known as *zemidjans*, which means 'get me there fast' in the local Fɔn language, and this is anything but a misnomer. That said, it's a handy way to travel and I doubt I've ever waited more than 30 seconds for a '*zem*' to appear from somewhere. No crash helmets, of course ("those things just get in the way," the drivers tell me). Instead, they sport the mandatory 'Chicago Bulls' baseball cap, a pair of cool shades and the occasional pale blue *Air France* eye mask – worn over the mouth and nose in a vain attempt to block out the inevitable pollution which perpetually chokes the city. "Spending a day in Cotonou," says the Lonely Planet Guide, is like "being locked in a car with a chain-smoking speed freak."[2]

Needless to say, accidents are common – I've seen one almost every week since living here. That said, considering the sheer volume of *motos* and how they drive, it feels as though there should be more. I've travelled on many a *zemidjan* and – I'm grateful to say – have never had an accident (besides burning my right leg on the exhaust pipe when wearing shorts). I tend to avoid *zem drivers* wearing thick glasses, for fear that they may not be able to see the road as well as I can. Another tip: if you get a particularly crazy driver, just tell him, "Stop, I'm getting off here!" (which is very true), then, once he's driven away, hail down another and hope this one has a tad more road sense than the last. That said, I can safely say I've prayed more on the back of a *zemidjan* than aboard any other form of transport!

I've just about made it out of the city limits of Cotonou now, and the quantity of motorbikes is gradually diminishing. However, once you've conquered 'the scourge of the swarming *zemidjans*', things have only just started to get interesting. Obstacle number two: the potholes. All the major roads in Benin are now tarmacked, which has significantly diminished journey times from the olden days of red *laterite* dirt tracks. However, the fresh, new tarmac soon got worn down by heavy lorries, resulting in holes – large and small – in the road surface.

After passing a few teak plantations, undulating hills and a large sawmill, I reach Allada, a former ancient kingdom and home to one of the country's largest Catholic basilicas. No sooner have I left the town than the onslaught of large, deep potholes commences. The next hour's driving – a distance which ought to take half as long – will be constantly punctuated by bumps, swerves and emergency braking. Brace yourselves, folks!

In some sections, there seem to be more potholes than actual road; in others they have been patched up with tarmac so many times that there are now patches upon patches, making the surface desperately uneven. However much you try, it is virtually impossible to avoid every pothole; I've tried keeping to the left, keeping to the right or straddling them, but nothing works when there are *this many* holes!  Furthermore, on potholed roads, the already lax driving rules take a turn for the worse: oncoming vehicles will happily swerve into your path a few feet ahead in order to avoid a particularly nasty hole, forcing you to brake suddenly or even dodge off the road onto its sandy verges.

My seventeen-year-old Land Rover Discovery is coping admirably with all the obstacles.  It's a wonderful vehicle: battleship grey, three door, turbo-diesel and, although it has definitely seen better days, it is still a pleasure to drive.  The worst thing is that when it breaks down (an ever more likely eventuality), parts are tricky to find here, especially in francophone Africa.  Most of the time, Freddie, my French mechanic in Cotonou, has to send one of his men over to Lagos in Nigeria for the part.  This is a three-hour journey with a tricky border crossing and way too many checkpoints for my liking.  I'm grateful for Freddie's assistance when this happens, but the parts are neither cheap nor always available.  More than once I've had to order parts from the U.K. and have them DHL-ed out here, and at least once, I confess, I've paid more in postage than the cost of the part itself!

In spite of all this, the Land Rover's driving experience is second to none.  The upright seating position for excellent visibility, the huge suspension which bears the brunt of potholes with ease, its *three* differentials allowing it to go almost anywhere, and the permanent four-wheel drive for added control all add up to a great experience behind the wheel.  I've heard many folk criticize Land Rovers, but I love mine!  I've driven 4x4s by Toyota, Nissan and Mitsubishi and they're all good too, but I end up feeling tired after a few hours of driving.  In the Land Rover, I have driven nine or ten hours in a day and still arrive feeling refreshed and stimulated.  All of the above, along with the tractor-like engine noise and the sheer power of the machine, led me to christen this car '*The Beast*'.

It's mid-morning and after three hours' driving I've made it to the *Auberge de Dassa*, a pleasant and comfortable hotel located on the main junction of four roads bang in the middle of Benin.  The Auberge – 'hostel' in French

– is like my second home on journeys such as this; its comfy seats, tasty meals, friendly staff and satellite TV providing just the break needed from this already tiring journey. There are also nice rooms for the night, but as it is barely halfway to most of my destinations, the Auberge most often serves as a stop-off point for me. Specialities on the menu here include some unusual dishes, such as ostrich steak or crocodile, and for dessert there is mint ice-cream containing real mint leaves. Mmm – refreshing indeed!

There's a weak but usable mobile phone signal in Dassa, so I take the opportunity to text my family from here; in more remote areas there is often no signal at all. That said, mobile phones have revolutionized communication in Africa and the majority of town-dwelling Beninese own at least one – often two, or even more. In fact, most have by-passed having a landline altogether. Scratch cards to top up phone credit are on sale almost anywhere and all the main towns in Togo and Benin have a decent signal these days. I think back to the early 90s when I was first in West Africa, teaching missionaries' kids. There were no mobiles and even phoning home conventionally cost a small fortune and often had a delay of up to seven seconds. Now, I can text the UK for around ten British pence and the message arrives almost instantaneously. Amazing, really.

I'm always keen to make my Dassa break last an hour – no more, no less. This is just enough time to recharge for the rest of the journey. So I sink into one of the comfy faded red armchairs and order *un sandwich omelette au fromage,* whilst catching up on the news on *TV5 Monde.* The *sandwich omelette* is a regular favourite of mine at the Auberge, though I confess the concept of eating an omelette inside a French stick was alien to me before coming to Africa.

About 90 minutes north of Dassa, I cross the border into Togo. This is one of the easiest border crossings I know. You leave the main road to the left and cross a rickety bridge, literally made from a row of tree trunks slung across a ditch. On the other side there is a building with one or two uniformed guys sitting outside. Most times, you simply wind down your window and give them a quick wave and – voilà – you're in another country!  I've never known anything like it elsewhere, but it certainly helps improve my journey time!  The journey will also feel an hour shorter when I arrive.  Here's why: although Togo and Benin together measure no more than 150 miles east to west, their border happens to be where the time zone changes from 'Senegal Time' to 'Cameroon Time'.  So before continuing, I put my clocks back an hour, making today a 25-hour day!

From here, it's still a good four hours' drive to Gando, with an overnight stay at our centre in Kara, an important city in the north of the country. Like Dassa, the Kara centre has also become something of a 'home from home' for me; a beautiful place surrounded by bright red flame trees and picturesque mountains.  It's a kind of conference centre with accommodation for a few dozen people plus a large meeting room, lounge, library, TV room, table tennis – the works.  The rooms are basic by Western standards, but do have electricity and cold running water.  However, I have a feeling this will be luxury compared with where I'll be tomorrow night!

The next day, after an early-morning drive over a mountain pass and through one of Togo's national parks (very little fauna any more, although there used to be elephants and monkeys here), I finally turn off the tarmac onto a bumpy dirt road which has no signpost but which, I hope, will lead me to my final destination.  After a few minutes of continuous twists and bumps, I begin to doubt that this can possibly be the right way, so pull over beside a couple of ladies carrying wood on their heads.

"*S'il vous plaît, c'est la route de Gando?*"

"Eh?"

Doesn't look like they're catching my drift.

"*La route de Gando?  C'est ici?*"

"Eh?"

These African ladies working in the fields are, alas, not much help.  They don't speak a word of French, let alone English!  I point frantically forwards.

"Gando?  Gando, *ici*?!"  I persist.

"Gando!" one of them replies triumphantly, pointing forwards. This, I fear, is the closest to an affirmative response I'm going to get this morning, so I continue ever onward. It's a good hour of rough red dirt, with large sections of 'washboard' surface. This is caused by rainfall creating even channels a couple of inches deep running parallel across the road every foot or two. Between each of these dips is a narrow ridge, which is what causes the bumpiness. Driving on this kind of surface makes the whole vehicle vibrate, and finding the optimum speed is important: too slow and you feel every single bump separately – a nauseating experience indeed; too fast and you're likely to slide off the road as the tyres cannot find enough to grip onto.

After an hour of bumps, turns and slides, the huge cloud of dust in my wake choking passers-by, I finally arrive at my destination. Gando is a sizeable town with cracked mud buildings, huge baobabs, semi-naked children, dirt paths, yellow grass and every kind of farm animal wandering freely, devouring the refuse and pooping wherever they wish.

Gando, and the villages surrounding it, are home to the Gangam people, who total around 46,000 in Togo. Language research, literacy and Bible translation have been going on here for several years, but the entire Gangam Bible (or even the New Testament) is still a good way from being completed. In the 'olden days' (before computer technology) it would take around 20 years to translate the New Testament and 50 years for the whole Bible. Nowadays, thanks to technology, I've heard of whole Bibles being finished in less than 30 years.

The centre where I'll be working is a small compound with a tin-roofed house and a couple of round huts. A missionary and his family used to live here, but it is now the Gangam Bible translation office. Deep pink bougainvillea hangs over the high boundary walls of the compound and a clump of spindly cacti is growing out the front. The compound has its own small water tower – undoubtedly one of the highest man-made structures in the town – and a pair of sturdy wooden gates. I push these open and drive in.

"Good morning! Is Kandembe here?" I ask one of the employees.

"No, he is not. Who are you?"

Oh dear! This isn't looking good. My contact, Kandembe, is not even here! I explain who I am and what I've come to do here, and the fact that the workshop was all arranged several weeks ago. They know nothing about it! Now, I admit I've had trouble getting through to Kandembe in the past week or so, but as it was booked and agreed, I assumed it would still be taking place. In Africa, however, advanced bookings of anything are quite rare and, even when they do happen, it is often the confirming phone call a day or two before that means the event actually happening.

"We can contact Kandembe for you," he continues.

"Thank you. That would be good." I perch myself on a rugged, wooden bench and wait as he makes the phone call, chatting away in Gangam. The conversation ends and he summarizes its content:

"Kandembe's child is very sick, so he needs to go to the clinic immediately. He'll call by here first, though."

A few minutes pass and Kandembe turns up, holding a decidedly ill-looking son. He has, it would seem, semi-forgotten about the workshop, but promises to round folk up for me as soon as he can, in spite his current family health issues. I take the opportunity to quickly check his phone number with him and – somehow – I have the wrong number. No wonder I haven't been able to get in touch with him!

Around half an hour later, my first two 'customers' arrive. I greet them and they take a seat in the hot, dusty meeting room. We all just sit and wait for quite some time. Life in Africa entails plenty of waiting around; a general rule is that it is entirely acceptable to wait 45 minutes for anything here. Whilst waiting, I make the most of the time by learning some greetings in Gangam from my two guests. To say 'Good morning', you say: '*A guamlè?*' which literally means 'Are you awake?' When addressing more than one person, this becomes '*Ni guamlè?*' The response is '*Awun gɔn mà le*' ('Yes, I am awake'). As ever in Africa, there follows a long string of questions – always asked – about family and work. Thankfully, the response to every one of these is '*Lafiɛ*', meaning 'Peace', which makes it easy for me to respond to all their questions, even if I haven't a clue what they're actually asking:

"How's your wife?"

"*Lafiɛ.*"

"How are your children?"

"*Lafiɛ.*"

"How's the mother-in-law?"

"*Lafiɛ.*"

"How's your work?"

"*Lafiɛ.*"

"How are your goats?"

"*Lafiɛ.*"

"And the chickens?"

"*Lafiɛ.*"

By 11:00am we have five people, one of whom is wearing a 'Britney Spears' tee-shirt. I begin to wonder what to do – should I just cut my losses, cancel the workshop and head home right away? Five is barely enough, but I guess we could do something. I make a start (aware that lunchtime is fast approaching), talking generally about what the workshop will entail and hoping more people will arrive. By 11:30, we have *eleven* people, which is not bad, so we go through the usual preliminary introductions and discussions about the use – and benefits – of local music styles.

Research has shown that using Western melodies in an African context at best hinders comprehension, and at worst gives a completely false meaning to the song. There are some amusing examples of hymns translated into Swahili, where the rhythm and pitch of the Western tunes used entirely alters the meaning. A notable example is a hymn including the phrase: '*Woga wa kufa*', meaning: 'those who fear death'. However, the Western melody changes the meaning to 'those who fear being good'.[3] Oops! Just a slight change there then. This is why indigenous melodies are always best; they not only ensure clear communication, but are also more quickly accepted by the local folk. Across Africa, the trend for local music has been developing for decades. As early as 1955, the Pope wrote the catchy-titled work, *'Musicae Sacrae Disciplina'*, encouraging missionaries to promote indigenous music in worship.[4]  However, this did not happen immediately and the Protestants were much slower to take the idea on board, some still considering African music as 'evil'.

The purpose of this workshop is to create Bible-based songs using Gangam music. This will enhance worship in the church and make it more relevant to the Gangam, as well as encouraging Scripture usage and knowledge. One of the first things to do in a workshop like this is to elicit a list of traditional *song genres*. In African culture, each genre is linked to a different event or occasion. So there are specific genres for weddings, funerals, circumcisions, hunting, fishing, going to battle, building a house, sowing seeds, harvesting and so on. Each of these genres is easily recognizable by those in the culture, in the same way that most Westerners can differentiate 'blues' from 'reggae' or 'rap' from 'R & B'. Each genre will have a different kind of melody, a different rhythmic accompaniment and a different dance – and these three are practically inseparable.

So, we list genres which exist in Gangam culture and the occasions when they are used. This will help us choose the most appropriate styles when composing the Bible songs and hopefully make for a varied set of recordings. Without this process, people are more likely to merely stick to the one or two genres they know the best or – worse still – use a Western melody. A by-product of my work is the preservation of musical heritage through the compositions and recordings. So the greater the number of genres used, the more of their own culture will be conserved and promoted through the songs. Here are some highlights from our fascinating – if a little unpronounceable – list of song styles:

> *Ijiguyuon* – for beating millet
>
> *Icɛncɛncienyuon* – for flattening the earth before building a house
>
> *Inɔpuogbenyuon* – for women to rejoice
>
> *Ikɔnyuon* – for the rite of passage to adulthood

*Inɔkpɔnyuon* – for hunting
*Ikɔkɔlyuon* – sung when building up a mound of earth around yams
*Ikpɛñunyuon* – for ploughing fields
*Ibuyuon* – for traditional fetish worship
*Ikɔnduunyuon* – for weddings
*Itelnyuon* – for story-telling

A great selection, I'm sure you'll agree. As we're in a rural location, the list is much more extensive than in many urban areas, where local music is no longer as significant a part of the culture. You may also have noticed that they all end in '*yuon*', which simply means 'song'. So these genres, although they look complicated, actually just mean 'ploughing song', 'hunting song', 'wedding song', and so on. One of their genres is rarely used these days. "We don't play that one often – the rhythm is *un peu difficile,*" they tell me. Thankfully, we have three old ladies in the group (though, strangely, no old men), and they remember the less common genres more clearly and are able to help others learn them.

As it's early March and the middle of dry season, it hasn't rained anywhere for at least three months and will not do so for a few more weeks. So no need for a brolly this time! It's particularly dry at the moment thanks to the *Harmattan* – a cool, dry wind blowing south from the Sahara. The Harmattan is both a blessing and a curse: the drop in temperature and humidity it brings is a welcome respite from the otherwise incessantly sticky African heat. However, the accompanying dust can be really quite unpleasant, as well as seriously affecting long-distance visibility in any direction. "Grind your teeth together during the Harmattan," folk say, "and you'll feel the dust." Furthermore, with humidity levels plummeting to 20 or even 10 per cent, I'm losing moisture from my body with every breath I take. It also means I don't *feel* like I'm sweating, even though I must be; the air immediately dries it up, sometimes leaving traces in the form of a salty residue on the skin. Thankfully, I have lots of bottled water with me and expect to consume several litres today, thereby avoiding the ever-present risk of dehydration.

Lunchtime comes around quickly and, whereas meals are provided on site for most of my workshops, in this case everyone lives locally and can return home for lunch. Considering they didn't even know they were attending the workshop until a couple of hours ago, I guess they already had lunch plans anyway. I tell them to be back by 2:00pm to continue.

A member of the translation team takes me to my hotel, where lunch has been prepared. There is only one hotel in Gando, made up of three buildings: the bar, the restaurant and the rooms themselves. The menu is simple: rice or spaghetti, with or without guinea fowl. Today it's rice and guinea fowl. This bird is quite common in West Africa and, I always think, resembles a good-looking turkey, with a speckled grey body and a black and white head, but none of those ugly dangly bits you find on a turkey. They also have a reasonable amount of meat on them most of the time and today is no exception.

After lunch, I am shown to my room, which contains three items: a bed, a table and a chair. That's it. There is, I'm glad to say, a mosquito net over the bed and even an electric light bulb and a socket. No power at the moment, mind. "It will come on later," the lady in charge assures me. Through my tiny, square window I can see open countryside, all very yellow at this time of year, but punctuated with green trees. A herd of off-white cattle, each with a big hump on the back of its neck, wanders slowly past my window. Towards the horizon, a couple of ladies are singing as they draw water from a well, the midday sun beating down on their covered heads. Enough discovering, time for a short siesta…

The participants' time of return is an improvement on this morning, with the first few back at 2:30pm and everyone by 3:00pm – only an hour late. I figure not many of them have watches and, even if they did, I'm sure most could not tell the time.

As folk filter in, I take the opportunity to learn a bit more Gangam. Knowing how to say 'Good morning' is useful up until lunchtime, but every language I know has a different greeting for the afternoon, and Gangam is no exception. 'Good afternoon' is: '*A taajuɔku lè?*' (literally meaning: 'Where is the evening?'), with the answer: '*A juɔre mà lè*', followed by another string of *lafiɛs*. We now have fifteen participants, and continue with Biblical exegesis and teaching on composition methods, in spite of the blistering heat outside. A couple of the ladies present are breast-feeding their babies as I teach; I've got used to this, although it shocked me to begin with. In African culture, it is perfectly normal and is not the slightest cause for embarrassment. In some parts of Africa, the average number of births per woman is over seven. If they were to hide away in a hut every time their baby got hungry, they'd be spending a significant chunk of their lives in solitude! 'Needs must' as they say, and so an African mother will happily flop out one breast inches in front of me and stick her baby onto it, blissfully unaware of how much I'm concentrating on *not* looking shocked!

For the songs, I was asked to choose verses from Psalms and Revelation – a curious combination and I'm not even sure why they chose these two! However, I always like to have a common theme running through each set of compositions, so we start off with a set of references about God's greatness. They are as follows:

Psalm 34:2-4: 'Glorify the Lord with me; let us exalt His name together.'
Revelation 15:3-4: 'Great and marvellous are your works.'
Psalm 145:8-12: 'All your works will praise you.'

A great selection of inspiring words! I'm already excited at the thought of how they'll make use of these verses in their songs. Each has certainly inspired European hymn-writers in the past, so I'm hoping they will do the same for these Gangam believers.

I divide the participants into three groups, each of which is allocated one of the Bible references to work on. Splitting them up like this makes each group a more manageable size and means we will get three songs done in the time it would take to compose just one. I make sure there is a mixture of men and women in each group as this will allow for more variety in vocal sound. It will also give them access to genres sung by only one gender, as well as gender-specific musical instruments (of which Africa has many). In addition, I've been careful to put one literate person in each group (as very few can read and write here), and to have at least one older person per group, to assist with the more obscure genres.

It's always good to get the song words actually written down too, and this makes it easier to check the words for accuracy (of grammar *and* content). The Gangam Bible translation team is on hand to help and, although these books of the Bible are not yet published in Gangam, they have translated each of the passages especially for the workshop, which is great!

Tee-shirts are always fun to observe in Africa, and this workshop has a particularly interesting range, likely to amuse the average Westerner due to their sheer incongruity if nothing else. As well as Britney, we also have ones displaying 'Nelly', 'Thailand', 'Chelsea FC' and 'Vote for Fauré Gnassigbe' (who is now the President of Togo, so I guess the tee-shirt worked!). The majority of these are donated by Western charities (who, presumably, have way too many to sell in their shops). They arrive in Africa (along with other clothing) in huge bundles, which are sold to market stall holders, who will then sort through and price each item for their stall. What it says on the tee-shirt is of little interest to the Africans themselves, but they are a constant source of hilarity to foreigners. Elsewhere, I've seen folk sporting tee-shirts saying (in English): 'I am the evil twin', 'Mind your own business', 'Yes, you can buy me a drink', 'I'm in a good mood' and 'Just shut up and dance'. Those wearing them probably have no idea of the message their attire is communicating. Moreover, some of them – which I will not share here – contain downright vulgar slogans!

Composition is underway, and these folk compose at lightning speed: literally within minutes, songs are emanating from all corners of the compound. You could almost say that, for the Gangam, composing and improvisation are one and the same – they sit down, familiarize themselves with the text, and then just start singing.

The songs are all done by the end of the afternoon, and we gather together in the small, dark classroom to share the fruits of today's labour. Each group sings its new song to the rest of the participants, who then offer encouragement or suggestions for improvement. This is a good way of checking the quality of a song and also of getting the best results in the end. The songs sound great and all use the African 'call and response' style of singing. This is rare in the West, but is almost exclusively used in indigenous African music: a 'leader' strikes up with the song and then everyone else chimes in singing a reply. Like in the old spiritual, which goes: 'When Israel was in Egypt's land ... Let my people go'.

Two of the songs have a fascinating driving 6/8 rhythm unlike anything I've heard elsewhere. However, the Revelation song has no drums or percussion – just voices, which is rare in African song. I realize that this is probably because they chose *Ikɔkɔlyuon,* a song style traditionally used in farming – and you wouldn't want to lug all your drums out to the fields as well as your tools, now would you?

We're all done by 5:00pm, so wind up and disband for the night. I remind everyone of the prompt start in the morning (7:30am), in the vain hope of getting underway before nine. One of the Gangam team points out that this is the time when the local schools start, so if they see school children heading out, it's time for them to leave home too. We'll see whether this tip actually gets them here on time tomorrow!

I head back to my pound-a-night hotel for a shower. The toilet block here is basic to say the least, comprising two mud-walled cubicles. One has a proper-looking 'loo' in it (but no running water); the other is for showering and is no more than a small, square room with a hole in one corner for drainage. The water itself is stored in a large clay pot in the tiny courtyard outside, and is filled up each morning by a local lady, who brings it in a smaller pot on her head. So, to take a shower (or 'flush' the toilet) I fill up a bucket of water from here and take it with me into the respective cubicle.

*Bucket showers* are kind of fun, although the first pouring is the most tricky as the bucket weighs so much when full. I tend, nevertheless, to lift the entire thing above my head and then pour about a third of its contents carefully over me. In some places, the bucket comes equipped with a large plastic cup to make things easier, but not here. This is the most basic accommodation I've stayed in, probably *ever*. It's also the cheapest, so I'm not complaining!

After dinner (guinea fowl and spaghetti), I take a wander to explore and discover more of Gando than the hut I've been in all day. Looking out from a small hill near the hotel I have a clear view of the surrounding countryside, such as it is. As far as the eye can see, there is nothing but flat land covered with yellow grass and punctuated with round, green trees, which look like upturned pieces of broccoli from this distance. Besides that, nothing. I am suddenly struck by the sheer remoteness of Gando: we are literally miles from *anywhere* with no mains electricity, and water from wells alone. There is, however, a mobile phone signal…

Breakfast the next morning is a simple but satisfactory affair: a large metal mug of Nescafé to drink, along with a tin of condensed milk – delicious stuff: ludicrously sweet and decidedly moreish. The Africans love this thick, oozy concentrate, most having a considerably sweet tooth, especially when it comes to hot drinks. If there is no condensed milk, most Africans will happily add six or seven sugars to their tea or coffee and think nothing of it. I guess they do not get as much sugar in the rest of their diet as the average Westerner, yet most do a whole lot more physical work than we would. With my coffee, there is a thin loaf of locally made bread attempting to resemble a French stick. On the bread is a pale yellow substance which I logically assume to be butter. I take one bite and pull the most horrendous face.

"Aarggh! They've only gone and put mayonnaise in my sandwich!" I say out loud.

Strange indeed, and I can't help wondering why or how this tradition has occurred – have there been *Belgians* in Gando at some point?  I carefully scrape as much of this vile condiment from my bread as I can and attempt to eat what is left.  Dipping it in my coffee takes most of the mayonnaise taste away, but does little to improve my beverage.  I'm halfway through a mouthful when my phone rings.

"Monsieur Robert, where are you?" says a voice at the other end. "We're all here waiting to start!"

Oops!  Admittedly, it is 7:45am, and we'd said 7:30 to start, but T.I.A. (this is Africa) and virtually nothing starts on time.  Also, given their track record yesterday, I figured I had a good half hour to play with.  Our wee tip about watching the school children leaving must've paid off after all.  Thankfully, it's only a three-minute drive to the centre, so I dive into *The Beast* and whizz off down the dusty track.

As I arrive, a few of the musicians are having a bit of a *jam session* in the courtyard.  Two younger men are playing small barrel-shaped drums, carried over their shoulders by a length of blue rope.  Beating out two different syncopated rhythms using a stick, they use their other hand to stop the sound at regular intervals.  The overall result is exhilarating.  Suddenly, as though choreographed, an older, skinny lady moves into the circle and begins playing a most intriguing idiophone.  As she throws the large egg-shaped instrument from one hand to the other, it makes a loud shaking noise.  Once the pod has been thrown into the other hand, this hand quickly lifts it up and down, to create two further shaky noises.  She then throws it back to the other hand, then up and down again.  The resultant 6/8 rhythm comprises three rapid movements lasting no more than half a second altogether: throw across, lift up, lift down, throw back, lift up, lift down and so on.  Her instrument is made from the fruit of the baobab tree, hollowed out and filled with stones.  I remember this lady – and her fascinating instrument – from a previous workshop a couple of years back.  At the time, I worked hard to master her rhythmic pattern and, in spite of my percussion-playing background, it took me two days to master.  Very tricky indeed!  In fact, that time I ended up dropping the pod on the floor and cracking it, so I hope she's forgotten about that by now.  A second lady joins the trio, smiling all over her face and clapping her opened-out hands in front of her with great joy, and in time with the others.  She then strikes up with a song, and the whole spectacle is a delight to the eyes and ears – an unforgettable start to the day.

Straight on with more Bible teaching and preparation for the next set of songs.  It's getting hot already and the sun seems ludicrously high in the sky for the time of day.  The second set of verses I give them has to do with the nature of God:

Revelation 7:12: 'Praise and glory and wisdom and thanks and honour.'
Acts 2:25-28: 'The Lord is constantly before me.'
Psalm 23:1-4: 'The Lord is my shepherd.'

We have a couple of hitches in the composition groups today: firstly, one of the old ladies doesn't arrive until late morning.  The rest of her group – all very young – are pretty lost without her and make very little progress.  As an older person, she knows the local music best of all.  That's why it's always important to have some older folk in workshops like this.

The second hitch is interesting: one of the groups composes a song which has the *identical* melody to one of yesterday's.  Now, it's true that in parts of Africa two songs can have the same tune whilst still being considered as different songs.  However, for our recordings it is not a great idea for this to happen, and this group may not actually realize what they've done here.  Thankfully, help is at hand: whenever a group is composing, I always try to make a short, informal recording of the song (no more than a minute long). This is mostly in case they forget how the tune goes the next day – then all I have to do is play the extract to them as a reminder.  But today it comes in really useful in a different way:

"Did you realize that your song has the same melody as one of yesterday's songs?" I ask the group.

"Really?" they reply (via an interpreter all the time).

"Yes, listen!" I take out my digital recorder and play them the song from yesterday (composed by one of the other groups). They gather round attentively and listen to the song. They then discuss amongst themselves and admit that it is virtually identical. And so they agree to rework their song to come up with something different.

*Pod-shaking lady* proudly continues to use her simple yet ingenious instrument, passing it from one hand to the other, and the sound really enhances and enlivens her group's song. Although she only speaks Gangam, I motion to her in a way which says: "Can I have a go with your shaker now?" She looks at me sternly whilst shaking one finger at me and utters something in Gangam, which I can only imagine means: "Not on your life, matey!  I remember what happened last time you played it."  Oh well, not to worry – it was worth a try at least.

After lunch, we tackle the final set of verses, centred around the Gospel message to do with God's forgiveness through Christ's death.  This way, there is also a progression through the three sets of songs: 'God is great' then 'God's nature' and finally 'God's plan for the salvation of mankind.' This means that even the many illiterate Gangam people will be able to recite – and understand – a range of key Bible truths and, of course, many non-believers will also hear and even sing these too.  Here is the last set of verses chosen:

1 Timothy 2:5-6: 'There is one God and mediator.'
1 John 1:8-10: 'If we confess our sins he is faithful and just to forgive us.'
John 11:25-26: 'I am the resurrection and the life.'


I arrive back at the hotel that evening to find the cook lady in the process of plucking tonight's guinea fowl.  I think I'll have it with rice tonight, just for a change.  As dinner is clearly going to be a while, I take a stroll into town, passing tidy mud buildings with busy courtyards, huge, spooky baobab trees, open fires, children playing, and handsome white donkeys pulling carts.  Towards the centre of town is a large open square with a tall metal water tower.  Here ladies are queuing, large metal bowls on their heads, to collect water. I guess this is much easier than pulling water up from a well, although it must've been pumped up to the top at some point. As well as the bowls, I notice dozens of plastic yellow jerricans with red stoppers and wonder whether this water-filling ritual is a daily occurrence or only happens occasionally. Probably the former – we take clean, running water so much for granted in the West that we don't realize how much of it we get through in the average day (and that's in a much cooler climate). And yet these ladies are lucky compared to some: the water is available metres from their houses and is coming straight out of a large pipe. I imagine this one was set up by one of the many charities working in this part of the world and it's great to see it being used to improve the quality of life of so many Gandoans.

Within the same square is a curious-looking tree with gourds growing on it. "So, that's where the ever-useful gourd comes from," I naively think to myself. The gourds may be growing *on* the tree, but they are not growing *from* the tree. The gourd plant is more like a vine, and climbs up anything it can to spread out and get more light. The tree itself looks pretty dead, but there are at least 15 pale green gourds growing on it, each around 14 inches in diameter.

From here, I head for the market, passing more impressive baobab trees. Baobabs can be found across the African continent and are truly enormous trees, their angular trunks often measuring 10 or 20 feet across. These ones are about 12 feet in diameter at their widest point, so already quite large. An African legend says that the baobab was planted upside down so that the roots grew upwards. Looking at these creepy trees, their huge trunks giving way to relatively small, thin branches and then even thinner, spindly ones like fingers, I can certainly see the inspiration for the legend.

Beyond the baobabs is Gando market. No trip to an African town or village would be complete without a visit to the market, so I have a quick wander before it gets dark. It is quite well stocked – always plenty of to-matoes, onions and okra in this part of the world, as well as all the usual stuff: second-hand clothing (including tee-shirts), household goods, joints of meat swarming with flies, live chickens, goats and guinea fowl. A couple of items catch my attention, though. Firstly, there are cassettes of African 'pop' music: various artists from Togo, Benin, Côte d'Ivoire and beyond and they're all reasonably priced. The second thing which I notice – and which shocks me somewhat – is a stall selling large posters of topless white women. How very strange! I cannot help but wonder what the local men (and women) think of this, or how on earth these found their way to this remote part of Africa. However, on reflection, I figure the locals probably don't even see this as anything unusual. Since arriving in Gando, I must've seen a good dozen topless African ladies – old and young – preparing the dinner or sweeping their courtyard, and this is not seen as particularly vulgar – or attractive – in the local culture. So, in the minds of Gando's inhabitants, maybe these white ladies had been busy with the housework and were just feeling a bit warm.

That reminds me of an amusing cultural story told by my mate Eric, a missionary in West Africa. Eric was visiting a village in his early mission days and saw three African ladies preparing a meal together.

"Could I take a photo of you, please?" he asked (it's always good to check first). The ladies looked at each other doubtfully, then one replied:

"Wait a moment – we don't have our heads covered. We must cover our heads before you can take your picture."

And with that, the three ladies removed their tops and wrapped them round their heads, ready for the photo! In great embarrassment, all Eric could do was to take a 'pretend' photo of these three bare-chested ladies and thank them for their trouble. True story. Culture is indeed a fascinating thing!

Tiredly wandering back to the hotel, I observe a gorgeous sunset in the distance and take a minor detour to see it more clearly. The sun looks like an enormous grapefruit, its rays fanning out across the heavens towards me, the majestic sky gradually changing from deep orange to a greyish blue. The sunlight catches the edges of tiny clouds high up in the stratosphere, as swooping hornbills are silhouetted against this glorious backdrop. I pause for a moment, remembering one of yesterday's songs:

> *Great and marvellous are your deeds,*
> *Lord God Almighty.*
> *Just and true are your ways,*
> *King of ages.*
> *Who will not fear you, O Lord,*
> *And bring glory to your name?*
> *For you alone are holy,*
> *All nations will come and worship before you,*
> *For your righteous acts have been revealed.*

That night, and halfway through another delicious – if predictable – dinner of freshly-slaughtered guinea fowl and rice, the power goes off. Electricity is by no means a 24-7 facility here, and is something I've learned to consider more as a luxury when it *does* happen than an inconvenience when it does not. The hotel staff (of one) provides me with an old paraffin lamp – perfectly adequate for finishing the meal. However, having left my torch in my room, I'm left to fumble my way back there in total darkness, an eventuality which seldom occurs in the West. It's only a few yards though and, in spite of the rough terrain, walking in a straight line behind the restaurant should get me there. As I tentatively edge my way forwards, hoping there are no snakes or scorpions underfoot, I cannot help but notice another impressive spectacle before my very eyes: the African midnight sky. An entire hemisphere of millions of clear, bright stars surrounded by nothing but darkness, continuing all the way down to the ground in every direction. Phenomenal. Thanks to the power outage in the whole of Gando, the lack of any significant pollution here, and a particularly clear sky, I am able to see stars I scarcely knew existed. The moon has not risen yet either, which makes the whole sight even clearer. I pause for a few minutes, admiring the celestial dome above me, each star a sun millions – maybe trillions – of miles away, decorating an entire uninterrupted 180 degrees of African sky. I am struck by the vastness of the universe and the sheer awe and wonder of God's creation. And yet, at the same time, He loved us enough to send us His son.

I'm up bright and early next morning to make sure I'm not late again. Today is recording day. Once all the songs are composed, rehearsed and ready, they need to be recorded, and that's my job too. I've searched all over for a good recording location, but this is a busy village with people, animals and vehicles around every corner. So, in spite of possible echoes from the walls, the compound itself is the best we can do. The type of walls (not overly smooth or clean) combined with their position and the dirt floor means there will actually be very little echo.

For making the recordings, I generally work with five semi-professional microphones, a portable, battery-powered mixing desk and a small digital MP3/WAV recording device. Modern technology has meant that field recording equipment which would previously have filled the entire rear of a car can now be carried in a small back pack. It is only the microphone stands which take up space, and even these are lighter and more compact than in days gone by.

The musicians arrive and I arrange them in a vaguely circular formation: choir at two o'clock, soloist(s) at seven o'clock, percussionists at ten o'clock, with a muddy wall conveniently located between the drummers and the choir. This will help isolate the sound of each group; if the drums are too close to the singers, then their sound will 'bleed' onto the vocal track. That said, they can all still see and hear each other, which is important. I use a unidirectional microphone for the soloist, to further isolate his/her voice from other sounds. This means that it only records what is immediately in front of it (give or take a certain angle) and nothing from behind it. And so the soloist's track will be clear, without even a hint of drum sound.

We have nine new songs in nine different genres, which is great news! Four of these genres have never been previously used in church, so this is ground-breaking stuff. All too often, traditional African rhythms have been written off as 'evil' or inappropriate for Christian worship, but this is seldom the case, in my experience. There are no evil rhythms. There are no evil drums. There are only rhythms and drums associated with traditional practices seen as evil, and these can – with time and perseverance – be redeemed for church use.

Over 50 years ago, Paul Jans gave the following advice to folk engaged in missions in the then Belgian Congo:

> *"Do not suppress* anything other than that which goes against the dogmas of the Church, against morals or against a sound moral order.
>
> *Do not suppress* anything without the greatest care, and not unless that which is to be suppressed would have caused irreparable damage.
>
> *Do not introduce* anything other than what is necessary, avoiding stifling that which is valuable to the civilization in question, even if it does not completely measure up to our own norms and standards."[5]

It will be interesting to see how other folk react to the new song styles and how these go down in church. Due to some past missionary influences, folk here may also reject these, considering them undignified or unworthy for church use. Time alone will tell, but the fact that this group has been willing to use these genres is half the battle already.

I'm always eager to have as broad a range of musical instruments and styles as possible, so as to accurately portray the culture's musical heritage in the recordings. This makes the recordings more varied and more likely to attract the attention of local people ("Listen, they're playing *our* tune!")

A highlight of today's recording session is the arrival of a pair of old blokes from the village, who were drafted in at the last minute to play their traditional three-holed flutes. Common in this part of the world, this narrow, 'V'-shaped flute has two holes, one on each side, near the top and a third hole right at the bottom. To play it, you blow across a larger hole at the top, changing the pitch by placing fingers or thumbs on the holes. A very nice sound, although it has a limited range of available notes and so is used almost more percussively than melodically. One of the guys is tall with a wrinkly face, distant yet piercing eyes and is wearing entirely grey, Western clothing. The other looks considerably older: a small, wrinkly chap sporting a bright green and pink traditional outfit along with a half worn-out baseball cap displaying the American flag, the word 'baseball' in faded capital letters just visible across the front.

They play their flutes beautifully, not in unison, but two complimentary parts, usually a third apart. As African music tends to be dominated by percussion, it is great to find and add some wind instruments whenever appropriate. These guys do a great job and their melodious interludes really enrich the recordings.

From each microphone used, there is a long, sturdy 'XLR' cable leading to the small mixing desk. Once mixed and balanced, the combined sound is then transferred to the digital recording device via yet another cable. At the moment, I'm using an 'Edirol R1 MP3/WAV recorder'; a great piece of equipment, although a little thirsty on batteries, I've found.

By 11:00am, the sun is already high in the sky and, whilst my musicians are all in the shade, I have had to compromise and sit in the sunlight in the middle of the courtyard. I attempt to counteract the heat with a hat, but I'm still warmer than I'd like to be. At one point, I press 'play' on the *R1* to listen back to a recording, but what I hear sounds more like an alien trying to communicate than the African song I have just recorded. Blips and bleeps galore, but nothing intelligible. Oh dear! What has happened here? Are all of this morning's recordings ruined now? I listen to earlier recordings of the day – they too are wrecked. If we have to start again from scratch, this is going to be a decidedly long day!

As this kind of thing has never happened to me before, I figure it may be something to do with the direct heat and sunlight the equipment has had to endure all morning. Quickly moving the boiling hot *R1* into the shade, I call for a brief break in proceedings so I can figure out what to do. Whilst they all 'take five', I put my headphones back on and listen again to the recording:

*Bloop-blip-zip- bip-bop-zip-zop-zoop.*

Oh dear – that's not Gangam! I wait, fanning away at the *R1* in the hope of cooling it down. Five minutes later, and not holding out much hope, I listen again. Remarkably, the aliens have departed and the recording sounds perfect.

Listening back to the other recordings, they too are free of 'space invaders'. Phew – what a relief! I call the group back together and we soldier on with the next track, once I've moved myself into a slightly more shaded area.

Thankfully, the rest of the recording session continues without hitches. A couple of dozen local children have been peering through the compound gate for most of the time, eager to see what's going on. Fortunately, they've not been particularly noisy, which is a good thing. Once all nine songs are 'in the can' and the copyright form signed, the musicians say a warm 'Au revoir' and 'Merci' and are on their way, each shaking my hand warmly as they depart.

"Can I have your baobab pod?" I ask a certain lady as she passes. A frown and a quick shake of the head confirm my fears! Not to worry.

It's just about lunchtime and so, after another plate of freshly slaughtered guinea fowl with couscous at my 'luxury' hotel, I load up *The Beast* and head back to Kara for the night. It all seems to be over so quickly – the workshop which almost didn't happen.

The journey home the next day is like almost any other: the usual dangerous trucks, potholes, goats, dogs and motorbikes to avoid. In England, we pray before eating a meal; in Africa, we also pray before driving our car any distance – a good habit in any country, but particularly necessary here.

I make it back to the *auberge* in Dassa for lunch and notice an interesting item on the menu: *crocodile au gingembre*. I can't say I've ever eaten a reptile before, so jump at the chance. I'd love to be able to tell you how delicious it was, but I'm afraid that this particular piece of croc was far from it. There was a small round bit of meat in the centre, which tasted and looked a bit like lamb. Then there was a large white piece, looking more like fish than anything else. This part was edible but bland. The rest was almost entirely fat, which I didn't fancy eating. So, although I can now say: 'I've eaten crocodile with ginger', I certainly cannot say it was a particularly enjoyable experience!

# Chapter Two

# Millet Beer and Madmen

*The Nawdm People of Northern Togo*

"I'm really sorry, officer. I don't seem to have my driver's licence with me."

"No driver's licence! Then I cannot let you across the border."

"Please, I simply forgot it, but I have it at home…"

"Out of the question. No licence, no entry. How do I even know you can drive?"

Oh dear! I'm at the Benin-Togo border once again and have made a terrible omission. To make things worse, I'm travelling with my good friend Ken, visiting from England. Disaster! Our plan is to make it to the centre in Kara by nightfall, but this is looking less and less likely by the minute.

Our two-hour journey this far has not been without its setbacks; even before we were out of Cotonou a nasty-looking red light on the dash came on. Alternator trouble! Now, this wouldn't have stopped *The Beast* from going, but meant the battery would eventually have gone flat, making it impossible to start the engine. We carried on regardless, hoping the light might miraculously go off again. It didn't, and so we stopped in a village north of Ouidah at a mechanic's shack by the roadside. (You're never far away from a mechanic in Africa and they pop up in the most unusual places). The problem was quickly diagnosed: a broken alternator belt. Thankfully the young mechanic had one just the right size – I guess that kind of thing must be pretty generic. He tinkered around under the bonnet for twenty minutes or so, his thin arms reaching ably through the small gaps.

"*C'est fini!*" he then said triumphantly. "Start the engine."

The engine growled into action, tractor-like as ever, but the red light was now off. Result!

"How much do I owe you?"

"*Deux mille francs*." Two thousand CFA francs (the currency in Togo, Benin and several other West African countries) is less than three English pounds! Seems very reasonable, but also a decent enough rate by local standards.

An hour later, and here we are stuck at the border – a different border from the one I crossed in Chapter One (there I'd have breezed through with a wave and a smile, with or without my licence). Today's border is three hours further south, nearer the coast, and we're coming this way to make an interesting detour. It has certainly been interesting so far, but not in the ways I'd planned.

I think of ideas which might work, so address our austere, portly guard once more:

"*Excusez-moi, Monsieur*. I could phone my wife and she could give me my licence number so you can fill it in on your form."

Most border checkpoints have a big book full of details given by drivers crossing them – page after page of 'car colour', 'car make', 'number plate', 'coming from', 'going to' and 'licence details'. I often wonder what they do with these books when they're full – is there a big room somewhere just full from floor to ceiling with old records such as this? Remarkably, the guard agrees to my suggestion:

"Make the call, Monsieur."

I pick up my mobile to call Lois. No signal. I try again. Still nothing.

"There's no signal, but I can keep trying," I say, as if time alone is likely to rectify the absence of any coverage.

"Yes, keep trying," he orders.

So I sit down and try again, to please the border guard if nothing else. Time passes, but the only thing to do in situations like this is to remain calm and just wait; try arguing or challenging them and your chances of getting across rapidly decrease. As it is, our chances seem only just above zero, but I continue silently praying all the time – I'm sure Ken's doing the same too. The thought of turning round and returning to Cotonou for my licence has, of course, crossed my mind. However, that would take at least four hours there and back, and then we wouldn't stand a chance of reaching our final destination before dark.

After a few minutes, a new border guard turns up, maybe to relieve this one, I hope to myself. He's younger and thinner than the first guy and has a pleasant look about him. As though by force of habit, I greet him in his native language of Adja, asking him how he is:

*"È le nyuiɖe a?"*

*"Aɛ, ŋ le nyuiɖe!"* he replies, with a smile not so big as to undermine his authority.

*"Sɔ́ bɛ́ dɔ?"* I ask, continuing the local greetings.

*"Dɔ y sɔ̀!"* he replies, looking more pleased by the minute. Then, as if by magic, the first guard stands up, looks straight at me and utters the words I've been praying for:

"Okay, Monsieur, you can go across."

Remarkable! Was it because of the local greeting or the arrival of his colleague? I don't know and I'm not too bothered which; the fact is, we're through. We now put our clocks back an hour to Togo time, so at least it feels as if we've got back the time wasted at the border.

"I never thought we were going to get through!" says Ken, whose first trip to West Africa is turning into a bit of a baptism of fire. I arranged this workshop for these dates with Ken's visit in mind, as he's an adept percussionist if ever there were one. Although he now works in renewable energy in the U.K., he still gets plenty of chance to drum. In fact, that's how he and I first got to know each other.

Now, the conventional route from this point would be to head due west on the road ahead, eventually intersecting the main north–south road from Lomé on the coast all the way to Kara. However, I've planned something a bit more fun with my mate Ken in mind. A short distance from the border we turn right and head due north on a bumpy dirt road running parallel to the Togo-Benin border. We pass through tidy-looking villages lined with mango and eucalyptus trees. Most of the buildings are concrete with tin roofs, but some classic round mud huts can be seen now and again. There are piles of firewood stacked up by the roadside, boundaries marked out by straw fences, covered areas made of branches and banana leaves, old men trundling by on rickety bicycles, ladies tending steaming cooking pots, small children pushing old bike tyres along with a stick, and plenty of animals to avoid. Remarkably, I now have a signal on my mobile phone, so call Lois and ask her to scan my driver's licence and e-mail it to Ben & Linda, friends in Sokodé, a sizeable town further north. I can then pick up a printout on the way through and at least have some kind of proof that I can drive, should I be stopped again.

Although we have only around sixty miles on this road, the going is slow: we are averaging around twenty-five miles per hour, due to the unevenness of this dry, dusty surface. On the plus side, it is a pleasant and interesting drive and with no traffic to speak of. Ken is enjoying the whole experience, clicking away with his camera as we chat our way northwards, catching up on news since we last saw each other. We played a lot of music together in the past, he on the drums and I on the piano. There are some drummers with whom one never really 'clicks' and so it becomes a chore to make the music work. With Ken it was the exact opposite: from the very first time we played together it just worked, and after six months or so, we could virtually read each other's minds. I love it when that happens! It helped that Ken was – and still is – a phenomenally good drummer: nifty, dextrous and ingenious, as well as lots of fun. We played together in our church worship band on many a Sunday morning, as well as dabbling in jazz now and again – we even made an album together once. Happy times!

To one side of the road, we notice a line of electricity pylons leading off towards the horizon; this is an encouraging sign, given where we're heading. Then finally, after what seems like an interminable bone-shaking fest, we arrive at the reason for our three-hour detour: the *Nangbeto Reservoir* with its hydroelectric plant. As Ken works in the renewable energy business, I knew this would interest him.

The large raised barrage appears in the distance and suddenly everything changes: the road becomes smooth and tarmacked, there are signs and speed limits everywhere, and we ascend a steepish slope followed by a ninety degree turn to the left. We're now on the dam wall itself and the view is stunning: a vast lake on one side and a low but broad tree-lined river flowing serenely away on the other. The whole area is surrounded by lush green vegetation, even though it's the middle of dry season. We find an appropriate point and pull over to admire the vista – and the hydro station – in more detail. A security guard approaches us suspiciously.

"What are you doing, *Messieurs*? No stopping allowed on *le barrage*."

"Sorry, sir, I didn't know. Can we stop for just two minutes? My friend here, it's his first time in Togo and he really likes your reservoir."

"Okay, two minutes, no more."

We park up by a monument commemorating the inauguration of the hydro-electric station in 1988. It reads:

> "*Opened on 5<sup>th</sup> May by their excellences Gnassigbe Eyadema, President of the Republic of Togo and Mathieu Kerekou, President of the People's Republic of Benin.*"

An interesting bit of history, as Eyadema died a couple of years back (replaced by his son, Fauré). Furthermore, Mathieu Kérékou was replaced last year by Yayi Boni, an upright, astute president, who is tough on corruption and also an evangelical Christian. A friend of mine – an African pastor – regularly goes to his house to pray with him. Amazing!

We walk over to the turbine housing, where the water passes to make the electricity. Ken is delighted and intrigued by how this compares with the ones he knows so well back home. There are several enormous metal flood gates, curved from top to bottom and equipped with a complex leverage system to move them up or down as necessary.

"Those are way too big," says Ken.

"What do you mean? Don't they *need* to be big?"

"Yes, but look at their height compared to the land around. The water level would never get that high."

Now I'd never have noticed that. Thanks Ken. He eagerly takes a few pictures – to show to the guys at work back home. Our two minutes is up, so we head back towards the car. The guard is still standing beside it, as if to make sure it does not outstay its welcome.

"Have you seen our hippos?" he asks, pointing down the river. We carefully look and, sure enough, downstream near the left bank there are four brownish dots. In the absence of any binoculars, I look through my camera's zoom and they can be easily identified as hippos. Nice! Ken is particularly pleased to see his first wild African animals besides birds and lizards.

Moving off, we head due west on a remarkably well-surfaced road to Atakpamé. We're there in under an hour and, as it's already gone midday, we stop at a small, rustic hostel and order lunch. As soon as we step out of the Land Rover, we notice a significant change in climate: here in the north, the humidity is much lower than down on the coast and the dry, dusty air makes you blink and turns your hair into straw in a matter of seconds. The main cause of this stark contrast is the Harmattan, bringing a cool, dusty and very dry feel to the weather up north. Just like in Gando.

Lunch has arrived: omelette sandwiches and coffee: predictable, but a much-welcomed break for both of us. The restaurant is small with three or four tables and a telly blazing away in the corner. The food comes quickly and is cheap and cheerful. Can't stop for long, we have our deadline of nightfall to meet, and – of course – that's an hour earlier in Togo.

What I like about driving north through Togo is that it is split up into nice, manageable chunks separated by sizeable towns. It will take an hour or so from here to Sokodé, then about another hour from there to Kara. Ken, a dynamic yet placid chap, is forced to comment on my driving in this section, and how he's a little scared. This is partly due to the huge quantity of potholes on this particular section, but mainly because of the coffee *and* Coke I had in Atakpamé – I'm now on a serious caffeine high and am, apparently, driving under its influence! I've always been sensitive to the drug; a cup of coffee later than 2:00pm and I'm up half the night. Being naturally somewhat hyperactive means this extra stimulation tips the balance, so right now I'm wired!

"You are driving quite fast, Rob," he says, in a good old British under-stated way.

"Yeah!  But it's fun dodging all the potholes – woohoo!"

By the time we get to Sokodé there is, thankfully, a little more blood in my 'caffeine stream' and I'm feeling more subdued. We stop off at Ben and Linda's compound for a drink ("Just water for me thanks, Ben!") and to pick up the scan of my licence.  Ben has received the e-mail and has already made a colour printout for me; at least I stand a reasonable chance with this (but wouldn't advise you try it yourself!).

Togo is a 'stripy' country in terms of religion: the south is more Chris-tian, with a large proportion of both Catholics and Protestants.  Then, as you get towards Sokodé, Islam becomes the predominant religion.  North of here, in and around Kara, Christianity – more obviously the Catholic variety – becomes more dominant.  I've spent many nights in Sokodé.  It's is a town I have grown to like and one which I pass through to get almost anywhere in northern Togo.

The final leg of our journey to Kara is by far the worst: we need to cross the mountains on the infamous *Aledjo Mountain Pass*; a steep, winding road climbing a thousand feet or so and frequently plagued by slow, broken-down and overturned lorries. At the start of the ascent, large wooden chocks are for sale – for putting behind the wheels of broken down vehicles to prevent them from sliding down the hill.  Every time I make this journey, I fear for my life, and the potholed ascent is always littered with breakdowns of one kind of another.  On occasion, I've even seen whole trucks fallen over the edge of the steep ravine, their contents scattered below, with brave or foolhardy plunderers scaling the slopes to retrieve what they can.  Some-times the road is worse than pot-holed: whole sections of tarmac have been ripped up by the heavy trucks, or have enormous wheel-sized grooves in them, adding further challenges to this route. The most interesting part of the journey is the *Faille d'Aledjo* (the Aledjo Fault, pronounced: 'fie da-leh-joe'), located almost at the summit of the pass. Here, a huge section of the cliff has been blasted out to allow traffic coming south to pass through a narrow channel between the sharp rocks, with only inches to spare for the wider trucks. The northbound road passes around the outside of the cliff, and dangerously close to the edge, before rejoining the other carriageway after the *faille*.

Today, as it happens, we witness one of the worst delays I've ever encountered on the pass. Dozens of trucks are backed up for almost half a mile and I wonder what could have happened up ahead. I pass the stationary queue tentatively, given the width of the road. Drivers are out of their cabs, looking ahead for clues. Some have realized they're going nowhere for a while, whatever the cause, and are eating sandwiches or lying in makeshift hammocks hung beneath their vehicles.

Finally, we discover the cause of the hold up: just before the *faille* itself, a truck has completely overturned and is lying on its side, slightly overhanging the ravine. Meanwhile, another truck, heading uphill like us, has broken down and is unable to move either forwards or backwards. The gap between the two is just – but only just – wide enough for a car (or Land Rover) to pass. I edge my way carefully through, watching my wing mirrors all the way. Made it! Past the *faille* there is an equally large quantity of trucks queuing in the other direction. I feel sorry for them and expect they'll be spending tonight sleeping in the hammocks under their trucks.

We descend the pass and come to the sizeable village of Bafilo which, I'm told, once made it into the record books for the worst ever road traffic accident in terms of fatalities/damage. Apparently, a large truck's brakes failed as it came down the steep hill and it careered off the road, ploughing straight through the market place, crushing stalls and killing dozens of people in the process. A real mess!

Thankfully, the final stretch of our journey is straight and relatively pot-hole-free, but I am exhausted and delighted to see the picturesque mountains of Kara looming in the distance. Kara was the home town of Eyadema Gnassigbe, Togo's late President. This is one reason why the main road north was built via Aledjo in the first place: so that it would go through Kara. Although it's actually smaller than Sokodé, Kara feels more like Togo's second city and certainly has more weight in terms of importance. During his lifetime, Eyadema Gnassigbe survived several brushes with death and was even believed by some Togolese to be immortal. One time, his plane crashed near Kara, and he walked out of it alive. The very spot is now marked with a large building, covering this almost sacred site. Apparently, every time Eyadema made an important visit somewhere, a choir would precede him, heralding his entrance with a rendition of Handel's 'Halleluia Chorus'. Well I never!

We finally arrive at The Kara Centre, with its pleasant, sizeable compound, grassy areas and mango trees. We find our room and unpack. Although I'll be working in Baga, further north, we'll be staying each night here and commuting into the village each day; a more comfortable option, especially as Ken is new to West Africa. As I unzip my bag to unpack, I notice something curious – my clothes are all damp. What has happened to them? It certainly didn't rain on the way here and I can't see how any water could've leaked in either. Furthermore, I don't remember them seeming even damp when I packed my bag. Then I realize what has happened here: the relative difference in humidity from Cotonou (80%) to Kara (30%) is so great that the 'dry' clothes I packed there seem wet when I unpack them here, even though they have not changed; the air outside has. I've noticed that, going in the opposite direction, your clothes come out feeling warm and dry – as though they've just been tumble-dried. Fascinating!

Early next morning, we're up with the lark – or, to be more exact, up with the weaverbird – and off on a 45 minute drive to Baga. The road is very straight and well surfaced and the scenery is spectacular (though would be even more so were there no Harmattan). I say the road is straight, but a couple of miles out of town is former president Eyadema Gnassigbe's actual village, and no stranger is allowed to drive through it. Instead, the main road makes a sudden 90 degree turn left shortly followed by another to the right, then a two mile detour around the village. After this, the road undulates gently all the way to Baga, where we turn left off the main road. A couple of hundred yards down a dirt track and we have reached our destination: a large Catholic church on a substantial piece of land. In fact, there are *two* Catholic churches here: an older, smaller one to the left of the square and an impressively large, newer one on the right. Baga is a curious place in terms of Catholicism. Men are trained for the priesthood here, but apparently a disproportionate number of Catholic priests in Togo *all* come from this village and its environs; a sort of 'Sargasso Sea' for the Catholic Priesthood. I've been here a couple of times before, to record the local Catholic choir ("Have a beer, Monsieur!" "Oh, thank you, Father.") and also to record some Biblical passages in the local Nawdm language.

I park *The Beast* in the middle of the large and already busy square, next to a round *paillote*. Before I've even turned the engine off, I notice a very old man wearing a small hat gazing straight at us. "Must be *Le Vieux du Village*," (the village elder) I think to myself, and remember an important cultural detail, which I quickly share with Ken:

"Ken, mate. When you shake hands with the old bloke, hold your right forearm with your left hand as a mark of respect."

"Okey-dokey," says Ken, jovial and easy-going as ever.

We step out of the car, surrounded by the usual crowds, eager to welcome us and fascinated by their pale visitors in a metal box. Ken does a great job greeting the old man with a 'weighty handshake'. However, as the chap begins to speak, I realize he seems to be speaking a strange 'dialect' I've never heard before. It's not Nawdm – I'd recognize that by now – and certainly not French either. Upon further analysis, it seems to be a bizarre mix of French and gobbledegook! What's with this guy? I can't understand a single phrase he's saying! Then I realize: this is not *Le Vieux du Village*, but *Le Fou du Village* – the village madman! Could make for an 'interesting' day.

Greetings over, and we head into the old church building to commence proceedings. I notice one guy is wearing a red tee-shirt which reads:'ASDA Service Squad, easing the rush hour' in yellow lettering. Our aged friend follows us all into the building too, and sits at the back, spouting nonsense the whole time. Following the customary greetings and introductions, we move on to the song genres and the participants come up with a fascinating list:

> *Simpa* – for rejoicing and also played at funerals (but not for mourning in a Western sense)
>
> *Balance* – used in the same ways as simpa
>
> *Santm* – for rejoicing
>
> *Kukpalŋa* – for rejoicing
>
> *Kamgu* – for rejoicing
>
> *Dagabina* – sung after the death of an old man
>
> *Fɔkabina* – sung following the death of an old lady
>
> *Timbingu* – sung/played during a procession
>
> *Kajaaga* – for rejoicing
>
> *Bagu* – used during hunting
>
> *Habaara* – sung by ladies in the moonlight, as exhortation

This is a decent list, though still a tad on the short side. There ought to be specific genres for weddings, farming, building, story-telling etc. These may already have been lost from the culture, or may just not be known to those present. Also, the large number of genres cited as 'for rejoicing' would almost certainly have had a more specific purpose in the past, but this has doubtless been lost with time. *Kamgu*, they tell me, is rarely sung these days, so I hope they attempt to use it for at least one of their new songs, to help save it from extinction.

Once the list is formed, I ask the group to perform examples of the different genres. This helps me to see and hear what they are like and reminds everyone present of how these are traditionally performed. There is also a hugely important social side to doing this: once the group starts to sing and dance together, they almost instantly begin to gel, united by their common musical heritage. I never cease to be amazed at how easily Africans can just pipe up with a song and sing the whole thing from memory. I guess this is the only way songs have survived historically in what has been a non-literate society until recent times.

During the morning, an older French couple, Jean-Paul and Claudette, turn up to watch. They've been working on Bible translation into the Nawdm language for decades and are very *au fait* with the local culture and customs. Dressed in classic colourful African dress and matching head-piece, Claudette is a small, amiable lady. Jean-Paul has a thick, white beard hanging halfway down his chest, a balding head and a warm smile, making him somewhat 'Santa-esque', bar his clothing. "*Bienvenu à Baga, Monsieur Baker! Le voyage s'est bien passé?*" he asks, with genuine warmth.

In Africa, dance is not merely an 'added extra'; it is an integral part of the song, as much as the melody or the drumming. One mistake a lot of early (and even present-day) missionaries to the continent made was to forbid dancing – even drumming – in church. But telling an African 'do not dance to the music' is like saying to a Westerner 'sing me your National Anthem, but without the tune'; nonsensical and pointless, as one of the key elements of the performance is missing.

We work our way through a number of songs. Each time, one person strikes up singing a melody, and – within seconds – everyone else joins in with the 'response'. Soloist then choir, soloist again, then choir again, and so on all the way through the song.

We get to one particularly interesting genre called *habaara*, which is always performed by ladies only. Jean-Claude leans over to me and says:

"*Ah, ça, c'est très spécial!*"

"*Oui, oui. Intéressant celui-là,*" echoes his wife.

I wonder what they can be referring to, but find out soon enough. The *habaara* is reserved for nights when the full moon is out and, as far as I can tell, is a chance for the younger women to meet beneath this free light source and dance the night away, just for fun! It's an intriguing dance: the ladies all stand in a circle – as is almost always the case in African dance –

but then, at a given point, they energetically bang their buttocks into their partner's, with a kind of sideways thrust. As they do so, they sing a song of joy together. Fascinating, and somewhat intriguing to observe, although this is in no way an erotic dance, just a fun one!

The aim today is to create new songs based on the book of Philippians. On a previous visit to Baga, I recorded an entire reading of Philippians (all four chapters) in Nawdm. The idea now is to have some songs to go with these readings. That way, a cassette will be produced containing a reading of chapter one, followed by a song based upon chapter one, then a reading of chapter two followed by another song and so on. This gives the listener a break from hearing read text and, at the same time, the songs reinforce the message and are more easily remembered. Doing all of this will also help literacy: once the cassettes are made, they will be sold with a hard copy of Philippians. So folk can listen and follow along with the text, thereby improving their reading skills in Nawdm at the same time. This should work especially well with those who can already read in French, as most of the letters are the same, but will also be a great tool for those just learning to read and write.

A colleague from the translation team does some exegesis on each chapter of Philippians, to ensure they understand what it's about before composing. Throughout this whole time, *crazy old bloke* is still sitting at the back, constantly interjecting with his nonsensical mumblings; quite distracting I must say, but we soldier on regardless.

I split the twenty or so participants into four smaller groups and each is allocated one chapter of Philippians. This they re-read and carefully consider together before coming up with either a key theme or some key verses for their song. At this point, we finally manage to lose our doggerel-spouting septuagenarian, which − I must say − is something of a relief! With nobody at the front speaking to 'him', he loses interest and wanders off the compound, never to reappear for the rest of the workshop.

One group is a bit confused:

"Can we do five different songs, as there are five of us?" they ask. I explain that this is meant to be a *group* composition session and, besides, five songs would just be too many to rehearse and record. Quality is more important than quantity in this game.

We all gather beneath the large *paillote* (pronounced 'pie-ott') for lunch. These circular, open-sided gazebos with conical roofs are common across Africa and are handy places to shelter from the heat whilst still benefiting from any breeze. Resembling an oversized mud hut with most of the wall removed, *paillotes* traditionally have straw roofs. However, in the interest of 'progress' and easy maintenance, many roofs are made from corrugated metal these days. This is not necessarily an improvement in other ways: they become intolerably hot in the middle of the day, too noisy for words (literally) when it rains, and difficult from an acoustic point of view if you're an ethnomusicologist.

A couple of ladies arrive with large metal bowls on their heads: beef and sauce in one and *foufou* in the other. *Foufou* is made from pounded yams, plantains or maize. This, I think, is the yam variety, but it's often hard to tell. Ken, for all his energy, is one of the tiniest blokes I know: around five feet five, weighing less than eight stone (around 100 pounds) and with a waist no more than 28 inches. His eating habits match his build, and today he takes a tiny amount of food, which he nevertheless enjoys! However, in African culture, it is both normal and polite to take a large amount, and having second helpings is seen as a great compliment too!

"He has not eaten enough. He should have more!" says one of the ladies who cooked the meal. I'm not sure how to respond and Ken's tiny tummy is full up already. In Africa, a good way out of such a situation (without causing offence) is to make a joke out of it.

"*Il mange comme un pigeon!*" (He eats like a pigeon), I announce to the cooking ladies. They all laugh, nodding their heads avidly in agreement. I feel a bit sorry for Ken, now the butt of this joke, but he's just relieved he won't have to be 'force fed' any more food than he can manage!

After lunch, composing begins, and each group finds its own shaded space to gather and begin working; some indoors, others outside under trees. As they compose, I circulate to listen to how they're doing, but also try to hang back and leave them to it. I take this time to have a chat with Jean-Claude who, it would seem, is something of an expert on African trees.

"That one over there is the *ronier fourchu*," he tells me – a fascinating tree in the palm family, with several large hand-shaped leaves at the top, often called the 'ronier palm' in English (*borassus aethiopum*). But this one is the forked variety (*fourchu*) and the trunk splits halfway up, giving the tree two 'heads'. Never seen this before.

One group has chosen the genre *timbingu,* but is experiencing difficulty adding the correct drum beats to their words. The trouble is they have composed all the words and tune first, without giving the rhythm of the genre much thought. Yet the drumbeat will dictate – to some extent at least – the metre of the lyrics; that's why they really need to choose their genre from the outset. Still, with a bit of work and much discussion they manage to make it all come together.

There is a decent range of percussion instruments that folk have brought along. As is often the case, there's a pair of 'conga' type drums on a metal frame – almost cone-shaped, narrowing gradually off all the way down. Curiously, these two are made of metal rather than wood, which ought to make them less resonant. That said, their sound is still not bad at all. The second curious thing about these drums is that a *lady* is playing them. Even in the West it is something of a rarity to see a female drummer, but in Africa it is virtually unheard-of. Here, men play the drums, stringed instruments, flutes and horns; women play bells and shakers and sing a lot. It may seem sexist to you, but that's just how it is here, and it won't change overnight. This is why I'm particularly surprised to see this woman drumming – and she's good! Five feet tall and nicely dressed with short hair and an air of earnestness, she glides from one drum to the other and back with dexterity and skill. A refreshing change indeed! Ken is eager to learn and watches her rhythmic patterns attentively, copying them with his own hands in mid air first. Once he is confident with the rhythm, *drum lady* lets him take the helm and he's away in a flash! He does really well, but I can't help noticing the contrast between their two faces when they play: *drum lady*'s is relaxed and content; Ken's is wrought with concentration – almost discomfort – as he strives to maintain the complex syncopations.

In Africa, percussion is by far the number one type of instrument found. In ethnomusicology, we call these either *membranophones* (ones with a skin), or *idiophones* (ones you hit/shake/scrape). So a drum is a *membranophone*, but a bell is an *idiophone*. Today, they have also brought along a *double agogo* – two forged metal bells of differing size and pitch, joined together and played as one instrument. This is virtually identical to the kind used in a Brazilian *samba* band. There's a reason for that: samba has its origins in this part of West Africa and found its way to Brazil years ago via the slave trade.

Another interesting *idiophone* present is the 'gourd shaker' – a small gourd covered in a string net. On these strings, beads, small seeds or even cowrie shells are attached at regular intervals. These hit against the side of the hollow gourd to make a percussive sound – a bit like an inside-out maraca. There are several ways of playing this instrument; the most common in this part of the world is to cradle the gourd in one's upturned hands and gently throw it from one hand to the other in rapid succession, in a diagonally upwards direction. I think back to *pod-shaking lady* in Gando – the principal is similar, but hers was much more complex and impressive.

There's also an unusual curved clay drum, which looks more North African to me; basically a large pitcher with a skin on top. As the bottom end is closed off, the sound is quite dry and not as loud as other drums. Then there's a small, shallow drum, shaped like a Western snare drum but not as big. It almost looks like a child's toy and is hit with a wooden stick, whilst the other hand is placed on or off the drum skin to create two distinct tones. Finally, there is a wide, double-headed barrel drum with a single snare across the end (quite common in West Africa). A fascinating selection indeed, and it should make for some great recordings!

The group working on Philippians Chapter Three have chosen the captivating *habaara* as their genre, and begin singing the song and dancing at the same time. Like all the groups, this one is mixed, and so even the men get to take part in the *buttock bashing* routine; an almost unheard-of eventuality out of this context.

By the end of the afternoon, the songs are sounding good and a nice range of genres has been used. Ken is playing along whenever and wherever he can – it is all so much fun for a percussionist such as himself. The Africans are also impressed to see a white man with such good rhythm!

"*C'est un grand percussionniste!*" I tell them proudly, and they all nod in agreement, smiles beaming across their tired yet jubilant faces.

Most of the genres are also accompanied by clapping, sometimes just a straight beat, other times very syncopated. As they sing through more songs, I notice that many of them are *hexatonic*. This means there are six different tones in the scale, rather than the Western seven, or the more common African five. Upon further analysis, it would seem that the seventh degree of the Western major scale is missing, so theirs goes: do-re-mi-fa-so-la-do.

Today has been very dry and baking hot, so I'm feeling like a 'Baker' in more ways than one! The heat this afternoon has been almost unbearable, in fact. As we round up for the day, I realize a curious fact: during the past nine hours, I have drunk three litres of water, but have only 'taken a leak' once in the whole time! The power of evaporation, eh?

Now, you'd think my day would be over now – straight to bed for some well-earned rest. That may have been the case were Evan Davidson not living nearby. Evan is literally one of my favourite people in the world – a Cornishman by birth, now in his mid-forties, a confirmed bachelor and living in Kara doing linguistic research for a PhD. Evan is a gifted linguist and musician as well as being an all-round nice bloke. He plays piano exactly the way I don't (and vice versa): he's amazingly gifted in the classical realm, sight reads music at a moment's notice, and can memorize entire pieces. I, however, did the classical *thing* when I had to, but always gravitated more towards reading chords, improvising and generally *playing by ear.* Ask Evan to 'just make something up' at the keyboard, and he'll be lost. Conversely, hand me some sheet music and say 'play this, Rob' and I'll say: 'Give me a week or two' and only then if I really have to!

I already know that Evan and Ken – also a much 'nicer bloke' than me – will hit it off. Evan is intelligent and knowledgeable enough for a stimulating chat, but down-to-earth enough to be amenable and approachable. He is eccentric enough for a good laugh and a few crazy escapades, but wise enough to not let this endanger his acceptance within the local culture. Fluent in French and the local Kabiyé language, I know few Westerners as integrated into the culture as Evan. In fact, he lives in a fascinating house he had built on the top of a mountain near Kara. As he had already spent some time researching the language there, a local chief literally gave him the land in exchange for a bottle of scotch! Using explosives, a well was built – even at this altitude – and his house, consisting of several round huts in a circle, began to take shape. The round huts are surrounded by a boundary wall, and at the front of the property a large veranda overlooks the African plain.

Ken and I meet Evan down at the Kara Centre and he agrees to take us out.

"Shall we introduce Ken to some *chouk*, Evan?" I ask.

*Chouk,* or millet beer, is the local alcoholic brew, found throughout this part of Togo and beyond. Most cultures in Africa seem to have their own locally-produced tipple, and here it is made from the cereal millet; hence the name.

"Go on then! We can try and find somewhere down the road. It depends on where it is market day today, though." Markets in Africa tend to run on a four or five-day rotation system, whereby the day of the week on which it takes place constantly changes. I guess seven days is just too long to wait for your provisions in this climate. That's why Evan – an expert in the local way of life – still doesn't know which markets will be on today.

Now, I'm not a big drinker by any means and would never condone excessive consumption of alcohol, or anything close to drunkenness. However, this is a truly Togolese experience for Ken, and sharing *chouk* with the locals is a great way to understand their culture. We hop into Evan's bright red Toyota and drive out of Kara in search of a drink. After a couple of kilometres, Evan stops, winds down his window and calls out:

"*Labaalé!*"

I take this to be some kind of local greeting. He proceeds to converse in Kabiyé with the passers-by. I notice he uses the word '*solumm*' quite a lot (meaning 'drink'). The folks shake their heads – no help here. Further on, three ladies carrying large bowls on their heads are walking by the roadside.

"*Labaalé!*"

These three know a place where there is a market and where we can most certainly try out some *chouk*. After a lengthy conversation, of which I understand precisely three words, Evan gets out and opens the back of his car. The ladies put their bowls in the boot and, somewhat uneasily, get into the back seat (as Ken squeezes into the front with Evan and me). I wonder if this is the first time they've ever ridden in a car. Quite possibly.

We turn off the main road and along another bumpy track, parking almost immediately. Evan asks the ladies whether they need a lift back to where he picked them up. "No, we can walk back from here," they say. Helping a foreigner is almost a duty of honour in this part of the world, and these three women – in spite of all the day's hard work – were still happy to put themselves out to help three strangers. Amazing.

The market is up ahead and is unlike most markets in the world – even in Africa. There are no 'stalls' as such; people have merely placed piles of items on the floor, often on a sheet or cloth of some kind. Tomatoes, onions, peanuts, yams, fish, spices, household goods, tools – the usual kind of thing. The 'stall' holders sit on large, dark rocks, which seem to occur naturally here.

"Have you seen these new L.E.D. torches?" Evan asks me. "They've really revolutionized lighting for folk here."

He points out the metal barrel torches, which look like any other, but have around half a dozen small, white bulbs (light emitting diodes) in the end, instead of one conventional bulb.

"What's the difference?" I ask, intrigued.

"Well, the light is much brighter and yet the batteries last much longer," he replies. Sounds good to me.

We wander around the noisy maelstrom of people, through narrow aisles, past large trees, with many folk staring at us or smiling and greeting us warmly.

"Here it is!" says Evan triumphantly. In one corner of the market is a covered area with a dozen or so people – mostly men – sitting on stones in a circle, drinking from bowl-shaped receptacles. Upon our arrival, some folk stand up to vacate three stones so we can sit down. Evan greets them all warmly in Kabiyé, which makes us instantly accepted in the circle. The 'bowls' from which they are drinking are in fact hollowed-out gourds, cut in half to form a hemispherical bowl. The gourd (called *calebasse* locally) is a most versatile vegetable and is put to a thousand and one uses in Africa. I think back to remote Gando and its impressive gourd tree in the town square.

The millet beer is stored in a large clay jar and our gourds are filled by being dipped into it. We are each handed a half-filled gourd of millet beer, which costs 25 CFA francs – that's about three British pence! I've tried this stuff a few times before, and Evan plenty I'm sure. But for Ken, this is a new experience. It is quite potent stuff and bears little resemblance to Western beer. The taste to me is more like 'Scrumpy Jack' cider than any beer I know. The colour is a pale beige, and bubbles constantly rise to the surface as it continues to ferment. Ken isn't too sure about the taste, but is enjoying the cultural experience of it all: people laughing, shouting aloud in Kabiyé, asking us, "Is it good? Is it good?" and pouring their dregs into the dusty earth beneath us.

We've all finished our first 'pint' – very refreshing too! You never drink the last half an inch, though, as that's pretty thick and yeasty.

"You have to pour your dregs out into the ground," says Evan.

"Really?"

"Yes, it's traditionally for the ancestors and how you pour it matters in the local culture."

Evan goes on to explain that, holding the gourd in one's right hand, the dregs must be poured out in a straight line *away* from your body. I try it and end up pouring it back towards myself instead. Whoops! The locals look on and laugh; they appreciate the effort I've made, even if I did fail abysmally. Ken does somewhat better, but declines partaking in a *second round* (and for someone his size, one is really plenty!)

It's still only just after nightfall, so Evan drives us up the steep and rocky mountain road to his house. To call this a 'road' is a bit of an exaggeration – a narrow, steep, bendy track of uneven rocks and gravel would be a more accurate description.

"It was built by a Catholic priest some years ago," he tells us, as we bump our way up and round a sharp bend, inches from a steep ravine.

Sitting on Evan's veranda, we enjoy a welcome glass of cool water and a good chat for a couple of hours, looking out over Togo as the moon shines down on us. A perfect way to end a hot, busy day.

Back in Bago the next morning, we begin by singing through yesterday's songs. The words for each refrain have been written up on the board so that everyone can sing along in Nawdm (or the literate ones, at least).

The Philippians songs have come out well and are jolly, catchy and authentically African in sound. Nawdm music is generally fast and very rhythmic, not only in the accompaniment, but also in the melodies themselves. In some, the soloist's words are so fast I wonder how on earth they fit so many syllables into each line. I'm also intrigued to hear that their second song has three beats in a bar – very unusual in African music, which almost always has four beats.

The Nawdm language seems decidedly short on vowels, but is rich in consonants. Yet, of all the African languages I've worked with, it remains one of the most beautiful to listen to for me. I'm not exactly sure why, but there's just a certain rhythm – a percussiveness in all those consonants – which makes it pleasing to the ear in a musical kind of way. The word for 'refrain' in Nawdm is '*sogdgm*', (roughly pronounced soh-guh-duh-gum) and I'm hearing it said a lot today, which can't be a bad thing. Other

Nawdm words I pick up are '*Saŋgband*', which means 'God' and '*Sabeerma*', meaning 'Lord'.

For the rest of the day, we run through the same process with the book of James, the only difference being that it has *five* chapters, not four. So we create a fifth group this time. Teaching is followed by composition in groups, then everyone comes back together to share the results. The first song has quite a Western feel to it – with clear I, IV, V harmonies coming out (if that means anything to you). A nice song, but somewhere along the line these people have been influenced by non-African music and so this song stands out from the others like a sore thumb. It is also less likely to be universally accepted by the Nawdm people, especially those who have no church background.

We're all done by 5:00pm and we say our goodbyes and thankyous and leave for the night. Before returning to Kara for the evening though, there is one more place close to Baga I must take Ken to: *Codhani*. It stands for '*Coopération des Handicapés de Niamtougou*', and is a centre which enables disabled people to have a job in textiles. In the car park are numerous disabled tricycles, the African equivalent to a mobility scooter. Two wheels at the back and hand-operated pedals at the front which drive the front wheel; an efficient way to get around, but tiring on the arms, I imagine. Inside the workshop, people of varying degrees of disability are painting designs on cloth, dying it in huge vats and hanging it out to dry. The gift shop is full of clothing, towels, wall-hangings and postcards in a range of colours and designs. Not the cheapest way to clothe yourself, but it's for a good cause and they're all very nice to look at. I try and get a shirt here whenever I'm passing and hope Ken will too.

Purchases made, we wend our way back to Kara. Ken has loved every minute of the workshop, but is looking pretty tired today: the new country and hot climate along with all the exciting sights and smells have rather worn him out. With no energy for another millet beer session tonight, we settle for dinner at *Marok's*, a fantastic African restaurant on the outskirts of Kara, which does delicious food at great prices: succulent steaks, roast chicken, pork chops, pizzas – the works. We're joined, once again, by Evan and enjoy another good old chat accompanied by a tasty dinner.

As it happens, there's a partial lunar eclipse tonight, so when we return to the centre after dinner, Ken and I grab a coke from the fridge and sit outside on a concrete staircase. Gazing into the atmospheric night sky, we both reflect on the many thrilling sights and sounds of the past two days. Has it really only been two days?!

Now, I've made so many field recordings in Africa that I no longer ask myself: 'Will anything happen to hinder the recording session today?' Rather, I think to myself: 'I wonder *what* will hinder our recording this time.' You see, there is always something that does; be it goats, motorbikes, chainsaws, parties, children or chickens. Today, it is the wind: although we'd scheduled recording for early this morning, the Harmattan is blowing so strongly that we have to wait. As if the wind itself were not enough, the *paillote* where we plan to record is surrounded by acacia trees with dry seed pods hanging from them. These rattle away in the wind making such a din that there's no way we can make a decent recording. In vain, I search for an alternative recording location, but everywhere I look there is either no shade or echoey walls. So we wait patiently as the groups run through their songs one more time.

By 10:30, the wind has died down and we can begin recording. I've chosen to use the round *paillote* for recording as it provides good shade. Its tin roof is not ideal, though, so I'm careful where I place the singers (and microphones) to avoid unnecessary reverberations. The percussionists have to go just outside of the *paillote* though: there is no way they can join the singers inside, as their sound would interfere with the vocals too much.

We set up the microphones once again and Ken helps me do a *line check*, then we're ready to record the first song. When it comes to field recording sessions, I have a couple of rules I always announce, just to make things run more smoothly and to get the best results. These, I explain before recording begins:

1. Silence before we begin. I will signify I'm ready to start by putting three fingers in the air, then two, then one. Once the countdown is done, I lower my arm to show that recording has begun and they can start.

2. If anyone makes a serious mistake during the recording, then rather than wait until the end, they should call out: 'Stop, stop!' immediately, so that we can start again. Otherwise, time is unnecessarily wasted.

3. At the end of the song, they should wait until I give the signal before starting to talk again. This I do by saying: '*Okay, c'est bon!*' out loud.

So, I raise my hand in the air to signal for silence. Three, two one, and we're off! This first song is based upon Philippians 1:18-24, and talks about how Timothy 'takes a genuine interest' in the welfare of others.

Shortly after recording this song, we have our second hindrance – another 'mad' person, this time a lady, wanders into the *paillote* screaming maniacally. Thankfully, it is before I've pressed the 'record' button and someone calmly ushers her out and off into the distance before we begin. (I'd like to say this is my last encounter with a 'crazy' person in this book; it is not). Africa doesn't always have the same level of psychiatric care that one finds in the West and so, sadly, coming across people like this is all too common. To compound this is the fact that African traditional religion would tend to put her illness down to some kind of spirit possession or even a curse.

We finally start the second song, which is based on Philippians 2:3-8: 'Do nothing out of selfish ambition or vain conceit, but in humility consider others as better than yourselves…' – great words to edify the Nawdm Christians; the non-believers too, I hope.

A chap from the village arrives with a traditional three-holed flute (a bit like the ones in Gando). A couple more instruments have turned up today too: a harmonica (mouth organ) and a recorder!! Very unusual, and somewhat incongruous in this context, but they seem intent on using them! Strangely, they fit reasonably well with these songs, but again I wonder what folk in other Nawdm villages would make of this curious Afro-Western fusion.

For one song, some of the ladies strap shakers to their legs, made from woven palm leaves filled with stones or seeds. The result is a line of small chambers over a metre long, which looks more like a Christmas decoration than a percussion instrument. This is then wrapped around one leg several times to make a shaky sound as they dance. It rather reminds me of *Morris Dancing* back in England, although that's done by men dressed in white, with straw hats, who prance around with hankies in their hands and metal bells around their ankles. So a bit different really.

I notice that two of the ladies have put their shakers around their right legs, but the third lady has hers on her left. Is this purely down to chance, or is she left-handed/legged? Or perhaps it's for musical reasons, to create a more interesting rhythm. So busy with the logistics of field recording, I'm afraid I didn't get chance to ask!

At various points during the recordings, women will spontaneously *ululate*. It sounds painful, but this just means a long, high-pitched cry (of joy) in the middle of a song. I've come across two basic varieties of ululation in Africa: the first is a 'warbling' kind of effect, often using the tongue (or even the hand) to create a 'Cowboys and Indians' type sound, usually ending with a downward pitch slide. The second kind is more of a pure, solid sound, with only occasional pitch changes. The latter is the kind the Nawdm women use, and theirs tend to finish off with three short downwards pitch slides, each one beginning slightly lower than the previous. Most uplifting, but I have to make sure that whoever is spontaneously ululating does not do so directly in front of the microphone, or the other voices singing will be totally drowned out. To avoid this, I ask any ululating women to turn their heads to the rear first – this gives more or less the right balance of sound: she can still be heard ululating, but the choir is audible too.

Third hindrance coming up: and this one is my fault! Some of my microphones run on what is called *phantom power*. Sounds spooky, but this just means that a small current of electricity has to travel up the cables into the microphones in order to make them work. Unfortunately, I accidentally set the phantom to the wrong voltage: 18 instead of 48 volts. This makes the choir sound much too quiet and the sound quality very poor. It's getting close to lunch and we're all tired and hungry. We do a retake on this song, but I can tell that some of them are getting a bit grumpy by now.

The first four songs are all done by lunchtime, so we're pretty much on schedule. The third song is based on Philippians 3:8-9 ('I consider everything loss compared to the surpassing greatness of knowing Christ Jesus my Lord…') and the fourth on Philippians 4:4-7 ('Rejoice in the Lord always…').

After lunch, the folks return in a jolly, jovial state; they've all been drinking millet beer with their lunch! Not something I wouldn't have recommended when we have accurate recordings to make, but at least they're more cheerful than they were this morning! They offer me a gourdful, but I politely decline: not whilst I'm working and, besides, I've got to drive *The Beast* back to Kara when we're done.

At this point, one of the priests comes over with a potential *fourth* hindrance: the *paillote* we're using is needed at three o'clock for a catechism class. It's half past one now, so we're on a bit of a race against time to get all the songs 'in the can' by then.

Three o'clock arrives and, thankfully, the catechists are all late ('on African time' we call it). Two more songs to go, so we're in with a chance. The priest arrives and his pupils filter in one by one. We're done by 3:30, which doesn't seem to bother them too much (after all, this is Africa, and waiting is often part of the culture!) We move away from the *paillote* to let the class begin and to get the copyright form signed: this is basically a form which lists the names of the songs, when they were composed and who was involved. The group has to choose one person to sign on their behalf. In signing, they retain the ownership of the songs, but authorize me and my organization to use the songs in teaching and raising awareness in other parts of the world on a non-profit basis. This also includes radio broadcasts, making cassettes or putting the songs on the Internet.

For our last night in Kara, we have another delicious meal at *Marok's* and Ken shares some startling news with me:

"This has been one of my best holidays ever."

It's an early start the next morning. Back over the infamous *Aledjo Pass* as the sun rises, and down to Sokodé. Here, I take my usual route back, heading southeast to the easy border crossing at Prékété. The guys are sitting outside their office and just about manage to muster up a wave as we drive past. No need even to stop (or show them my technically illegal driving licence).

Ken has been great company on this trip and continues to be on the long journey home.

"I know, Rob. Let's play a guessing game," he says, and we pass an hour or so with this. Later, Ken shares some tips from an advanced driving course he recently took: how to do what he calls a 'police overtake', where you move out onto the other side of the road, check whether it's clear and then move off. Another tip he mentions is to start accelerating *before* you move out into the road, so that the time passing a vehicle is less and therefore safer. A final tip was 'you're responsible for the distance in front of your car', and that you can always hang back and be safer, rather than staying close behind, even if it means someone behind overtakes you and fills the gap. Now, I don't know if these comments were a result of his intense fear at my driving, or whether he was just being helpful. Either way, what Ken probably doesn't realize is that I have remembered and used this advice on many occasions; he may even have unknowingly saved my life! Thanks matey.

Unfortunately, his advice is not enough to keep me from slipping up as a result of overtiredness today: a minor disaster strikes on the outskirts of Cotonou. I'm just busy chatting away to Ken, not realizing how tired I really am or how busy the traffic has suddenly become. Overtaking a parked lorry, there is a sudden SMASH! What just happened?! Did someone throw something at the car? Did someone drive into me? No, what just happened is that I was too close to the lorry I was passing and the metal cover on its rear indicator has scraped the whole side of the Land Rover, from the front windscreen pillar all the way to the back — and there's a line to prove it. The smashing sound was the side window at the back shattering, and there are now thousands of tiny pieces of glass in the back of the car and no window left to speak of. Disastrous! What was I thinking?! I remind myself to have a break in future, just before the crazy onslaught of Cotonou traffic begins. After all that driving – not to mention the workshop itself – my spatial perception was hindered; I had no idea I was so close.

"I don't know what you were doing," Ken said later. "You were just way too close to that lorry."

Meanwhile, the lorry driver is unhappy with me. I have, apparently, bent the metal cover on his rear left indicator and he wants compensating for this. "He should worry," I think to myself, but I know how things work here, especially when a *yovo* (foreigner) is involved.

"*15,000 francs!*" he says, demanding a ludicrous eighteen English pounds for the repair. I look at the sturdy metal cover: I could bend it back myself if I had a wrench.

"That's too much. It's not a big job."

"*Donne-moi 15,000 francs!*" he orders. He's getting angry – shouting, gesticulating, ranting. I know that here in Africa there can often be a huge discrepancy between what is 'right' in principle and what actually happens. I know he's wrong, and I could carry on arguing this for the next half hour, tiring myself out even more. However, there are times when, for a quiet life, it's just easier to pay up and move on, so that's what I do. Before we move off, I pull out all the loose bits of glass from the broken window; even the rubber surrounding comes off in my hands.

The last half an hour of the journey is very subdued as I ponder over my blunder and how, had I been another inch further to the right, it could have been much worse. Still, on the plus side, the ventilation in *The Beast* is very good now.

Back in Cotonou the next morning, I take *The Beast* straight round to Freddie the French mechanic hoping he can mend the broken window. I have another trip up north next week, so it has to be done quickly.

Freddy is a likeable chap and, in many ways, typical of the multitude of world-wise expatriate French living in West Africa: smokes like a chimney, knows all there is to know about 'surviving' in Africa and could talk the back wheel of a Toyota Hilux. In his mid 40s, Freddy has spent much of his adult life in Africa and really knows the ropes. It's also clear when talking to him that he loves the freedom and thrill which living in this part of the world affords him. Not only an excellent mechanic, he's also a serious *petrolhead* and adrenalin junkie. Besides his numerous gripping stories about crossing the desert, fording huge rivers or almost breaking the sound barrier in a nitrous oxide-powered Peugeot, he also flies a motorized hang-glider in his spare time.

"*Ecoute*, Robert: One time, I was flying my *ULM* over the Pendjari National Park," he once told me. "I came down low, just above the ground and chased a herd of elephants into the river." Some people spend their weekends shopping; Freddie spends them experiencing the thrills and spills of extreme sports, usually involving some kind of mechanical contraption.

This morning, though, Freddy takes one look at the smashed rear window of my Land Rover and exclaims:

"*Zut alors, Robert! Qu'est-ce que tu as fait cette fois?*" which basically means: "Sorry to hear about your misfortune, Rob." (He actually didn't say '*zut*' – hardly anyone does anymore – but something a tad more colourful. However, I'll save you the ordeal of having to 'pardon his French' on these pages!)

By the end of the same day, he's put something called *Plexiglas* in the gap, as real glass would be expensive and tricky to do during my two-day turn around. It's basically plastic, but looks just like the real thing and certainly does the trick. "Drive carefully this time, Robert," he bellows as I carefully reverse the grey Land Rover out of his small, cluttered workshop, ready for my next adventure.

A typical day in Cotonou's crazy traffic.

# Chapter Three

# Watermelons and Woodcutters

*The Tem People of Northern Togo*

**From:** Ben & Linda

**Date:** 26 September

**To:** Rob Baker

**Subject:** Literacy music!

*Hi Rob,*

*We would love to create an alphabet song, a song about writing the two aspects used most often, and maybe a couple to cover some tone basics.*

*When would you be free to come up to Sokodé after the New Year?*

*Thanks,*

*Linda*

I was immediately intrigued – and excited – by this e-mail from my friends in Sokodé. What on earth are the *two aspects* she mentions? Must go and find out! And besides, alphabet song-writing could be fun! We all know some kind of 'A B C D E F G' type song from our childhood and it surely helped us understand the alphabet – even learn to read more easily. As literacy levels are still relatively low here, this could be a marvellous way to get the message across, especially if we use musical styles which the local folk know and love.

After several e-mail exchanges with Ben & Linda, we agreed on a date for the workshop and on what it would entail: a literacy song-writing workshop, to help people understand the orthography and grammar of the Tem language. *Orthography* is a great word, banded about by linguists worldwide. It's basically a posh way of saying *spelling*, but say that to a linguist and they will disagree: "No, the two are quite different!"

The first category of songs to be composed is *alphabet songs*. The plan is that these songs, reciting the Tem alphabet, will catch on and be sung by children and adults alike, spreading from village to village and thereby reinforcing literacy. Music is a very powerful tool for communicating in this way: it can be heard from far away, attracts listeners, is pleasing to the ear and sticks in your memory in a way that speech alone does not. Think of the Western song which says: 'Now I know my A, B, C, next time won't you sing with me?' It may be nauseating, but it is also catchy and, because you can't get it out of your head, you remember the letters of the alphabet.

The next category of song has to do with the tone rules. Tem, like most languages in West Africa, is a *tonal* language. This means that the pitch of your voice matters when speaking. If you inadvertently use a high tone in place of a low tone – or vice versa – it totally changes the meaning of the word. This could lead to serious communicational errors, like calling someone's brother a dog, or ordering a plate full of worms for lunch. Tem only has two tones – high and low. *Fɔn* in Cotonou has three. Mandarin Chinese, apparently, has *four* tones, which is hard to imagine. I wonder if being tone-deaf there constitutes a speech impediment…

The third category of song is concerned with the complexities of Tem grammar, and the tone combinations used to express different tenses. Don't ask me – I'm just glad *they* understand how these work!

So, once again I'm heading out of Cotonou early one morning, navigating the crazy *zemidjans* and avoiding numerous potholes along the way. Another obstacle one has to contend with on such a journey is the seemingly endless convoy of trucks, all on their way north like me, from Cotonou's busy port to northern Benin and beyond to Burkina Faso, Niger and even Mali. Noisy, rusty, dirty, smelly, dreadfully slow and – of course

– overloaded, these thundering behemoths belch out acrid black smoke as they rattle their way northwards on bald tyres and wobbly wheels.  On an average morning departure from Cotonou, I have a good score of them to overtake, holding my breath all the way (for more than one reason), honking my horn to ensure my presence is duly noted, and hoping there are not too many potholes until I get past.

It is far from uncommon to see overturned trucks by the roadside anywhere from the outskirts of Cotonou to the Burkina Faso border.  As well as those on the treacherous *Aledjo Pass* in Togo, others are to be found at regular intervals: broken down, burnt out, or fallen into a ditch somewhere. I'd say that, on an average eight-hour drive up north, I see at least two or three overturned trucks – and it's not the same ones each time.  This happens for several reasons, most of which are due to financial limitations.  Firstly, some trucks are poorly maintained – bald tyres, faulty steering, axles out of line and so on.  Secondly, they may be carrying more weight than they were designed to and, thirdly, the drivers are not necessarily trained to the high standards one would expect when piloting eight tons of metal at high speeds for hours on end.  Add to this the blind optimism of many Africans: "It won't happen to me," or: "If I die it is God's will," and it's not hard to see why there are so many accidents.

Some of the lorries I pass have signs on the back saying things like 'Trust in God' – a good plan for anyone behind the wheel of one of these monsters!  I've also seen ones which read '*Dieu sait tout*' (God knows everything), '*Etes-vous Dieu?*' (Are *you* God?) and I even recall once seeing one which read: '*On va tous mourir*' (We are all going to die).  Doesn't bode too well, given their track record…

After numerous dicey overtaking manoeuvres and even more potholes, I arrive in Bohicon, an intriguing little town, the entrance to which is marked by a gilded statue of four men holding a cooking pot in the air.  It is here that I remember one crucial part of my equipment which I have forgotten to bring with me (and it's not a cooking pot!)  After composing and recording the songs, I will be duplicating a large number of cassettes to leave with the folks in Sokodé.   For this, I brought my fast tape copier with me, but omitted to bring a cassette deck for making the master copy of the tape.  Poo!  This is a problem and could mean a serious delay in the production of the cassettes.  So, rather than turning right at the 'golden pot people' and onto the bypass, I head straight on into town, hoping to find an electrical store in Bohicon to bail me out.  Thankfully, I find one on the way back out of town and pull in to have a look.  The shop resembles almost any other electrical goods store in the country: a wooden 'shack' about ten feet square with a large counter at the back.  There are shelves all around containing tape players, speakers, random wires and cables, even a few televisions.  Headphones, mobile phones, batteries and more cables hang randomly from the dust-stained walls in this dingy grotto.  Loud African pop music, linked to a stereo system in the shop, booms from two huge speakers strategically positioned out front.  A single strip light, hanging crookedly from visible red and black wires, provides lighting in the shop.  Two thin, youngish Beninese men chewing wooden sticks are sitting behind the counter.

*"Mi fɔn gangi à?"*

I greet them in the customary way, asking them whether they woke up well this morning.  The answer is always the same:

*"Een, un fɔn gangi!  Hwé ló?"* Apparently, they did!

*"Un fɔn gangi!"* I reply, letting them know that I too woke up well this morning (if a little earlier than usual).

"I'm looking for a tape recorder, but it must have the audio input sockets in the back."

"This one is good," he says, recommending an enormous beast of a system way out of my budget range.

"Something smaller, perhaps?  What is the cheapest you have?"

"This one, Monsieur."

They hand me a tiny cassette/radio which, amazingly, does have the sockets in the back I will need.  I take a closer look: it is so small and tin-ny-looking that I really cannot see it being up to the job, and a bad master cassette means all the copies will be the same.

"Do you have anything else?"

"Only this one here, which is playing the music."

He shows me a square, black unit which takes one cassette, typical of the kind found in hi-fi stacking systems of the 90s. That said, it looks relatively new and in good shape and I'm impressed by its 'soft eject'.

"Would you consider selling me *this* one?"

He thinks for a few moments.

"Sixty thousand francs, Monsieur!"

Now, 60,000 CFA francs is about seventy English pounds. Seems a little pricey to me. However, I've lived on this continent long enough to know that the price stated is almost never the price they are aiming for. And so the usual charade is necessary to reach an agreed amount .

"*Non, non, Monsieur. Trop cher!*" I respond.

"Okay, fifty-five then," he concedes.

"Still too expensive. I'll give you thirty."

"Ah! Be reasonable, Monsieur, fifty thousand francs."

"Thirty-five?"

"Forty-five!"

"Forty?"

"*D'accord, donne l'argent.*"

Deal done, for 40,000 CFA – that's about £50. The throbbing, Ivorian pop ceases as he immediately unplugs everything and hands me the dusty unit in exchange for four purple banknotes. I'm happy, he's happy and – I'm guessing – his neighbours are pretty happy too!


The fourth and final obstacle for anyone driving north through Benin is the animals: chickens, pigs, guinea fowl, goats, cows, sheep and ducks; all happy to 'share' the road with oncoming traffic. The occurrence of these is, thankfully, inversely proportional to that of the *zemidjans*, so you seldom encounter large numbers of both at the same time. This is a small consolation, however, as each of the creatures listed will cross the road without prior warning or, worse still, just stand there staring at you until you screech to a halt in their path. The worst of all are the dogs, who will often just lie there in middle of the road, enjoying a snooze in the sunshine. However loudly you honk, they will not get up and move. Eventually, they may raise their head and glance vaguely at you as if to say, "Do you mind? You're ruining a perfectly good siesta here. Can't you wait half an hour 'till I'm done?"

Across West Africa, there is basically only one breed of dog, which can be divided into two subsections: (i) The light brown, floppy-eared mutt of low intelligence and (ii) The black and white floppy-eared mutt of low intelligence. Combinations of the two also exist, and most come with a multitude of flies hovering around, and landing on, their red-raw ears.

The silver medal for hindering motorists goes to the goats, and it's a very close second, I assure you. For some reason, they see a car coming and decide that it is a good time to *start* crossing the road. To add insult to (inevitable) injury, they seldom work alone; once one goat has started to cross, there will invariably be another half a dozen to follow. Now, this may be a bit unfair to the goats, as some of the culprits might actually be incognito sheep: in Africa, the only way to tell the difference between the two is that goats' tails go up and sheep's tails go down. Otherwise, they look almost identical.

I confess I've killed one or two chickens on my travels and even hit a goat once. It made a large CLUNK as it hit the front of the vehicle, but then wandered off the road in a slightly less than straight line. Call me heartless, but I didn't stop to see what became of said goat.

At Dassa I once again take the left branch at the junction, but not before enjoying another delicious *sandwich omelette* at the *Auberge*. The road then heads northwest for a time, before turning northwards at the pointy mountain peaks of Savalou. Around 80 minutes after leaving Dassa, I arrive at Prékété and cross over into to Togo. Of course, I have my driver's licence with me this time, but they don't even ask for it at this border crossing!

As ever, I put my clocks back an hour to Togo time. It's now about fifty minutes' drive northwest to Sokodé. The road is undulating but very straight and virtually traffic-free.

I reach Sokodé, my final destination, by mid-afternoon – *The Beast* has done me proud this journey, with no hitches or breakdowns of any kind. This is good news and, in the light of other trips related in this book, an almost unheard-of occurrence.


Sokodé is the second largest town in Togo, after the capital of Lomé. However, as the Lonely Planet Guide says, "it doesn't feel like it."[6] It is one of the longest and thinnest towns I know: driving on the single main road through Sokodé seems never-ending, but take a left or right at any point and you'll soon be out of town. It is not far from the Beninese border, but then that could be said of almost anywhere in Togo; a narrow country by all accounts. Neither Benin to the East, nor Ghana to the West, are ever more than a couple of hours' drive away.

Ben and Linda live on a small compound towards the edge of the town, which comprises four flats – two upstairs, two down. I park up just outside their compound, beneath some pretty *bougainvillea,* and ring the doorbell on the wall. A tall, dark-haired, bearded American in his thirties answers the door, saying, in a decidedly deep voice:

"Well, hi Rob! Welcome to Sokodé. How was the journey?"

It's Ben, who invites me to join them for a drink and a chat. Their upstairs apartment is small but sufficient for a family of three.

"Hi Rob. Come on in. Would you like a drink?"

It's Ben's wife Linda, small and blonde, wearing an African outfit; even the matching headpiece. Their toddler son, Kyle, looks at me and smiles, but doesn't talk much yet. As we drink and chat, he puts various objects on his head as he's seen the Africans do and even speaks a couple of words of Tem. For the first two nights, I'll be staying in their guestroom downstairs. After that they have a short-termer arriving, so I'll be turfed out for the latter half of my stay.  I'm shattered now, so after a short meeting and a delicious dinner, I hit the sack.

Early start next morning – I'm up at 6:00am, although it feels like 7:00am to me, thanks to the Benin-Togo time difference.  After a classic yoghurt-with-bananas breakfast, Ben and I head off to find the location for the workshop: a craft centre specializing in local weaving techniques. After 100 yards of bumpy dirt road past a very nice bakery, we turn onto Soko-dé's main street near to the market, which is already grinding into action. Men in full length, pale blue robes wearing round hats make their way back from early prayers at one of the town's many mosques, whilst women in colourful outfits ascend the hill towards the market, large baskets perched on their heads.  The road is lined on both sides with deep open drains so characteristic of West African towns.  As if to add insult to injury, these are often full of all kinds of rubbish as well as the acrid, foul-smelling effluent oozing through them.  Interestingly, there are wooden huts selling second hand clothing built directly over the top of one drain - I really hope their floor planks are good and solid!

We turn off the road opposite the somewhat incongruous 'Total' petrol station, its imposing red and white signs visible from afar.  At the turning there are a number of ladies under a tree selling huge watermelons for about a pound each.  It's that time of year and the melons are so huge that some would be hard for one person to lift.  This is not my favourite fruit, I have to confess; they may be cheap, but all you get is a mouthful of seeds and some watery, almost tasteless, red flesh.  In a country which has delicious bananas, luscious mangos and juicy pineapples, why would anyone opt for such a bland alternative?

The weaving centre is just a few yards from the main road.  Thinking ahead, I'm hoping we'll be far enough from the noisy traffic to make decent field recordings at the end of the workshop.  About two acres in size, the compound contains a number of well-kept buildings; offices, classrooms and

– not surprisingly – rooms containing huge looms. I'm always fascinated by these devices and it's something you don't see much anymore in the West.

Near the compound entrance, and next to a large, round *paillote*, is a small shop, selling clothing, bags, mats and other woven goods at prices which would seem to be aiming more at a tourist market. The stripy blue, red and grey design of these tempts me to make a purchase, but just then I notice several folk arriving and rush to greet them instead. There are still a good fifteen minutes until the scheduled start time, so it is impressive to see around half of the participants here already. But these are educated folk who can read, write *and* tell the time; three skills which cannot be taken for granted here. Of course, I wouldn't even be here today if everyone in Sokodé were already literate.

Another thing which immediately strikes and impresses me is that several of these folk are sitting on shiny, brand new motorcycles, all identical but in either *electric blue* or *racing red*. Maybe this is how they all managed to arrive early! I'm intrigued by these and ask Ben how they all ended up with matching bikes. Apparently, they recently received them from a Swedish charity to help them get around for their literacy work. Handy.

Once everyone has arrived and the mandatory greetings and handshakes have been given and received, we make our way to the sizeable classroom. It is far bigger than we need, has long, screened windows on either side and several of the usual white, three-bladed ceiling fans (which I hate – you'll find out why in Chapter Four).

Proceedings begin with each participant giving their name and why they are here. One guy is called 'Salami', which makes me smile. To him it's just his name and comes from the Arabic *'salaam'* meaning 'peace'; a nice name to be called, really. A more pertinent question here would be how on earth this term was given to thin, spicy sausages in the West!

We have ten men and four women taking part; a small but workable number. (I like to have a minimum of twelve on such occasions, and anything over thirty becomes too cumbersome). Most of them are Tem literacy workers and, surprisingly, only two actually describe themselves as musicians. This could be interesting – I usually have at least half the group being 'actual musicians', preferably more than that. I'm hoping that their level of education and advanced knowledge of the Tem language will compensate for any lack in musicianship. In any case, this is Africa and virtually everyone *does* music, whether they would classify themselves as an actual musician or not.

Following introductions, we go through the song genres which exist in Tem music. Here are the main ones listed:

> *Siríníya* – for praising someone
> *Kétékpé* – for rejoicing
> *Gúḿbe* – for rejoicing
> *Kewɔɔ* – for mourning/exaltation
> *Láwá* – for rejoicing
> *Simpa* – for rejoicing

Now, experience tells me that this list is way smaller than it ought to be, partly because we are in a larger town rather than a village, and partly because we have fewer musicians present. It is not uncommon to come up with at least thirty genres, and ones more closely linked to specific events than the above list (as was the case in Gando, even Baga). Nevertheless, it's a starting point and we can certainly make use of these genres for the new songs.

I note each genre on the board as they state them, doing my best with the *orthography*, but often needing their help in this. All the time, I am encouraging them to branch out and use some of the song styles they would not normally choose. I usually work with groups where there is a healthy mix of old and young, but this time they are almost all under thirty. This demographic will make it more tricky to resurrect some of the lesser-known traditional genres, as it tends to be the older folk who know and remember these best.

Once we have our genre list, I talk to them about composing and, in particular, how to create a good alphabet song. The aim is that even small children will be able to sing it, so it needs to be simple and catchy. It should also be a song which can be understood upon first hearing and which can easily be passed on to others. A key way to do this is to create an ear-catching refrain with a clear and simple message to draw people in.

I go on to suggest *three* types of alphabet song they could try. The first one is the classic 'Sesame Street' style:

> *A is for apple*
> *B is for book*
> *C is for cookie*

Secondly, they could do a song which requests a response:

> *What's the first letter of apple? A!*
> *What's the first letter of ball? B!*

The trouble with this (and the first type of song) is that not all letters of the Tem alphabet can be used at the start of a word, but there are ways around this, as you'll see later.

The third possibility would be to recite the different sounds of the alphabet in order. I do this kind less frequently, as you don't actually *learn* as much from it, especially if you are entirely illiterate to begin with.

As usual, I divide them into three groups and off they go to different locations around the compound to begin composing their songs.

The work of an ethnomusicologist during a composition workshop has been compared to that of a midwife during labour: you do everything you can to ensure a successful 'birth' and to make the whole process as painless as possible. However, you cannot *give birth* yourself; only wait patiently and be there to help out.

Many groups I've worked with compose very quickly; however, this is not the case today. The Tem are discussing, planning, thinking, writing down every word and – eventually – making musical sounds. It is indeed a slow delivery, but the end result will be all the better for it, I hope.

By midday the weather is beautifully sunny and hot – the kind of enveloping heat you can almost touch; penetrating your entire body and bathing you in warmth and light, something I've never experienced back in the

UK. Bulbuls, one of the most common – and bland – of West African birds, peck around on the path or soar up into the branches of the surrounding trees. Insects of various shapes, sizes and colours buzz and crawl everywhere, including on me!

The groups are still busy composing, but there has been little sound of any music yet. By lunchtime, the first three songs have more or less taken shape, so we reconvene to share the fruits of their labour. In order to check the songs' effectiveness, I hand out a sheet containing ten self-check questions for them to ponder upon. I gleaned this from a colleague who spent many years in Cameroon doing ethnomusicology, and have always been very grateful for it:

1.  *Is the song easy to learn and easy to sing?*
2.  *Can it be sung by men and women alike?*
3.  *Can children sing it too?*
4.  *In your opinion, will people enjoy singing it?*
5.  *Are the words easy to understand or are there ambiguities?*
6.  *Should the song be accompanied by dance or other gestures (such as hand claps)?*
7.  *Does the choice of genre work well with this song?*
8.  *What instruments could be used with this song?*
9.  *What do you learn when singing it?*
10. *Is the song too long or too short?*

The idea is to have a 'yes' answer to each question (except for the last three, where some kind of constructive answer is hoped for). None of this is rocket science, but the questions help iron out any potential pitfalls at an early stage and make for a better end result.

Each group has come up with a different kind of song in a different genre, which is great news. The first says: 'How do we read the letters of the Tem alphabet?' and goes on to list those occurring at the beginning, in the middle or at the end of different words. For example, *the sound 'B' is found in 'table'* or *the word 'bread' ends in 'D'*. Nice idea.

The second group has gone for a fun song which elicits the letter from those listening — always a good educational technique: 'The first letter of Apple is…A!'

The third song, though, is the most memorable by far, probably because it has a simple, catchy refrain which you cannot get out of your head. Because of this, I expect it to be the most successful and most widely used in the future. It goes like this:

> *A gɛ alaa*
> *B gɛ baba*
> *C gɛ caweele*

The 'C' here is pronounced 'Ch', like in many African languages. It means:

> A is for women
> B is for daddy
> C is for tortoise

This is the refrain, but the song continues through the entire Tem alphabet, listing three different items in each verse before returning with the refrain. Here are the next few for you – the choice of words used speaks volumes about the local culture:

| | |
|---|---|
| *D gɛ liiḍeé* | *D is for money* |
| *Ɖ gɛ ḍeére* | *Ɖ is for horse* |
| *E gɛ Elíya* | *E is for Elijah* |
| *Ɛ gɛ téɛré* | *Ɛ is for morning* |
| *F gɛ féḍɛ* | *F is for hoe* |
| *G gɛ gaarí* | *G is for ground cassava* |
| *Gb gɛ gbégídi* | *Gb is for bucket* |
| *H gɛ háma* | *H is for hammer* |
| *I gɛ ivéléwu* | *I is for witch* |
| *ɩ gɛ ɩzíre* | *ɩ is for eye* |
| *J gɛ jenté* | *J is for a 25 franc coin* |
| *K gɛ kéké* | *K is for peanuts* |

On the back of the euphoria which the creation of three great new songs has brought to the group, we break for lunch (under the *paillote*). After eating, I grab a few minutes to walk up the hill, past the watermelon ladies, to the market. If the song-writing goes well, we may begin recording tomorrow. I have just about enough batteries to run my equipment, but would like to get a few extras in case. (There is electricity on site, but this should never be relied upon in such circumstances).

A market, I find, has a similar atmosphere wherever you go in the world: the way the stalls are laid out, the parallel aisles, the noise, the size of each stall, the variety of what is on sale — these are all pretty similar from one country to another. However, there is still something very distinct and exciting about an African market. It stimulates all the senses: there are sounds, sights, textures and — most of all — smells. Many of these are less than pleasant and change every few seconds as you wander through its muddy labyrinth of stalls: onions, fish, soap, peanuts, urine, rotting vegetation, grilled chicken, lady's perfume, body odour, charcoal, raw meat, sewage… a veritable olfactory marathon! Eventually, amidst the hubbub, I find a stall selling the square nine volt batteries I need. Fake Duracells — hmmm, worth a try at least. They don't come cheap, but needs must and I leave with four in my pocket.

We continue work in the afternoon with the second category of song — tone patterns in Tem. The idea of these songs is to explain the idea of tones in speech so that Tem speakers understand how this works. As there are only two tones in Tem this shouldn't be too difficult, but their melodies will have to go in the same direction as the tonal words. An acute accent (like in *paté*) is used in Tem to denote a high tone; the lower tone then doesn't need any marking.

The first group composes a song about words which have a high tone followed by a low tone, such as *yélɛ* (egg), *páya* (pear) or *háma* (hammer). Another group does the opposite (i.e. low to high), with words like *milá* (millet) or *jenté* (a 25 franc coin) and the last group does words which are *high-high* or *low-low*. Now they're in the swing of things, they compose these songs faster than the first set and are just about done by the end of the day.

The next day is Friday, a holy day for Muslims, and the day breaks with calls to prayer resounding from each of Sokodé's numerous mosques. My students, punctual as ever, whizz in through the gateway on their shiny motorbikes. Some seem a little unsure when riding their new acquisitions and, as I watch one of them swerving slightly as he attempts to control the bike, I wonder whether the Swedish charity provided them with driving lessons too.

The tone songs are finished and the participants are eager to begin work on the third category of songs: Tem grammar. For these, I am indebted to experts present (including Ben and Linda), who are able to explain the Tem rules to be included in the songs; not knowing the language myself means I cannot easily do this. Furthermore, the complexity of the rules makes them somewhat baffling to me. Here's the briefing I received prior to the workshop:

> *For an accomplished action, an 'n' precedes a high tone. For an unaccomplished action, an imitating vowel with an imitating tone followed by a high tone (the vowel becomes identical to the preceding vowel, as does the tone. The floating tone is placed on the following syllable).*

All clear now, then?! Good!

Thankfully (and somewhat astonishingly), my participants understand the rules and get straight on with the task of composing. By mid-morning, the songs are done and we gather under the *paillote* for 'show and tell', once again referring to the list of ten questions. We get to question five ('Are the words easy to understand or are there ambiguities?') and one of the composers makes an important statement:

"Monsieur, we understand the meaning of the song very well, but that's because we're literacy workers. What we don't know is whether everyday folk on the street will understand it."

Fair point – I hadn't thought of that. I've scarcely begun to think of a response to his question when another guy pipes up with:

"I've got an idea! Why don't we go and find an everyday person on the street and invite them to come and listen to the song?"

I've heard worse ideas and, although it will cause a bit of a disruption, I figure it will be a good way to test out the effectiveness of the songs. Before I can say, 'Great idea, mate', he's off on his shiny red *moto*, on the quest for an 'average person' from the streets Sokodé. We await his return, singing through the rest of the songs to pass the time. After a good half hour, the roar of his bike is heard coming up the driveway and he reappears with a youngish, skinny, everyday-looking kind of chap. "He's done a good job!" I think to myself.

"It was really hard to find someone," he says apologetically, "as most people I asked didn't want to leave their work." That's understandable, especially when it means riding pillion with an under-experienced, turbo-charged motorcyclist you've known for barely thirty seconds. Our *everyday fellow* is probably around twenty-six years old and dressed in jeans and a tee-shirt. I can't imagine how overwhelming it must be for him as we avidly quiz him to make sure he's not a closet linguistics expert in his spare time. We find out that he's actually an electrician by profession and that he can neither read nor write in Tem. Perfect! Just the kind of person we're looking for (although I hope he does learn to read and write one day soon). The group sings him one of the songs, after which he's 'grilled' about its content. He thinks for a moment and then mutters a few phrases to the group in Tem. I'm eager to know if our experiment has worked:

"What's he saying? What's he saying?"

"He says that the song talks about unaccomplished actions and that you need to put the letter 'n' before a high tone."

Result! Onto the next song, and the next. For each one our human guinea pig comes up with the goods, showing a clear understanding of the main points in the songs. Everyone is very happy, even blokey himself. In fact, as a token gesture of gratitude, we invite him to stay for morning break, where he enjoys a complimentary bottle of *Fizzy Pamplemousse*.

Once break is over, and whilst the groups are refining their nine songs further, I take a walk around the compound. After a slow start, the composing has happened quickly and so I'm planning to begin recording this afternoon. It's always wiser to start this sooner rather than later, even if it means setting up and taking down the equipment twice. You can never tell what hitches – technical, musical, animal or meteorological – may hinder recording, but, as you know by now, something usually does!

I wander round the compound clapping my hands loudly in strategic places to get a feel for the acoustics. Too much echo will make for a poor quality recording, so I'm looking for a place with as *dry* a sound as possible. Of course, an indoor location would seem a more logical choice in some ways (less outside noise, fewer hindrances from the weather, no direct sunlight). However, African halls, churches or large rooms are generally a poor choice for recording, as the bare walls, tin roofs and cement floors all create way too much reverberation. So, unless you travel with a couple of dozen mattresses or several hundred egg boxes, it is probably best to avoid such locations. I wander over to the *paillote,* which could have been an option, but it is still a bit too echoey because of its tin roof. It is also a little too close to the main road with its noisy, honking vehicles.

Finally, I settle for a grassy area right at the back of the campus away from the buildings (whose walls can create an echo, even from the outside). There are also several large trees here, so we can have shade – very important with midday temperatures of over 30 Celsius. The only possible fly in the ointment I can see is the presence of lots of crunchy, dry leaves on the ground. However, once people are in place this shouldn't be a big problem, as long as they stand still.

I have the equipment all set up after lunch and try out my new nine volt batteries by putting the two terminals on my wet tongue: if I get a small electric shock, they are good! I try the first one: nothing. Second battery: nothing. Third and fourth: nothing! They're all complete duds. I look at the 'best before' date on them and it is two years ago! I've been done, hook line and sinker (and, in Africa, virtually no chance of a refund – you just put it down to experience). The musicians arrive and we're ready to roll. I set them up so that everyone has shade from trees and we do our first practice run. Once the sound is mixed, it's time to record.

We've got a decent percussion section, including a couple of rectangular frame drums, held at the back with one hand and played with the other hand. It reminds me of the Irish *bodhrán* in its construction and how it is held (although the shape and playing technique couldn't be more different). This kind of drum is quite common in West Africa, its shape giving more of a low *thud* than the bright, clear sound achieved by a conventional round drum. It's all to do with *tension,* which can be evenly applied to a round skin but not to a square one, because it has corners – it's the same principal which dictates that aeroplane windows are round. As though to compensate for this lack of contrast in their sound, the two frame drums are of different sizes, to give two distinct pitches: the larger one, resting on the player's knee, reaches all the way up to his bottom lip; the smaller one scarcely reaches armpit height.

As well as these two, there is a selection of other percussion instruments, not all of which are played for every song. A pair of tall painted blue *congas* on a metal stand, a small goblet-shaped drum (a bit like a *djembe*) and a larger double-headed drum with a single snare across one end. Finally, there is the *talking drum:* one of the most interesting, and commonly found membranophones in West Africa. Shaped like a sand-timer (but up to two feet long), it is placed under the arm and squeezed against the player's ribcage using the upper arm – rather like a bagpipe player would squeeze his windbag. At the same time, one end of the drum is hit with a curved stick held in the opposite hand. The squeezing tightens a few dozen leather chords running the length of the instrument, and these in turn cause both heads of the drum to tighten, thereby raising the pitch of the instrument. The opposite happens when the player stops squeezing. The tighter you squeeze, the higher the pitch! It is called a talking drum because of the pitch undulations, which resemble speech. It is also known as the *pressure drum* or even the *armpit drum.*

Ben and Linda have been popping in and out throughout the workshop and turn up this afternoon with a young, newly arrived short-termer, fresh off the bus from Lomé. Cathy, I discover, is from Cambridgeshire in England, a stone's throw from my home county of Bedfordshire. A fellow Brit, how exciting! Shame there isn't a teapot and some crumpets handy, really.

Cathy has come here to work on creating a Tem dictionary for the next couple of years. I have to be unsociable for most of the time, as we're in full swing with the recordings, but we manage to exchange greetings and chat a bit between songs. I begin with one of *the* most predictable questions for such an occasion:

"So, is this your first time in Africa?"

"Yes, kind of. But I also spent a year on an island called Reunion, in the Indian Ocean."

"*La Réunion?!*"

"You've heard of it?"

"Heard of it? It's one of my favourite places in the whole wide world!"

*La Réunion*, or Reunion Island, is a tiny volcanic island between Madagascar and Mauritius, and is now a French overseas department. I know it well as I spent a year of university there, studying French as well as music at the conservatoire. A truly amazing place, with gorgeous beaches, an active volcano, waterfalls like paradise and fascinating Creole people – but all that is for another book some time. I'm just surprised to be meeting someone else who's been there or even knows it exists! And I don't imagine there are more than a couple of hundred Brits on the planet who've ever visited 'my island in the sun'! Cathy and I reminisce about this wonderful island, the places we visited, the food, the language, the people, the delicious cuisine. We even muster up a few Creole greetings for each other:

"*Oté mo' ti caf! Koman y lé?*"

"*Lé là! Douceman, douceman, mo' zanfan!*"

("Hello matey! How are you?" "I'm fine, take it easy kiddo!")

Meanwhile, we have a couple of songs in the can already and the recording is going well. The sound of the calls to prayer from nearby minarets echoes out at various intervals and we have to just stop and wait. These never last more than a minute or so, allowing us to quickly resume recording. By the end of the day, we have four of the nine songs recorded, which is a good start.

Tonight I'm staying in a local hotel as Cathy will be moving into my old room at Ben & Linda's. My hotel is just round the corner from the weaving centre, which will be handy, although by car the road is rough and steep, punctuated with gullies and rocks everywhere. No sweat for *The Beast*, mind…

The hotel is fairly typical of any mid-to-low priced African hotel I've stayed in: basic but comfortable, with dark narrow corridors and the room numbers painted in white on matt grey doors. I've never understood why so many hotels here paint their doors grey – it is, after all, the dullest 'colour' one can imagine. Maybe grey paint is cheaper, or perhaps it seems like a good neutral choice to them. It certainly doesn't show the dirt like white, or even black, would.

I take hold of my key, with its typically enormous carved wooden fob, and unlock the door. My room has a somewhat gloomy feel to it: mouldy-looking walls, a small window and, in the corner, a large, dark wardrobe of almost Narnian proportions. The low, double bed looks comfy enough, but – alas – is not equipped with a mosquito net. The long, thin en-suite has a classic African shower made from a metal pipe running up the wall. I try it, and the water works, although the single cold tap on the sink is a tad wobbly and there is neither a towel nor any loo roll (two shortcomings quickly rectified by the hotel staff, I'm glad to say).

Because of the lack of mosquito net, I have a somewhat torturous night. To make matters worse, there is no mesh screening on the window either, and so the wee beasties feast away on me all night. I've lit one of those green spiral-shaped mosquito coils, which smoke for hours and are meant to repel the evil insects. However, these mozzies seem impervious to the smoke, even if I'm coughing and spluttering with it. I once read that burning one of these coils in your room equates to having a chain smoker sitting by your bedside, lighting up seventy times throughout the night. I'm just hoping it's a friendly chain-smoker who doesn't make too much noise drinking beer at the same time! I try pulling the sheet over me, but it is so hot I just end up sweating profusely, which attracts even more mosquitoes. Aarrgghhh!!!

I awake the next morning feeling somewhat jaded and covered in nasty bites. Thankfully, we have a later start today as it's Saturday, so I enjoy a much overdue lie-in once my nocturnal biters have gone away to sleep off their sanguine banquet.

Breakfast time and it's the standard Nescafé with bread and jam. This is one of the ways of differentiating between a budget hotel and a slightly more upmarket one in Africa. In a 'posher' place, you'd probably get an omelette and maybe some pineapple or mango. You'd also stand a reasonable chance of having filter coffee, rather than a sachet of instant powder with a jug of warm water. Air-conditioning in your room is also a prerequisite in the nicer hotels, whereas I had just a floor fan. I've stayed in both kinds of hotel – and in ones far worse than this – so I'm not complaining. It's all part of the rich experience of life on the African continent!

I'm the only person in the dining room this morning; a large open space with dozens of chairs stacked in one corner and, at the other end, a television is talking to itself, chuntering away in French about the latest goings on in Israel, Sudan, America, Iraq…

I saunter on down to the centre around ten o'clock and the folks are busy doing orthography checking of the five remaining songs. They're almost done, so we plan to start the second session of recording as soon as possible. I return to yesterday's location to set up the recording equipment once more. As usual, I carry virtually none of it myself as Africans are always quick to help a white man in this way, almost as if they consider us incapable of carrying anything heavier than a briefcase.

I'm halfway through setting up when a minor disaster occurs: in the adjoining compound a very loud chainsaw grinds into action. I rush to the boundary wall and peer over – a couple of guys are cutting up large pieces of wood on a building site. Oh pants! What are we going to do?

I'd never envisaged *this*. My able helpers are still with me and a couple of them volunteer to go round and ask whether the builders could possibly stop sawing for the next couple of hours. I wait patiently, whilst continuing – in faith – to set up the equipment. Five minutes later, my blokeys return.

"They said they cannot stop the sawing."

"They can't?!" I reply.

"No, they say it's their job and that they cannot simply stop working for two hours, or their boss won't be happy."

"Fair enough, I suppose, but what are we going to do about the recording?"

Silence. What an absolute disaster. How can we even attempt to make a field recording with this row next door? I think of alternative options: find another location…wait until the evening…try and edit the saw out post-recording. No, that would never work. Then one of the guys pipes up with:

"They did say they'd be having a lunch break from twelve till one…"

"An hour's lunch break?"

"Yes, that's what they said."

"And no sawing the whole time?"

"I suppose not, Monsieur."

I do some more thinking: the maximum number of songs I usually get done in an hour is four, sometimes only three. But this is with run-throughs, mistakes and technical hitches. If we were really organized, we could just about get all five done in an hour, I figure.

"Okay, go and tell the musicians to get themselves into position ready for recording as soon as possible."

So, by 11:15 or so, they're all in place and ready to record. Whilst the chainsaw rasps away over the wall, we sing through the remaining five songs one by one and I mix the sound as best I can in anticipation. At 12:01 precisely, the sawing stops. I wait a few seconds, in case it starts up again, then, when I am convinced this is actually their break, I say:

"*Okay, tout le monde.* Let's do song number five right now!"

Recording has begun at 12:02 and the first song is in the can by 12:07. For most songs I record, five minutes is a good duration. If it gets too long, I give a hand signal that they should start rounding up – this could be particularly useful today. We soldier on and, remarkably, all five of the remaining songs are done by three minutes to one. I think the urgency of the situation rubbed off on the musicians and they knew it was a *now or never* situation. Seconds after completing the last song, the chainsaw whirrs back into action and our silence is shattered. Nobody minds this time, as the work is done and the songs are finished!

Ben has organized a closing ceremony for the afternoon, where friends, colleagues and family members can come along and hear our new songs. We choose one song from each of the three categories and perform to them. This is followed by speeches – an almost mandatory requirement in Africa. I give one too, of course, thanking everyone for their willingness to be involved in this important project and for all their efforts during the workshop. They thank me back for mine and hand me a small gift: a stripy woven zip-up bag to put my equipment in (wonder where they got that from?!)

After dinner that evening, I crack on with editing the songs, transferring them from my digital recorder to my laptop computer and then working through each song using an editing programme called 'Audacity'. The recordings have come out well, with no glaring errors or glitches to speak of. This makes my job much easier, and means I really only need to make sure the beginnings and endings are tidy and check the overall sound level of each song. This takes about an hour. Now the real work starts: before leaving tomorrow, I will make eighty cassettes of the songs, using my fast copier. But before doing that I have to make a master cassette, which is done in 'real time'. So I rig up my newly-acquired tape deck from the shack in Bohicon and get started. Once this is done, I put the master into the fast copier and four blank cassettes into the remaining slots. It's an amazing machine, which makes the four copies in under five minutes (both sides at once). Very clever, but to make eighty will take me a further couple of hours, so I'm in for a long night…

Sunday morning and, once again, I wake covered in mosquito bites.  I must remember to bring my own net with me in future.  I make an early start to avoid the traffic and heat on my six-hour drive back.  *The Beast* has been parked in the gated hotel courtyard, so the guard opens the gates for me.

"Monsieur, I washed your car for you last night."

A hint for some cash, without a doubt, but to me the grey Land Rover looks as dirty as it was four days ago.

"Are you sure?"

"*Oui, Monsieur*, I cleaned your car for you.  *C'est bon, n'est-ce pas?*"

It's first thing in the morning and I haven't even had breakfast yet, so I'm in no mood for triflers.

"No, you didn't clean it.  It's still dirty."

"Monsieur, I got up early and cleaned your car."

Deadlock.  I have two choices: I can just drive off as he clearly hasn't done the work, or I can give him the benefit of the doubt and pay him something (as he may, conceivably, have shown a grubby cloth to the paintwork for a few seconds).  I hand him a smallish coin and drive out, down the gullied road and left at the watermelons.  Past the incongruous Total station, up the hill with its rancid open drains and out of town, saying goodbye to the market which will always remind me of dud batteries and random electricians.

Back in fumy Cotonou two weeks later, I go down with malaria.  I've had the disease four or five times before, so am used to the symptoms: the shivers, the aches and pains, the sweats and fevers, along with a total lack of energy.  It's never a pleasant experience, but modern medicines mean that – with prompt diagnosis and treatment – recovery rates are good and, thank the Lord, I do recover in order to continue the adventures in this book.  However, I can't help wondering whether one of those Sokodé mozzies was the culprit which brought me down.

# Chapter Four

# Tin Roofs and Trance Drums

*The Bogo People of Western Togo*

Did I ever tell you about the worst day of my life?  It was just horrendous, but the whole family was grateful for God's grace and protection during such a traumatic event.  More about that later…

My final destination this time is in *southern* Togo, so I've taken a different route, heading west along the coast from Cotonou all the way to the Togolese border, then on to Lomé, Togo's capital.  It's a decidedly wet morning and *The Beast* is splashing along all the way, bouncing in and out of puddles. The road is pretty well-tarmacked, mind, and relatively obstacle-free compared with the northern route (at least, once I'm out of the crazy urban sprawl of Cotonou – almost as bad whichever direction you take).  It's only a couple of hours' drive to Lomé, but the border crossing often takes a good 45 minutes, partly because of the sheer volume of vehicles and pedestrians using this route, and partly due to the somewhat cumbersome set-up of the place.  I've got it all sussed out now, but it was decidedly tricky to begin with.  In fact, the first time I came this way, a colleague drew me a map of the entire border zone, with detailed instructions of what to do where! Without such a guide, I really don't know how any newcomer would have a clue.  It goes something like this:

1. *Pass through the first barrier and park on the left, perpendicular to the road.*

2.  *Go into the small hut across the road and show your passport (make sure it gets stamped).*

3.  *Now go and sit in the larger hut, also to the right, and give your personal and car details (which will be written in a large book).*

4.  *In the same building, go to the small window at the rear and show your driver's licence. That is the end of the formalities for the Benin side.*

5.  *Now get back in your car, drive fifty yards over 'no man's land' stopping at the barrier which is 'automatically' raised by a man in an adjacent hut pulling on a rope.*

6.  *Now park up again, this time in the middle of the road but always between the white lines.*

7.  *The Togo side (slightly more streamlined than the Benin side) has two buildings: The one on the left is for passport details (sit on one of the long, wooden benches and await your turn, beneath an almost life-size photo of 'Son Excellence Fauré Gnassigbé, Président de la République Togolaise').*

8.  *Once your turn comes, the border police officer in charge will hand you the book and you have to fill in all the details yourself. (Name, nationality, profession, coming from, going to, address in Togo, purpose of journey etc.)  When travelling with my whole family, this takes quite some time!*

9.  *After this, the building to the right is for giving your vehicle details. You can now enter Togo.  Phew!*

Early on in my border crossing days, I remember queuing for a good ten minutes at this last hut. When I finally got to give my car details (Land Rover, 1990, grey, one on board), I was then asked my destination.

"Lomé."

"Lomé?" came the surprised response.

"Yes."

"Then why did you stand in *this* queue?"

"To give you my vehicle details, as required."

"Monsieur, you should stand in *that* queue there for westbound traffic; this one is for eastbound traffic headed for Cotonou."

So, back to square one, more queuing and more details. The two log books ('east' and 'west') are right next to each other and there are no signs telling anyone where to stand for what; that would make life much too predictable!

The torrential rain I've had to endure on the journey so far is actually a help to me at this point; the border crossing is faster than normal, to avoid people getting drenched whilst queuing. I'm grateful I brought my brolly, though, which keeps most of the rain off me and my documents.

On the other side of the border, the road immediately becomes bumpier and the whole place seems more dreamy and, in some ways, less developed. It nevertheless has a more aesthetically pleasing feel, with groves of palm trees, pretty lagoons and tumbledown colonial buildings, today with rain gushing from their semi-dilapidated roofs. It's less than an hour's drive from here to the capital, and I'm feeling ready for my breakfast!

Entering Lomé there are several large factories, including a huge one producing cooking oil ("it smells like a *chippy* from miles off"), followed by the bustling port with more smoky lorries precariously edging their way in and out, splashing through the deep, muddy puddles in the process.

Although Cotonou and Lomé are two West African capitals very close to one another, they could scarcely be more different in many other ways. Cotonou is a fast-growing, dynamic, chaotic mass of commerce and enterprise; Lomé is a provincial-feeling, tree-lined *small town* sort of place in need of much repair. People used to say: '*Lomé la belle, Cotonou poubelle*' (Lomé the beautiful, Cotonou the dustbin), but that was a good couple of decades ago. Democracy and the ensuing political stability in Benin have led to huge investment in the country as well as the involvement of dozens of charities.

Peter Biddlecombe described Cotonou as "a giant jigsaw puzzle with half the pieces missing,"[7] but that was back in the early 90s, and now most of these pieces have been filled with hotels, banks, restaurants, supermarkets and apartment blocks. Meanwhile, Lomé – once known as one of the jewels of the West African coast – seems to have lost many of the pieces it once had and is, today, a shadow of its former self. Hotels which look as though they haven't seen a lick of paint since 1970, old tin-roofed shacks, more potholes and very little sign of new development anywhere. Compared with Cotonou's upbeat optimism, Lomé has an air of slight despair and all the dynamism of a cold rice pudding.

In terms of layout and sheer charm though, Lomé still wins out. Its road system, designed by the Germans, is – predictably – well thought out; a semi-circular road runs from the coast to the far west of the city, up through the town and back down to the sea on the east side, forming a sideways 'D' shape with the coast road. Known locally as *Le Boulevard Circulaire* (in spite of being only half a circle), all the main roads run off it, like spokes on a bicycle wheel. Clever!

I pull into the Hotel Sarakawa, a lovely place located in the middle of the straight line of the 'D'. (If you've been following so far, you'll know that this means it's by the beach). I battle through the torrential downpour and make my way to the bar area in the huge, high-ceilinged hotel vestibule. Time for breakfast!

"*Un grand café au lait, un croissant et un pain aux raisins, s'il vous plaît.*"

"*Tout de suite, Monsieur.*"

I tuck into my delicious pastries and warm, strong coffee, admiring the wooden carvings and wall hangings that adorn this, the *poshest* hotel in Togo. Given the one-hour time difference between Benin and Togo, it is still only 8:00am, even though I've been on the road for three hours already!

My journey from here will be another four or so hours north to a small village near the Ghana border, to work with the Bogo people (who speak Igo).

A few weeks ago, I received the following e-mail inviting me to work there:

**From:** Isabelle Kwadi

**Date:** September 22

**To:** Rob Baker

**Subject:** We need you!

*Dear Rob,*

*We are interested in the work you are doing, and will be very pleased to work with you next year…We are the smallest ethnic group in Togo (about 6,000 people) and are losing our traditional songs in favour of Ewe songs. We will be giving you details of what we really want to do, depending on your availability.*

*Warm greetings in Him,*

*Isabelle*


I was immediately struck by the potential impact I could have on these people; so few in number and their local arts are slowly dying out. A visit from me could therefore fulfil at least *four* goals:

1.  To create new songs in the local style.
2.  To increase Biblical knowledge and understanding through the creation of new songs.
3.  To preserve the local music from extinction.
4.  To celebrate Bogo art forms and cultivate an attitude of pride and ownership towards these.


The village of *Sassanou* is located in a small valley in the southern half of Togo, only 500 yards from the Ghanaian border. Today, I will travel as far as the Baptist Hospital in *Tsiko* (pronounced 'Cheeko'), at the base of the mountain range which separates it from *Sassanou*. Early tomorrow I will meet Mrs Kwadi at the hospital and we will travel together to the village, a good hour's drive from there.


The road north to Tsiko is pretty decent and getting out of Lomé isn't nearly as chaotic as leaving Cotonou. Passing through numerous small and somewhat waterlogged villages, I finally reach the pretty town of Kpalime, surrounded by picturesque mountains and lush greenery (particularly so today). Kpalime has a pleasant main street with a pretty Catholic church at one end. There's also a centre where blind people learn arts and crafts, and a few nice eating places. I opt for lunch at *Chez Fanny*, a delightful little place run by a Frenchman. It's not the cheapest place in town, but the food is always good and the welcome warm. *Chez Fanny* is also a small hotel, with a handful of comfortable rooms for travellers such as myself. I'm hoping to stay here on my way back home, but decide not to book a room as I am not yet sure of which day I will be passing through. Hopefully, there will be space when I do. After a succulent *steak au poivre avec pommes sautées*, it's time to continue my journey.

Shortly after leaving Kpalime, I turn left and head due west down a narrower, more bumpy road. After about half an hour, I arrive at the *Hôpital Baptiste Biblique*, an amazing hidden treasure, quite literally in the middle of nowhere. It has a pleasant guesthouse with air conditioning, good meals, tap water you can drink, a nice lounge area with a piano (of sorts) and even a small swimming pool! My family and I have come here a few times on holiday and have always had a wonderful time.

However, our first visit to the hospital was not for leisure purposes, but for an emergency visit with our then six year old daughter, Ruth. Whilst at a conference at the centre in Kara, a teenage boy was playing with Ruth and accidentally lifted her up in the air directly beneath a quickly-rotating metal ceiling fan. The rest of the family was sat next to the fan eating dinner and it took us a few seconds to realize what had happened. It was when Ruth began to cry that I noticed the blood pouring from the top of her head and the reality of what had just occurred hit me.

"Quick, someone call an ambulance!" I desperately called out.

Of course, there were no ambulances in Kara, but thankfully there was a missionary doctor living just over the road. We rushed Ruth into the adjacent kitchen, lying her down on the large central table, blood still pouring everywhere, looks of concern and horror on the faces of colleagues and friends. My wife, Lois, fainted almost as soon as the accident happened and was laid out on the kitchen floor unconscious for almost half an hour! I tried to comfort Ruth as the doctor took a razor to her head to clear away some hair. Thankfully, some colleagues had taken our other two, Madelaine and Micah, away to watch a film in their room. Ruth was uncomfortable, but – somewhat surprisingly – not in too much pain. She also seemed to be fully conscious and aware of her surroundings, which was good news.

Upon further examination after clearing away the hair, we could see that her head had two deep semi-circular cuts: one just behind the forehead, the other on her crown, each about two inches across. The doctor lady had initially hoped to use adhesive strips to pull the wounds back together. However, she could now see how deep the rear cut was and that stitches were definitely going to be necessary.

The nearest decent hospital was the Baptist Hospital in Tsiko, but this was a five-hour drive away. Driving at night in Togo can be dangerous and is not recommended, so we had to wait until five o'clock the next morning before we could leave. Meanwhile, the doctor patched her head up as best she could with bandages and tape. Lois and I then took turns to wake every hour through the night and shine a light into Ruth's eyes to make sure her pupils were dilating – a sign that the brain is still working properly.

We made it to the hospital in *Tsiko* by ten o'clock the next morning and Ruth was in theatre by midday. The first thing the American surgeon did was to shave the entire central part of her head – giving her a 'balding man' haircut. It turned out that her head was cut right down to the skull in both places, but with no fractures. She needed 64 double stitches in total; 32 internally and the same number on the outside.

By the next day, Ruth was up and walking about, with a hat she would get used to wearing every day for the next few months. Amazingly, she'd only had to have one dose of *paracetamol* the whole time! Thankfully, both scars are beneath her hairline and she incurred no long-term damage.

It is strange that, at such times of trauma, God seems closer than ever and that, although it remains the worst day of my life, we look back on that time and know how much we were being held up in prayer by friends across the planet.

So, I arrive once again at the Baptist Hospital, get my room key and crash out, treating myself to an hour or two of air conditioning in this warm, humid environment. I wake up in time for the evening meal, and sit down around a dining table with some of the doctors and other staff from the hospital, all from the USA. It's nice to get to know these folk, who are always very welcoming and up for a good chat. We all tuck into our *sloppy Joes* – an American delicacy unknown in the UK. Like hot dogs but with minced beef instead of sausages. As we eat, the conversation – predictably – turns to medical issues, covering thrilling topics such as gall bladder removal ("the old fashioned way") and spinal tap insertion! Such an education for the non-scientific likes of myself, and all over dinner too! After eating, I play a few tunes on their slightly honky-tonk piano before heading back to my room. The beds here are not equipped with mosquito nets, but this time (not wanting a repeat of Sokodé) I've come prepared! I proudly erect my newly-acquired fold-up mosquito net – shaped like a small tent, with two curved rods holding it up. I place it on my bed and carefully unzip the side opening and crawl in. Should be in for a good night's sleep!

As it turns out, I wake up the next morning having had a lousy night indeed! No fault of the guesthouse (or the mosquitoes), but I think I'm still suffering from PMT: *Post Malarial Tiredness*! I had malaria again a week or so ago, and always find I suffer from headaches, neck ache, and general exhaustion for a good few days afterwards. Given the six-hour journey yesterday, it's no wonder I'm so tired.

Mrs Kwadi said she'd meet me at 10:00am at the hospital (not as early as I'd anticipated), so this gives me time to play some more tunes on the *old Joanna*. I end up with a mini audience around the piano, asking for requests and the whole thing turns into an impromptu sing-along!

Ten o' clock comes and goes, but Mrs Kwadi does not. I call her at 10:20am to see what is happening. Apparently, her car is overheating, so she has stopped near Kpalime to let it cool down. She hopes to be on her way soon and should be there within an hour. At 11:30am there is still no sign of her, so I ring again. The bad news is that her car has totally broken down this time; the good news is that it was obliging enough to break down just in front of the hospital! I rush to meet her there and we eventually get the hospital's mechanic to come and look at the car. The first thing he tries is turning the ignition key, but the car will not start. He then opens the bonnet, stares intently at the engine for literally five minutes, then removes the radiator cap and fills it up with water. Still the car will not start. He pumps the accelerator, checks the battery terminals and asks:

"Is there any petrol in the tank?"

By now it's gone midday and the villagers must be wondering where we are (as this constitutes a late arrival, even by local standards). The sun is hot and we're all getting tired. In the end, we decide to leave the car to be investigated (and hopefully repaired), whilst Mrs Kwadi gets a lift over the mountain with me in *The Beast*. Her 'assistant', Jacques, is also travelling with us; he's from the village and is therefore a handy chap to know. So, after transferring around twenty yams and a large sack of rice to my car, we're finally on our way.

Left out of the hospital entrance and the road immediately climbs uphill. The ascent is a steep one, but the tremendous view from the top makes it all seem worthwhile. This is definitely a 'first gear up, first gear down' mountain road, with narrow hairpin bends, uneven surfaces and poor visibility. Now, at least there are no trucks on this road (they'd never make it), but the sheer gradient and angle of the bends more than compensate! To make the climb even more exciting, vehicles coming downhill towards us tend to switch their engines off to save fuel. Cars and motorbikes alike, all coasting downhill, blissfully unaware of the hazardous effect this could have on their braking ability.

As I edge my way around one of the more acute bends, Mrs Kwadi lets me into a secret:

"Rob, the road back down on the other side is even worse than this."

Great! That's something to look forward to then.

We reach the top and the road flattens out. We're on the *Danyi Plain*, one of the prettiest parts of Togo. Even the villages you pass through seem well-ordered, pleasant places: square buildings made of earth, but with tin roofs and tidy wooden shutters, blossoming red flame trees, friendly stalls selling fruit and vegetables, pretty yellow hedgerows and majestic palm trees – it all seems very civilised. As we missed lunch due to the car incident, we stop at a small convent on the mountain and Mrs Kwadi buys ten yoghurts and some biscuits from the shop. I also buy some delicious sugar–coated peanuts, good for an energy boost and extremely moreish.

The road back down the other side of the mountain is indeed worse. For a start, it's about half the width; little more than six feet wide in places. Secondly, the surface is very poor, with numerous potholes and loose stones. At one point, we head through a complete tunnel of green, with a sheer drop to one side and a jagged, vertical rock face to the other. Rocks like this would have bolts through them or netting over them in the West; no such reassurance here – so I'm hoping they stay intact for the next few minutes!

As we descend the sinuous track, glancing down at the canopy of trees and vegetation beneath us, Jacques shares an interesting fact with me:

"The Bogo used to live up on the mountain, but the Ewe people drove us out."

"Really?"

"Yes. Now the Bogo all live in the valley instead."

"And when did they drive you out?"

"About 400 years ago."

So, hardly recent history, but interesting background information all the same!

By the time we finally reach the bottom of this lush, green valley, the tyres on *The Beast* have taken a fair beating from the road; the sharp stones have made gashes in the sides and I'm fearful they may not last the duration of my return journey. From here, it's not long before we reach the village of Sassanou. We pull in at one of the first houses in the village, a 'posh' concrete house with a flat roof and a garden at the front. Within seconds, the car is surrounded by a couple of dozen ladies, all singing and rejoicing, before I've even stepped out of the car! As I do so, they approach me, smiling, singing and clapping all the time. I can't help noticing that most of them are missing at least half their teeth. At the end of their jolly song, they all give out a high pitched 'Eeeee' and one of the ladies produces a large necklace made of round, whitish stones with dashes of colour on them. She proudly places it around my neck, as though I were an Olympic medallist, and they all begin to cheer. Wow – what a nice start to my time here! As this is rural Africa, nobody is tapping their watch or asking 'why are you so late?' They're just pleased to see us at last!

Festivities over and I'm taken through the village towards the church. This place really is idyllic: a small valley surrounded by abundant vegetation and magnificent mountains in almost every direction. Just one narrow lane runs through the village for traffic; a network of tiny footpaths provides access to the rest of the houses. As far as I can tell, mine is the only car in the whole place, although there are a few motorbikes about.

In Britain, a place of such beauty as this would be overrun with tourists. There'd be *Bed & Breakfasts*, tea rooms, pubs, and shops selling 'Camping Gaz', Kendal mint cake, waxed jackets and water-resistant trousers with way too many pockets in them. There'd also be a visitor centre from whence one could choose a range of carefully colour-coded footpaths of varying length and difficulty. Well, nice as such things are, I'm actually relieved that Sassanou has thus far been spared any tourism and, as such, remains virtually unspoilt.

The church is a long, rectangular building with a tin roof, situated a few feet from the main road up a slight slope, surrounded by palm trees, mango trees and teak trees. Behind the building is a small bell tower and to one side is a large, flat football field, identifiable by two white goal posts at either end.  I enter the long, echoey building, which quickly fills up with scores of villagers – more than I'd anticipated or planned for!

In one corner of the church, right at the back, is an old harmonium: a kind of simple organ, played by pumping bellows with two foot-pedals.  It has certainly seen better days – several of its keys are damaged or missing and the whole thing looks good for the scrap heap.  I doubt it has been played for several decades.  For a moment, I stop and imagine a young, keen, American missionary almost a century ago, making their way down the sheer mountain road to Sassanou with this instrument on the back of a cart.  And all in the aim of spreading the Gospel more effectively!  Well, I'm sure the organ did help reach people, but not in a way that would have particularly made sense to them.  Western hymns bear little resemblance to indigenous African music and often hindered people's understanding of the song words.  I'm here years later to help redress this balance, so that the people of Sassanou can finally worship God in a way which makes complete sense to them.

So, teaching begins and, as is often the case, I am working with an interpreter so that everyone can understand.  However, the lady translating seems to be saying about three times as much as I am; maybe it's just a long-winded language!  I quickly learn that the Bogo only have the four gospels translated into their own language.  Some of the verses I was going to give them were from other books of the Bible, so some last minute modifications will be necessary on my part.

We soon move on to discussing the song genres which exist in Bogo culture.  Now, as you've seen in the first three chapters, most ethnic groups can name at least a dozen different genres they know: songs for weddings, funerals, rejoicing, sowing, harvesting, hunting and so on.  Even a list of as many as forty or fifty different genres is not uncommon. Today, however, the Bogo come up with a grand total of four! And to top it all, two of them are for women only; the other two almost exclusively for men.  Here they are:

*Ikawo* - sung by women to express joy

*Iyaya* - sung by women at funerals to express joy

*Okpaja* - sung after hunting or after harvest, mostly by men

*Atungba* - used when a new chief is enthroned. Men sing and play whilst the women dance

This is quite sad; what has happened to all the other genres which surely existed in times past? The answer is that they have probably died out because nobody did anything to preserve them. You see, the *Ewe* (roughly pronounced 'eh-vay') are a much larger, more dominant ethnic group, occupying land from the coast all the way up to Bogo land and beyond. And so, Ewe culture has encroached upon Bogo culture, causing the latter to decline. Even in their churches, the Bogo sing songs in Ewe, not in their mother tongue, and they all speak Ewe as a second language. That said, they are also very proud of their 'Bogo-ness' and would, if they could, maintain all aspects of their own culture, as it is part of their heritage and very identity. So, I'm eager to make use of these four genres for song composition; not only will the songs enable Bogo people to understand the Bible in a relevant and clear way, they will also help preserve a key part of Bogo culture.

As the Bogo only have the four gospels, all songs composed will be based upon verses from these books. "Why can't you just get someone to translate verses from the other books?" I hear you ask. Well, firstly it would be less useful as the songs would encourage them to read books of the Bible that don't yet exist in their language. Secondly, Bible translation is not an 'off the cuff' affair; it can take up to fifty years to translate the entire Word of God into a local language. Even before beginning, much work is done to define the Biblical *key terms* – how to say things like 'saviour', 'holy spirit' or 'sin' in the local language. These need to be chosen carefully, so that the Bible is understandable in the local language and culture. Now, if an ethnomusicologist comes in and composes songs on verses not yet translated, and if these verses use the wrong key terms, this could ultimately affect Biblical understanding when the verses are translated properly. So now you know!

Participants will split into four groups, each composing a song on one of the following passages:

John 3:16: 'For God so loved the World.'

John 11:25–26: 'I am the resurrection and the life.'

Luke 10:27: 'Love the Lord your God.'

Matthew 7:15–20: 'A tree and its fruit.'

Due to the late start, it is already lunchtime, so after a hearty helping of rice and sauce, they split into groups and begin composing. As such a huge number of folk turned up, some groups now have as many as fifteen members: far from ideal for such a task. In practice, though, only four or five people are actually composing the song, whilst the rest are sitting around watching and listening.

The groups have dispersed so quickly that I don't actually know where they've all gone! Thankfully, a couple of young children offer to take me to each group, so that I can see how they're doing. As we cross the tiny village lane, a 2,000 franc note falls out of my pocket. One of the children picks it up and hands it to me. How's that for honesty? And 2,000 francs is a lot of money to a Togolese villager!

The songs are going well so far and, as it turns out, each group has chosen a different one of the four genres, which is great news! At the end of the day they share their songs as usual, before we wrap up.


Now, I could have stayed the night in Sassanou, but instead have gone for a more interesting – and slightly more comfortable – option: the monastery on the mountain. The only downside of this is that it means driving back up the sheer, jagged lane again. Thankfully, it is only a few miles and I am soon back up on the Danyi Plain and turn into the leafy driveway of the *Abbaye de l'Ascension*. It's a pretty place with a large green lawn in the centre. Straight ahead is the imposing round chapel, and on the other three sides are cloister-like walkways. I park up and find my way to a simple reception room. Two African monks are sitting quietly in one corner.

"*Bonsoir, Messieurs*. I'd like a room for the night please."

"Wait a moment."

I wait for what seems like an age; if waiting around is part of the culture in Africa, it must be even more so in a monastery!  Eventually a young, slim monk appears, dressed, like all the rest, in a light brown hooded habit.

"Come," he says.

I silently follow him down a long, resonant corridor; semi-open to the lawn on one side, doors to rooms to the other.  As I do so, I cannot help noticing that beneath his simple habit he is wearing a rather nice pair of white sports shoes.

"Here is your room.  Dinner is at 6:00pm."

And he's gone.  It's a simple but clean room with a walled shower compartment beside the door, a single bed, a table and a chair.  At the far end, there are windows and a door out onto a tiny veranda.  I switch the light on to see more clearly.  It flickers, buzzes, then goes out.  I try turning the switch off and on again, but the light is sporadic at best.  Time to go back and talk to the monks.  Interestingly, rather than change the light bulb, they simply show me to a different room, just a couple of doors further down.

A room for the night here – including all meals – is a mere 3,000 CFA francs (about four British pounds).  However, it costs 5,000 CFA for 'those who can afford it'.  Having pulled up in a Land Rover, I hardly feel I can pay the lower rate, even if I am entirely supported by gifts.  And besides, this is still a ridiculously low price for full-board accommodation, even compared with other West African hotels.

Dinner is, as expected, a simple affair. The sizeable dining room has a high beamed ceiling and long benches, rather reminiscent of the one in *Hogwarts*, though somewhat less grand.  I sit down opposite a couple who look like many other couples I've seen in West Africa: a portly, middle-aged white man and a young, slim, beautiful African wife.  In addition, a pale brown-skinned child sits between the two of them.  An interesting phenomenon indeed, but one which is far from uncommon in this part of the world.  It generally occurs for two simple reasons (like it or not): he gets what he wants – a stunning wife half his age; she gets what she wants – financial security.  Now, I'm not saying they don't love each other, but the factors mentioned certainly seem to play a significant role in their choice of partner.

"*Bonsoir.*"  I greet the man.

"*Bonsoir,* je m'appelle Laurent Dubois."

"*Enchanté.*  Do you live in Togo?"

"No, I did in the past, but now I live in France."

Curiouser and curiouser.

"Do you like Togo?"

"Oh yes, I love Africa.  In fact, I love Africa so much, this happened!" he adds, pointing his head towards his partner and daughter.

As we tuck into our soup, bread and butter, a bat enters and circles around the rafters above – this really *is* Hogwarts!  After dinner (and part of the reason staying here is so cheap), we all muck in doing the washing up together, as well as putting all the crockery and silverware away.  One monk is on duty, his watchful eye making sure we do things the right way.

The next morning, I'm up with the lark and heading back down the infamous mountain road to Sassanou.  Folk are already gathered in the church.  I greet them with a smile and in the customary Bogo way:

"*E ne i fáà?*"

"*A lɔ blô!*" they reply, assuring me they are indeed well.

Having composed the first set of songs on key doctrinal verses, the second lot are based on key bible passages for Christian living, namely:

Matthew 6:9-13 (The Lord's Prayer)

Mark 10:19 (The Ten Commandments)

Matthew 5:3-10 (The Beatitudes)

Matthew 28:18-20 (The Great Commission)

I spend a good while teaching on these as it is really important that folk understand what they are all about.  Of course, everything takes at least twice as long – or more – thanks to my long-winded interpreter!

In terms of instruments, there are some large barrel-shaped drums in the village, used for traditional ceremonies. Could these drums be used for the new church songs? I ask the group.

"There is no problem from our point of view," they reply. "These are our instruments too! However, we do not know whether the non-believers in the village would like it or not." They agree to ask the villagers what they think and whether it would be feasible to use these drums for the new compositions.

It's late morning and I make another tour around each group to see how they are doing. Crossing the village lane is more hazardous than I had expected; motorbikes coming off the mountain are still free-wheeling down at this point, their engines completely turned off. So I have to be all the more careful not to get hit by one of these silent two-wheelers. I listen intently to one of the groups; their song is sounding good, but they are still finalizing the words. As I'm listening to them, an older lady from the group with a lump the size of a grapefruit in her neck approaches me. She bends down and begins picking off seeds which have stuck to my trouser legs during the day. Such a humbling experience – I don't feel worthy of such treatment, but it's her way of showing hospitality to a guest, so it would be an insult for me to refuse her this right.

The songs are ready by lunchtime and we're hoping to record them this afternoon. I'm concerned about the gathering dark clouds above, though.

"Will it rain this afternoon?"

"No, tomorrow," they reply. I trust their judgment and we plan to commence recording in the afternoon.

I find a sheltered mango grove a short walk away and we agree to reconvene there after lunch to record the songs. By the time I get there, the whole area is teeming with people; maybe as many as a hundred. Amazingly, the village folk have agreed that my workshop people can use the traditional barrel drums, and say it is no problem for them. This is quite rare; it can sometimes take years before local non-Christian musicians agree to such a step – or even the Christian ones! This will really enhance the music and also make it something the people of Sassanou will be pleased to hear.

A group of ladies is dancing enthusiastically and singing one of the new songs, as the drums beat out their syncopated accompaniment. It is great to see the joy on everybody's faces – these people have never worshipped God in their mother tongue until now, and it shows! One lady shouts out: "*Jésus nous prend tout!*" meaning: 'Jesus takes everything which is ours'. In other words, even their local music can be used for His glory.

This is the point at which I realize: *I'm living through new and exciting events here – this is ground-breaking stuff! I must share these experiences with the world – it's a story too great not to be told!* And so from that very moment I resolved to make my ethnomusicological adventures into a book, so that others could share in my unforgettable experiences. This book, you are holding right now. Thank you God!

The large barrel drums from the village are about four feet long with a single head and are only used for the *atungba* genre. They rest diagonally against a large log with the base on the floor, and are hit with two bent wooden sticks. In addition, an old man from the village has brought along a ram's horn, which he plays to start some of the songs. Then several ladies are holding carved wooden sticks about eighteen inches long and three inches wide, which they beat together to accompany many of the songs; a simple but effective percussion instrument.

The fact that two of the genres are only sung by women, and the other two almost always by men may make for an unusual church service, with a session of men's songs followed by the women's songs (or vice versa). Eventually, the songs may become mixed, or they may not. If the culture says 'men and women do not sing together', then why should anyone impose a different tradition upon them? After all, there is no sin in singing in single sex groups; it's all about what you're used to.

Every one of the ladies' songs begins with an interesting call and response. The leader calls out a long and slowly descending:

"*Eeweeeee!*"

And the rest all respond with:

"*Eewaaaa!*"

And again:

"*Eeweeeee!*"

"*Eewaaaa!*"

Then the song itself begins. The men have a similar responsive call: leaning inwards the leader gives a falling '*Aah-aaah*', which is quite nasalized. This is then echoed by the other men. Fascinating indeed; I've never come across this sort of introduction before, but I like it!  Of course, this kind of thing is by no means unique to the Bogo; many cultures have devices for introducing songs, plays or stories – a kind of 'signature tune' to let people know it's about to start.  In the case of the Bogo, the introductory words don't actually mean anything; it's just another way of calling everyone to order.  But as it's part of their culture, we will keep these vocal introductions for the church songs; that way, it still makes sense to them and respects their way of doing things.

We begin recording. I've been provided with a small wooden table and a stripy folding garden chair to sit on – very pleasant!  The chair is a bit low though, so I perch on the end to regulate the sound on the mixing desk. Recording goes pretty well, but I have to tell a couple of men to stand more still when singing. This is often a problem in Africa – people love to move about as they sing.  However, when in front of a microphone, such movement is not possible as it will affect the recording.

At one point, there is a great deal of discussion about the *okpaja* genre. The participants don't seem to be getting the rhythm right to begin with, and have to stop playing to work it out.  Many folk offer suggestions and a long debate ensues as to how it should actually be played.  Caught in the crossfire, I just sit back and listen as they babble away in Igo for several minutes!  I'm used to this happening by now. Thankfully, they get there in the end and the song sounds great! The people are clearly enjoying the experience of using their own music in this way.

One guy, called Samson, has a fascinating instrument called the *zoho zaha*.  It's a percussion instrument, made up of three parts.  Firstly, there is a narrow wooden stick about three feet long with grooves carved into it. The second part is a hollowed-out spherical seed pod with two round holes on opposite sides. This is 'threaded' onto the stick and pulled up and down the ridges by the right hand to make a grating sound. But no musical instrument is complete without a resonator; up until now, this instrument works but would not be audible to listeners. So, the third part is another seed pod, this time a flatter, dark brown one. One end has been cut off to improve resonance. This pod is then held in the left hand at the lower end of the instrument and is systematically placed against the stick or removed from it to change the timbre. The result is a percussive scraping sound somewhat reminiscent of a person brushing their teeth!

The *zoho zaha* – thus named for reasons onomatopoeic – is not used with the village percussion ensemble as it would be too quiet. However, Samson has some solos he sings accompanied by the instrument and these sound wonderful! I make a point of recording one of these for the final album too.

Recording here, there is no need for me to turn off my mobile phone, as I often do at such times: there is no signal whatsoever in Sassanou – the deep valley sides and its generally remote location take care of that.

We're done before nightfall. The people are very pleased with what we have been able to achieve in such a short time and excited by the prospect of another day's music-making tomorrow. One guy comes up to me, buzzing with enthusiasm:

"You know, when they play those big drums for village ceremonies, it usually makes people go into a trance. But today there was no trance when we played them!"

Wow! I might have thought twice had I known this was a risk. However, I've studied trance quite a bit and – as a general rule – when the object of worship and the heart of the worshipper change, then trance will not occur. It's a big issue in redeeming 'pagan' music for church worship and one which has caused some churches to fear even trying to play local drums. With time, though, all of these can be redeemed for God's glory alone.

Tomorrow, we will tackle the last lot of songs: parables.

I arrive back at the monastery in time for vespers in the chapel – just what I need after a busy, hectic day's work. At the front of the church, a dozen or so monks are sat on the raised platform in front of the altar, wearing green, white or fawn-coloured robes. Singing is accompanied by four *koras*. The kora is a beautiful West African instrument, a bit like a harp. It has twenty-one strings in two rows, a long neck and a large half gourd at the bottom, with animal skin stretched across the opening. The Catholics have done a lot to develop kora usage in worship; much more than the Protestants so far, and the music tonight sounds truly heavenly! Towards the end of the service, everyone sits still in silence for about ten minutes. Well, everyone except one person: I can't sit still *and* quiet for that long, so make my way out after about four minutes – my 'still and silent' cut-off point!

It's the final day, a Sunday, so we're starting later due to the church service. After numerous echoes of: "*E ne i fáà?*" and "*A lɔ blô!*" we're ready to crack on with the parable songs. They are:
Luke 8:4-15 (The Sower)
Luke 10:29-37 (The Good Samaritan)
Luke 15:11-32 (The Prodigal Son)
Matthew 18:21-35 (The Unforgiving Servant)

Setting stories to music usually works well in Africa, and there is often a song genre specifically for story-telling. To aid the teaching, I recount each of the stories to the group, acting them out whenever possible. They listen intently and my interpreter copies many of my gestures, which is always fun!

Halfway through the teaching, yesterday's prediction comes true: the heavens open and, almost instantly, it begins to 'chuck it down'. Rainstorms in Africa are often accompanied by strong winds, and today is no exception. Almost horizontal rain is flying in through the windows down one side, drenching the church floor, and anybody in its path, within seconds. The windows are quickly shut, but not before a decent degree of dousing has already occurred!  As the church has a corrugated metal roof, the noise of the rain is amplified considerably. With no P.A. system in the church, it is impossible for me to carry on with my story-telling, so we all just sit down and wait, watching muddy brown streams gushing down the nearby hillside.

"At the service this morning, they prayed for rain," one participant tells me. Well, thanks!  Couldn't they have prayed for it to come *tomorrow*?!

Eventually, the rain subsides and we are able to carry on.  Into groups for composing, in spite of continuing light rain.  I'm grateful for my umbrella, which I brought with me just in case.  In Cotonou, as soon as rainy season kicks in, men appear on street corners selling these colourful but useful items. They are pretty cheap and – on average – last about a month before collapsing.  Looking on the bright side, this gives me a chance to try out a different coloured umbrella each time!  This one is red, white and green, which is always a pleasant colour mix.  No word of a lie, a man once greeted me in Italian when I was using it in Cotonou!  But I prefer to think of it as my *Welsh* umbrella, and today's weather – along with the surrounding landscape – certainly fits the bill!

The groups struggle with the parables, more than I've experienced in other locations.  Not sure why, but it partly seems to be the length of the songs and the amount of detail needed to tell the story from start to finish. This is much more than in the previous songs, where the same verse could be repeated *ad nauseum* without any trouble.

As I pass through the village to visit the groups, I notice an enterprising chap working hard under a covered part of his courtyard.  He's chiselling away at pieces of wood to make more sticks for the ladies to hit together. Did they order them, or is he just making the most of an opportunity pro-vided by the workshop?  I never did find out. Still, let's hope he gets them done in time for the recording session!

By early afternoon, the rain has stopped and the remaining recordings are made.  I'm eager to begin my journey home this afternoon, so packed everything into *The Beast* before leaving the monastery this morning. We're all done and I'm ready to hit the road by 3:00pm. The folks are, once again, teeming with joy and also sad to see me go. They offer me bananas, pineapples and coconuts as tokens of thanks. Oh, and I get to keep the necklace too!

Today, the high mountain plain is cloaked in mist and mild drizzle. In fact, the weather outside is cooler than the air conditioning inside *The Beast*, so I opt for a 'windows open' approach instead. Down the other side, and a dozen hairpins later, I pass the Baptist Hospital and continue on to Kpalime, hoping for a room at *Chez Fanny* tonight.

I arrive at *Chez Fanny* just as night is falling, only to find that their rooms are all fully booked. Oh dear! What shall I do now?

"Do you recommend anywhere else nearby?" I ask the receptionist, in desperation.

"Well, you could try the *J-Pines Hotel*, just round the corner."

With no other viable alternative, I decide to give it a try.

The *J-Pines* is typical of many mid-range, modern African hotels: a big, concrete building with shiny tiled floors and dark, echoey corridors. A large sign outside also boasts a 'karaoke bar'. The rooms are not bad, though, with air conditioning, en suite bathrooms and television. I notice there are no mosquito nets, but hope that the air-con will stop them sniffing me out in the first place. If not, I can always put up my folding mozzie net again, to avoid 'the Sokodé effect'.

I crash on the large double bed and switch on the telly: nothing much worth watching! As is often the case here, TV 'entertainment' is limited to debates or dancing! On one channel, important looking men in hats are sat around a table discussing political issues; on another, a fat African man wearing a medallion is singing and dancing in front of a shiny new *Hummer*, the mandatory sunglasses adorning his gangster-like face. On the third channel – oh dear: shapely lycra-clad African women are wiggling their fluorescent-coloured *derrières* inches from the camera and calling it 'art'. Time to make a swift exit!

Thankfully, *Chez Fanny* is still open for meals, so I decide to take refuge there, ordering a tasty and much-needed antelope stew. Yum!  I try to make it last as long as possible, hoping to spend most of my time at the J-Pines asleep!  When I finally get back there, the nightclub in the basement is grinding into action.  So the *karaoke bar* sign was for real!  I'm hoping to get to sleep soon, but the music is so loud that even my pillow is vibrating – and that's two floors up.  I briefly consider an *'if you can't beat them join them'* approach, but quickly realize the folly of such an idea: as almost certainly the only white man present, I'd get eaten alive down there.  And, besides, my night-clubbing days are over.  Come to think of it, they never really began!

So, attempting to ignore the booming below and the screaming guests down my corridor, I hit the sack. After just about managing to get to sleep, there is a power cut and so the air-con goes off.  Not to worry: the room is quite cool now.  The power returns after a while, but the air-con will not work anymore.  I consider just leaving it, but it is a warm, sticky night and – besides – the sound of the a/c does help mask the music (which is persisting well after midnight!)  In the end, I make my way down to reception and am given a new remote control, which works.  Back to sleep, for what seems like a good while.  I can still hear the music going 'Boom! Boom! Boom!' down below.  I look at my watch: 3:15am.  Do these people have no beds to go to?!

I wake again at 4:00am and all is quiet at last.  However, my nose is hurting and, just by looking ahead, I can tell it's larger than usual.  In spite of the air-con set to 22 Celsius, I have been bitten on my nose. The rest of me was under the sheets, so this is all that was left for the mozzies to nibble!  Much too tired to put up my folding mosquito net now, though…

Finally, after all the disturbances, I am about to go back off to sleep when a thought occurs to me: what did I do with my digital recorder?  I can't remember where I put it so turn out all my bags searching for it: no sign of it anywhere. Oh, dear! What has happened to it? Frantically, I lift the mattress from my bed, pull off the sheets and turn my bags completely inside out. It is nowhere to be seen! What am I to do? Did someone come in and steal it whilst I was out to dinner? It contains the only copy of the workshop recordings, which the people of Sassanou and I spent hours making. Where can it be? I continue searching, my hope of finding it diminishing with every frantic yet half asleep minute. After much searching, the device turns up: it has fallen inside the lining of my bag. Phew! That's such a relief!

Although it was a tad hair-raising at the time, there are a couple of things I learned from this experience:

1. Don't trust your judgement at 4:00am when you've hardly had any sleep.
2. Do keep valuables with you when you leave a strange hotel room, just in case.
3. The *real* work done at the workshop was in people's hearts and minds. Even if the recordings had been lost forever, the people of Sassanou had been changed and had these new songs within them now.

Next morning, I am delighted to leave the J-Pines behind, vowing never to stay there again. Now, all that remains is a six-hour drive home with a lengthy border crossing. Should be plain sailing!

Oh Dear! How early missionaries thought
African church music should look

Recording session with the Bogo people of Sassanou

# Chapter Five

# Biting ants and Bowls of clay

*The N'cam People of Western Togo*

*"Allô?"*

*"Monsieur Nukun?"*

*"Oui!"*

*"C'est moi, Robert. Je suis arrivé à Bassar."*

After another lengthy and not altogether uneventful journey across Benin and most of Togo, I've arrived in the westerly town of Bassar, about midway between the coast and Togo's northern border. Mr Nukun, my contact here, asked me to give him a call when I arrived so that he could come and meet me. At the time, I was somewhat unsure about this arrangement: supposing my mobile phone had no coverage there or somehow stopped working? We Westerners tend to think of the worst possible scenario – not entirely a bad way of doing things – whereas the African attitude is often *'Ça va aller'*, which basically means 'It'll all work out just fine'. And most of time it does, today being no exception. Five minutes after our call, Mr Nukun rolls up on his old but sturdy-looking motorbike. We've never met until now, so it's just as well that a white bloke in a Land Rover is an easy thing to spot in Bassar! Mr Nukun is a short chap in his mid-forties with large, gold-rimmed spectacles and a warm smile.

"Welcome to Bassar, Monsieur Robert!"

"Thank you. It's good to be here."

My journey here was not dissimilar from all the rest, so no need for me to reiterate the chicken, goat, dog, motorbike, and smoky truck stories. However, this time the fan belt on *The Beast* started screeching loudly shortly after my 6:10am departure from Cotonou. Thankfully, this slowly wore off as the journey continued; maybe just a bit damp, who knows?

The second fly in the ointment in terms of the Land Rover was the rear door, which was coming loose at the catch and so rattled incessantly throughout the journey. *The Beast,* it would appear, is becoming more and more like its apocalyptic namesake! And this is by no means the first time the car has done this to me – even back on the Gangam trip I had the same problem. Usually, I just take a screwdriver and tighten it all up and that's that (for a few days at least). This time, though, it's much looser and the screws just don't want to tighten any more (I think their thread has finally worn out). The risk of the tailgate actually swinging open is, thankfully, pretty slim, due to the design of the lock. The rattle is, nevertheless, disconcerting, and the longer it continues, the more damage may be caused.

My friend Delia, a vicar in Yorkshire, drives a similar Land Rover around her Dales parish and – surprise, surprise – has had the same problems with the rear door. She called the mechanic one time and he was clearly familiar with the quirks of Land Rovers: "Trubble wi' back door? Is it cumin' loose or stuck fast?" Yes, I've had the latter problem too, where the door will not even open! This time, I decided to keep going to save time, and made it here in one piece. I'm hoping to find a mechanic in Bassar before my return journey, though.

Also on the way up, I called in at my favourite *Auberge* in Dassa, for the usual omelette sandwich and coffee. The folk there greeted me like an old friend again – very nice after a long drive. But this time, I was also meeting with a chap called Dorothé. Yes, you read it right, the man is called Dorothy, and this is far from uncommon in Africa. Don't suppose he's ever been to Kansas, though…

I met up with Dorothé because we're planning a workshop in the Dassa area in a couple of months' time and Dorothé runs a small holiday centre a few miles out of town. So, we travelled there and he showed me around. The centre contained a series of buildings and huts, scattered across a large area. These included three hotel-type rooms with en suite facilities.

"You and your family could stay here. And over there are the dormitories where your musicians could stay."

"Okay, but we would need more than just the three rooms, as there'll be two families, making ten people altogether."

"No problem. Just over the road there's a house which is not being used. It has beds and furniture in it, so some of your family could stay there."

It all looked pretty do-able and meals are provided on-site too. I think we could make this work.

"I'm hopeless at music," he shared with me.

"Well, I'm pretty useless at sport," I retorted, to try and make him feel better.

"No you're not. You're walking really well."

Now I felt bad again – I know walking is not a 'sport,' but Dorothé has quite a limp when he walks, due to a hernia, he told me.

So, we verbally agreed that, given the facilities and the terms discussed, I hoped to run a workshop there in August. You will see in the next chapter how the reality of this actually panned out – not entirely as planned but, hey, T.I.A. (This *is* Africa).


"Follow me," says Mr Nukun, and promptly kicks his motorbike into action and whizzes away towards the centre of Bassar. I then follow him off the main road and onto a dirt track. About a mile further on, we cross a large football pitch and enter a compound through a sturdy, metal gate. This is where I'll be staying. The house is a single-storey place with the usual screened veranda and central wooden door at the front.

"I'll leave you to have a rest, Monsieur Baker. I'll be round later this evening to discuss the workshop," says Mr Nukun, who promptly disappears.

The house – clearly a missionary home in the past – has a concrete floor and wooden ceiling with a large white metal fan in the middle (which brings back unpleasant memories). The windows and door frames are, interestingly, painted grey and are adorned with the typically gaudy curtains hanging from wooden poles; curtains which – in general – don't quite meet in the middle. A large central room forms the lounge-diner with a kitchen behind it, blocked off only by a larger, equally gaudy curtain. To either side of the living room are two bedrooms, making four in total, and between each pair of bedrooms is a shower and toilet.  On the wall is a brightly-coloured, almost certainly Chinese poster of various fruits.  The dark, wooden entrance door is adorned with an out-of-date German calendar displaying picturesque alpine scenes.  A nice-looking television set sits on a small table in the lounge area, covered in a cloth which matches the curtains. There is a chunky wooden sofa and matching chair, both with velour cushions in a deep maroon colour.

The kitchen is reminiscent of that seen in many missionary homes I've visited: a big, square sink with a gold-coloured tap, an old-fashioned whistling kettle on the stove, a plastic water filter, a large fridge full of water bottles (filtered, no doubt), three different-coloured plastic waste bins with lids, and painted wooden shelf units with more curtains hung over the front.  If you're wondering about the three waste bins, the system is usually as follows:

> *Green bin:* biodegradable waste
> *Brown bin:* burnable items
> *Blue bin:* other rubbish.

This is how most missionaries manage their waste in remote locations. Biodegradable waste is composted, burnable waste is – well – burnt, and a deep hole (or 'long drop') is dug for the rest.  So now you know!

I'm in the first bedroom to the right, at the front of the building, and appear to be the only occupant of the house.  I unpack and erect my foldable mosquito net. Time for a shower. African showers, whilst similar to Western ones in their function, could scarcely be more different in every other way. Firstly, most are housed in a small, square room with a concrete floor. Then a metal pipe appears out of one wall a couple of feet from the ground and rises vertically about four feet before bending outwards at a right angle from the wall. Halfway up this pipe is a small tap and at the very end is a downward-facing circular nozzle, roughly seven inches across, which would look more at home on a watering can. That's it. Then in one corner of the floor (or sometimes even in the middle) is a drainage hole. No hot water, no removable nozzle, no electric 'power shower' pump, no shower curtain. Simple and effective, and just what I need after a long journey on this hot, sticky day in June. I turn on the shower tap. Nothing happens. Oh dear, there's a water cut! This is far from uncommon, and I've got used to it in some ways. Looks like I'll have to wait a while before I can smell nice again. Thankfully there is electricity, so I plug in my chargers to get plenty of batteries ready for the forthcoming recording sessions.

I'm just dressed again when there is a knock at the door. A large African lady in a typically colourful outfit is standing in the doorway. On her head is a tray holding two small blue saucepans, whose floral design makes them look more suited to a canal boat than an African household. I open the door, slightly stunned to have a visitor so soon.

"*Bonjour, je m'appelle Madame Philippe,*" she says in a booming voice. "I will provide your meals here during your stay."

"Oh, *merci beaucoup.* Come on in."

She sets the pans down on the long wooden table and removes the lids to reveal spaghetti, beef, green beans and the ubiquitous tomato, onion and oil sauce. Looks like I'll be well fed during my stay in Bassar.

"Do you have some of *your* water?" she asks, knowing that Western visitors usually bring shed loads of filtered water with them.

"Yes I do, thank you."

After eating what proves to be a very tasty dinner indeed, I try the shower again. After considerable gurgling and shaking, it actually produces water this time. That's a relief!

The aim of this three-day workshop, as usual, is to produce new Bible-based songs using the local language, song styles and musical instruments. Not foreign music, but music which belongs to the people of Bassar; the music which *they* play, sing, dance to and love. This is always a powerful way to communicate the Gospel message to people. Justin Ukpong gives the following three characteristics of *inculturating* our mission – in other words, evangelizing from within:

1.  The utilization of the resources of the culture being evangelized.
2.  The Good News of Jesus is pronounced to challenge and animate the culture.
3.  All this is done from the perspective of the culture and through the agency of an insider or insiders in the culture.[8]

What right have I, a foreigner in this land, to come in and impose my Western ways of doing things upon these people?  And besides, much of how I perceive this culture would – initially – be false, as I would be looking at it through a Western 'lens'.  I've heard missionaries, even to this day, say to me: "We can't sing *those* songs in church – they don't sound nice!"  To Western ears, maybe not, but to an African they sound exactly how they should – beautiful.

I'm roused from my daydreaming by another knock at the door.  Mr Nukun is back already – I must've been musing for longer than I thought.  With him are a couple of other members of the Bible translation team.

"*Bonsoir! Tout va bien ici?*"

"Fine, thanks.  Have a seat. There is water."

"Thank you."

Cultural greetings and welcomes over and it's time to discuss the workshop.  He shows me some Bible verses written in their language – also called Bassar, or Ncam (pronounced 'un-cham').  As I look over them, a familiar lack of vowels strikes me.

"Is the Bassar language related to Nawdm?" I ask, recalling my millet beer-swilling friends to the north.

He's impressed: "Yes, it is. There are many similarities."

I begin to wonder how similar their music will be, and whether they have the famous *colliding buttocks dance* here too!  Mr. Nukun continues with a slightly concerning statement:

"We have two *petits problèmes,* Monsieur Robert."

Oh dear. "What are they?"  I quickly ask.

"Well, firstly," he continues, "we cannot do the workshop on Saturday, as it's market day and all the ladies need to go and sell their goods that day."

It's Thursday tomorrow, so that would mean only two days for the workshop.  Sunday would be out, due to church, and I cannot stay until Monday.

"So just two days then?"

"Yes, Monsieur Robert. Two days."

Well, that's going to be a rush.  I usually try to do nine songs on a three-day workshop, but that may be tricky this time.

"Well, I'll do the best I can. What's the second thing?"

"Well, there are two different dialects of the Bassar language represented at the workshop, so we would like to have two different cassettes produced, one for each dialect."

This *is* going to be a challenge!  So, in two days, we need to record enough songs to fill two cassettes and in two different dialects.  It's going to be tough, but I'll give it a go!

Near the centre is a small African shop, known locally as a *'boutique'*. Similar to many across the continent, this small, square shack is made of wood and corrugated metal.  Behind a long counter sits the shopkeeper and behind him are shelves all the way up to the ceiling, stocked with tins of tomato puree and condensed milk, bars of soap in cubes, mosquito coils, margarine in tubs, powdered milk, biscuits, Quaker Oats and batteries. There are also bottles of mineral water – a common sight virtually everywhere in Africa these days – so I buy four: given the performance of the taps in the house so far, I could well run out of filtered water otherwise.  Now it's time for bed.

Next morning and the shower is shaking more furiously than ever. In addition, the loo is gurgling loudly. Fearing another water cut, I quickly get under the shower. About halfway through, the inevitable happens and I'm stuck there, covered in soap and with a head full of shampoo, but no water! All I have is the bottled water I bought last night, and that's been in the fridge for about nine hours. Brrrrr! It's the only option, but it certainly wakes me up fast!

Another knock at the door, and this time it's a man bringing me the usual bread, margarine and coffee for breakfast. Rather than the all-pervading Nescafé, this time it's *Maxwell House* coffee, which, according to the label, is '*Bon jusqu'à la dernière goutte*' (good till the last drop). Well, not as 'bon' as it might be; this is decaffeinated coffee – aarrrgh! Not what I was hoping for…

Before the workshop even begins, I've arranged for Mr Nukun to take me to a local mechanic, who can hopefully sort out the dodgy rear door on *The Beast*. It's a few minutes' drive across town, but we're soon there. Most African mechanics' workshops look pretty similar, especially outside of larger towns and cities, and this one is no exception: a sizeable open area littered with wrecked cars, old engines, and black oil stains carpeting the ground everywhere. There is a covered area too, often made from branches covered in palm leaves, but this one is covered in corrugated metal instead. There's a small shack to one side, which houses tools and, rather than an inspection pit, there are a couple of rickety ramps, which look like they're made of *Meccano*.

As the mechanic takes a wrench and screwdriver to my car, I glance around and my attention is drawn to an old-looking sign near the workshop. It points down the road and reads: '*Les Hauts Fourneaux de Bassar*', which means 'The High Furnaces of Bassar'.

"Monsieur Nukun, what are those?"

"*Ah, Les Hauts Fourneaux*, yes!" He responds with nostalgia. "The furnaces were way up on the hill there, but they've been closed for many years now."

"Furnaces.  So what were they used for?"

"We used to mine iron in this region, and the furnaces were used for smelting."

"So what happened?  Why did they shut?"

"Well, with colonization, cheaper sheet metal started to be imported from overseas and so our local mining and smelting industry went out of business."

"That's sad," I reply.  Sometimes I think Africa would be better off today if the West had never set foot on its shores.  Only sometimes, though…

Once the car is sorted, I pay the mechanic the princely sum of sixty pence for his trouble and we head straight for our workshop location – an unusual one this time.  It's being held in a hotel halfway up a hill overlooking the town of Bassar.  Sounds lovely, eh?  Well, I'm sure it was once upon a time.  However, the hotel has not been used for a good couple of decades and its general state of repair certainly reflects this!  Even the winding one-in-three road which leads up to the hotel is made up of more potholes than paving!  The hotel itself would once have been a wonderful place to stay, with a gorgeous view for miles across the plain.  Now, every room is coated in dust and rubble with broken windows and doors falling off their hinges.  Such a shame. Wandering through the dilapidated building, I peer through a round window in a door and see what would have been a decent kitchen back in the day.  There are still utensils hanging up, but everything is just one big mess now.

Outside, people are slowly gathering.  It's almost nine o'clock now, so we need to get started soon.  That's when I hear a noise: somewhere nearby, a man is shouting loudly and uncontrollably.  I look over and the person concerned is swaying around, wildly addressing random members of the crowd.  It takes me about a second to realize that this is another madman.  Oh deary me!  But, whereas my old mumbling chap in Nawdm land was irritating but harmless, this chap seems anything but.  He notices me and instantly turns on his heels and stares wildly at me.

"White man!  White man!  You come and eat some of this!"

I remain silent, glued to the spot.  He's holding a bowl of what looks like porridge.

"Come on!  Try some, white man!  Are you scared of dying?"

As it happens, right now I am!

"Have some!  I'm not scared of dying," he continues.

"No thank you," I reply, meekly.

"Come on, white man!  Eat!"

Suddenly, for a second or two, he is distracted by someone else in the crowd. This gives me just enough time to make a run for it.  Hiding behind the dilapidated door of what was once the hotel reception, I peer through its tainted, cracked windows and watch cautiously.  He scarcely seems to have noticed I'm missing, continuing with his crazed utterances.  After sereral more minutes of ranting, raving and gesticulating wildly, one of the larger men present manages to usher him onto the back of his motorbike and the two of them ride off down the hill to who knows where.  I don't really mind where, as long as it's a long walk from here!

So, the workshop begins and, as it happens, we meet in the ramshackle hotel reception area.  There must be a good forty people squashed in this tiny space, and I have to almost fight my way through to the board at the front before I can begin teaching.  I'm aware from the outset that this will be a demanding workshop in terms of time-management, so we get straight on with talking about song genres. Within minutes, various people are striking up with traditional songs they know and, in spite of the lack of space, some still manage to dance in the middle of the room!  Their list of song genres is similar to that found in most other parts of West Africa: songs for weddings, funerals, hunting, harvest and so on.  However, with my experience thus far, it is interesting to note some overlaps with neigh-bouring ethnic groups.  For example, the Bassar people have the genre *gúmbe,* for rejoicing after a good harvest, which is also sung by the Tem people in Sokodé, east of here. Then – sure enough – there's the moonlit, bottom-bashing dance for young women, known here as *abaal*. This very much resembles the Nawdm equivalent, which was called *habaara*, so even the names are similar. It's fascinating to see patterns like this emerging as I become acquainted with more and more ethnicities.

A final genre worth noting is called *dikpaŋŋool* and is sung after a hunt, but only when a ferocious animal has been killed. There is a 'conventional' after-the-hunt genre too, but *dikpaŋŋool* is used specifically if you've killed something fierce, like a lion or a cheetah. Traditionally, the hunter would chop off the animal's head, put it on the ground, and then the hunters would dance around the head in celebration! Of course, there are virtually no ferocious animals left in this part of Africa, unless you count snakes – and I doubt they would. Historically, though, there would have been lions, cheetahs, monkeys, hyenas – even elephants – in this area. Now the 'National Park' area between here and Sokodé contains little more than a few birds and maybe a warthog or two.

Because of the two dialects present, I split participants into *six* different groups: three for the Bassar dialect and three for the other dialect, known as *Tapu*. Various parts of the tumbledown hotel are used for each group (talk about 'health and safety' regulations!), and some groups are out in the grounds. They're already composing by ten o'clock or so, and this needs to be the case if we're ever going to get through everything before tomorrow evening! We begin with three classic verses I often use:

Psalm 34:2-4

Revelation 7:12

2 Timothy 3:16-17


The six songs are done by lunchtime and we crack on with the second lot straight after lunch, scarcely stopping for a breather. No surprises here either:

Romans 6:23

1 John 1:8-10

Romans 10:9-11

They soldier on throughout the afternoon and, remarkably, the second lot of songs are ready by around four o'clock. So, with the two groups that's twelve songs altogether, all done in about five hours. This is feeling like a production line for new songs!

To save time tomorrow, I make the decision to record some of the songs today; we're on such a tight schedule that we'll never manage to do them all tomorrow *and* compose another set of songs. They'd also be more likely to forget so many songs if we save all the recordings until the end. So I set up the equipment, as per normal, under some mango trees in the hotel grounds. Mr. Nukun and another chap from his church help me with the line check, and take great joy in saying '*Bonjour…bonjour!*' into each microphone and waiting for my thumbs up.

As usual, I've set my musicians up in a vaguely circular formation, to maximize on sound quality, whilst allowing them all to see and hear each other. So, soloists on one microphone, choir on another, the drums get a couple, and then the fifth microphone – because it's there – is used for a lady shaking a small gourd covered with beads. They play the usual kind of drums: two smallish barrel-shaped ones, a pair of goblet drums a bit like *djembes,* and the ever-present under-the-arm 'pressure drum', it's tones rising and falling like human speech. All very nice indeed and everyone seems happy and positive, which is good!

Between songs, they chat away in their language which, to me, sounds something like this:

"*B B B M M naa N ch G D N M B B aah.*"

Way too many consonants to be a European language! It sounds lovely, though, and I relish the melodic and rhythmic nature of this language, without being able to understand a single word.

As I record, I am drinking the bottled water I bought last night, to stay hydrated in this heat. One lady comes up to me between two songs and says:

"You must give me your water bottle when it's empty!"

"Okay," I reply, knowing this is just how people ask for things in Africa. I've no idea what she wants it for, but I'll have little need for it once the water is gone.

When I chose the mango tree to sit under, it seemed like a good idea. In fact, beneath a mango tree is generally my preferred choice for most recording sessions: they are commonly found, are large and provide good shade. Furthermore, their leaves do not make a lot of noise when they move. However, what I *didn't* realize was that this mango tree is infested with red ants, each about half an inch long! So, throughout the recording session, the wee critters are falling down the back of my shirt, landing on my head, and finding their way between the sliders of my mixing desk — most off-putting indeed. I incur a few nasty bites as a result, but recording must go on, so I carefully squish each ant which appears, or — when possible — flick it out of the way, careful not to move any of my sliding volume controls in the process.

A different, but equally irritating insect halts our recording session as dusk approaches: mosquitoes. They tend to bite more as night falls and, although we've only managed to record eight of the twelve songs composed, I decide to call a halt to proceedings: the mozzies are having a feast on my ankles and it's the malarial ones which bite after dark. In any case, I'll scarcely be able to see what I'm recording in about ten minutes' time as night falls quickly at this latitude. So we pack up and, after thanking them all for their hard work today, I head back for another delicious meal prepared by the fair hands of Madame Philippe.

Back at the house, there's a power cut, so I light an oil lamp to see my dinner. In addition, there is still no water, so I'll have to forgo a shower again tonight! Thankfully, there are two toilets in this house: one to the right side and one to the left. As I'm the sole occupant, I am able to alternate between the two, which helps, especially as both loos have filled cisterns to begin with. I hit the sack almost immediately after dinner, exhausted but satisfied after a full day's work. Tomorrow will be just as crazy, if not more so!

I'm woken the next morning by a young African boy urinating in a bush outside my window; I've never been woken in this way before, and maybe never again. There is also a man tending the garden (not remotely phased by the extra 'fertilizer' our young friend is providing). I can also hear drums and singing in the distance, which is always a good sign. It's 7:00am and I'm very grateful for the hour's time difference between Togo and Benin; it feels like 8:00am to me – a much more civilized hour to rise!

There is *still* no water in the house and so, once again, I use bottled water for a 'shower' of sorts and use the loo at the other side of the house, which has filled up since last time.

Everyone has arrived by 7:50 and we make a prompt start by singing through the remaining four songs from yesterday – two from each dialect. One of the songs uses the genre *kitamkpanbeeu* – quite a mouthful. This song style is accompanied by a single-stringed instrument, referred to by locals as *la guitare traditionelle,* although it bears very little resemblance to a Western guitar. This one has been painted pale blue with white writing on it, and the body – as usual – is made from half a gourd covered in leather. The neck of this chordophone is just a round pole almost three feet long. At the top of the neck, a strip of rubber (probably from an old inner tube) has been wrapped around the end to hold the lone string in place. On the very end of the pole is a nail which holds three metal lids from glass drinks bottles, so common here. As it happens, these are three different colours: red, green and orange – or 'Coke', 'Sprite' and 'Fanta', to be more precise. A nice touch aesthetically, and the lids jangle together during playing to add a bit of percussion to the performance.

After an hour or so, the last four songs are ready to be recorded, so once again I set up the equipment under the trees and we get cracking. Another interesting instrument (or instruments) is a pair of small clay bowls, known locally as *kibaŋi.* Each bowl is no more than five inches in diameter and with a slightly curved lip. Two ladies perform on these using half a small gourd to hit the opening of the bowl, creating a percussive sound. In fact, two different sounds are made: one by hitting the gourd on the rim of the bowl (giving a higher, sharper sound) and the other by hitting the gourd evenly across the entire opening (a deeper, more closed sound). The two performers then alternate these two sounds, playing one after the other in quick succession. The two bowls used also differ slightly in size, adding to the range of sounds produced (one higher, one lower). The resulting music sounds similar to a horse's hooves or a sound one could make using a couple of half coconuts. Very nice indeed! To record these, I think of a novel idea: pointing a unidirectional microphone at each of the two bowls, I can 'isolate' their distinct sounds. Then I 'pan' one of them almost entirely onto the left stereo channel and the other onto the right. In this way, anyone listening to the recording will be aware of the two different sounds, as they will appear to come from two different locations. In fact, listening with my headphones, one bowl is in my right ear, the other in my left – a curious feeling indeed as the incessant 'clip-clop' alternates on either side of my head!

As usual, we've acquired a bit of an audience for the recording sessions. I really don't mind this, as long as they make no noise. In fact, it can be a huge help in raising the profile of the whole event and the new songs created. However, we also have a few unwanted guests in the form of goats! These make far too much noise with their incessant bleating, and can also generally get in the way. Thankfully – for us at least – a couple of the musicians throw stones at the goats, which frightens them away.

One of the ladies approaches me between recordings:

"*Rob!*"

How does she know my name? And, anyway, I go by '*Robert*' in French.

"*Rob!*" she says again, pointing at the empty plastic bottle by my table. I quickly realize that the word '*rob*' in Bassar actually means 'bottle'. How about that – Bottle Baker, the ethnomusicologist! I hand her the bottle and she smiles and politely curtsies, bobbing her head towards me in a gesture of gratitude. I have no idea what she wants it for. Must find out!

In between recordings, I use a pair of small speakers to play the song back to the participants. They always enjoy this and it encourages them in their work as they instantly get to hear the fruits of their labour before continuing with the next song. Sometimes I also hand the headphones to certain individuals, as the sound quality on these is much better. Almost without fail, the person listening will approvingly nod their head and smile, saying: "*C'est bon!   C'est vraiment bon!*"

By lunchtime, the four songs are 'in the can' and it's hard to believe that, since yesterday morning, they have composed, performed and recorded twelve new songs!  However, we still have this afternoon free, so I may as well make the most of the time.  Before breaking for lunch, I give out the remaining three verses, namely:

2 Corinthians 5:17

Colossians 2:6–7

Philippians 2:9–11

Straight back into their six groups after lunch for the final composing session. Whilst they are busy working on their songs – and as they 'know the ropes' by now – I take a few minutes to climb up the hill which continues behind the hotel.  It's a pretty steep one and there's no time to make it to the very top today.  However, I get far enough to admire a truly impressive view of Bassar, way down below, and the plain beyond it: lush, green and flat, extending to the horizon, many miles away.  Parts of the distant horizon are marked by the undulations of tiny mountains, which I know are actually huge.  Bassar itself is a mass of rectangular buildings with rusty brown roofs and small windows, punctuated by mango trees, teak trees, even a good number of coconut palms.  The streets are long, straight and pale brown, and white smoke is rising from various locations across the town. Ladies are walking to or from the small market with bowls on their heads; muscular men, pouring with sweat, are chopping wood; children are playing with old motorbike tyres and old men are sitting in the shade watching the world go by.  Weary, world-worn donkeys are pulling carts through the muddy streets as motorcycles whizz by, and small clusters of wandering sheep – like tiny balls of cotton – roam aimlessly through the town.  Makeshift poles made from branches – not one of them straight – carry electricity to most homes, a mass of twisted cables dangling haphazardly between each.  In one place, a lorry is unloading large sacks of charcoal and in an open grassy area, young people are playing football with great energy. This strangely idyllic view is somewhat spoilt by two large antennae, one at each end of the town, both painted the usual red and white. It is only then that I notice how many homes are equipped with television aerials; one or two even have satellite dishes!

Refreshed from my few moments of peace, quiet and watching African life from a distance, I make my way back down the steep, rocky hill to the hotel.


It's around 3:30pm when we begin the final recording session, which is still not a bad turn-around. But the sun will start setting at six (and finish doing so at 6:15) so we must 'make hay' while it still shines.

In addition to the alternating clay bowls, the tribute-to-fizzy-drinks guitar and the general driving poly-rhythms of Bassar music, a group of five ladies have a fascinatingly syncopated clapping rhythm which accompanies one of the songs. Hard to describe in words, but there is a lot of alternating clapping between three of the clappers and the other two. Also some gaps and 'off-beat' clapping, all adding to this intriguing accompaniment. As in virtually every group I've worked with, these people have a rich cultural and musical heritage, showing a high degree of skill, ethnic identity and musicality. Awesome! To record my clapping ladies, I stand them close together in a circle. An omnidirectional microphone is then placed in the middle, facing upwards just below the height of their hands. This captures the sound of each performer equally.

Another lady comes and asks for one of my empty bottles. "You promised me it yesterday!" she adds defiantly. A while later yet another woman asks me for a '*rob*'. My curiosity gets the better of me:

"What do you want these bottles for?"

She replies, in a very matter-of-fact way: "To put things in."

Fair enough. Ask a silly question…

We have a slight problem for one of the last songs – the genre includes dancing feet, which also make a percussive sound integral to the whole music. As we're under mango and teak trees surrounded by grass and dead leaves, this looks like it isn't going to work. However, just a few yards away is the hotel forecourt, which is paved. We make the decision, time-consuming as it will be, to move all the recording equipment over to this area for the song in question, and will then stay there for the last few. Acoustically, this location is less preferable, as there are far too many walls about for my liking. Also, there is very little shade, but the sun is already on its way down, so that shouldn't be too much of a problem.

The feet-percussion ladies dance and sing at the same time, so I need to use two microphones: one pointing down at their feet and the other near their mouths to capture both sounds effectively. One lady – as if enough isn't already going on – is also attempting to breast-feed her baby whilst singing and dancing! No wonder so many African children grow up with such a good sense of rhythm!

We're all done by around 5:00pm and, as ever, I have planned a quick getaway to make a start to my journey home. Sokodé is about an hour's drive away and has a good number of respectable hotels. If I can get there before nightfall, it will make tomorrow's drive more bearable. Having already hoped for such an eventuality, I packed all my things up this morning after my water bottle 'shower' and am therefore ready to roll! After the customary closing speeches, mutual messages of thanks and signing of the copyright form, I'm on my way, passing through strangely named villages and crossing the equally strangely-named *River Koubousong*.

It is no longer watermelon season in Sokodé; neither does it seem to be wood-sawing season, which is good to know. However, the market is as chaotic as ever and the tuneful calls to prayer are still resounding from various corners of this bustling town. I've stayed in a few hotels here and like to try a different one each time. Today, I opt for the *Hotel Kadia*, which is on the main road near the junction for my onward journey tomorrow. It is a long, narrow, single storey building with a car park to one side. I step into the small reception area, littered as usual with touristic posters and wood carvings.

"*Bonsoir, Monsieur!*" a friendly young chap on reception greets me.

"*Bonsoir*. Could I see one of your rooms please?"

It's always wise to check the accommodation out before committing, just in case. More than once I've done this and then walked away! As it turns out, the rooms here are quite nice, although most have no windows to the outside – just one onto the interior corridor. The first room he shows me has a double bed and a small en suite bathroom. The second has a sizeable but slightly smaller bed and no hot water in the shower. I go for the latter option, which is slightly cheaper at 11,000 CFA (rather than 13,000). I don't need a double bed and usually have cold showers in this hot country anyway.

"I'll take this one."

"*D'accord, Monsieur*," and he hands me the key with its customary oversized wooden fob, my room number etched into its shiny surface. As a bonus, the room has air-conditioning at no extra cost – this is turning out to be quite a bargain! Interestingly, it has a pair of large, sweeping curtains – somewhat overly-ornate for the size and quality of the room. There is also coving around the tops of the walls and a small, white ceiling rose from which a mini chandelier hangs! No carpet of course, but a nicely tiled floor all the same. There's a decent enough television, which works well and has a record *four* channels: two in French, one in English and one from Côte d'Ivoire in a mixture of French and Jula.

Time for my first decent shower in three days! I switch on the bathroom light and it flickers violently and continues to do so. Better than no light source, I guess, and I'm pretty desperate for a shower by now! I turn the tap clockwise and nothing happens. A second later, yellowy-brown water 'explodes' out of the pipes, but then flows relatively smoothly, becoming clearer by the second. Wonderful to finally feel properly clean! I step out of the shower only to discover something I ought to have noticed earlier: there is no towel! Eek! Oh well, time for another 'drip dry in front of the air-conditioning' session. It's not the first time I've had to do this and it is actually quite refreshing.

All clean, dry and changed, I head for the restaurant, just across the corridor. I step into the empty room which contains half a dozen or so square tables. Two men appear from a door to one side.

"*Bonsoir, Monsieur.  Soyez le bienvenu!*"

"*Bonsoir, Messieurs*. What's on the menu tonight?"

They look at each other, slightly taken aback.

"Well, Monsieur, there's not really a menu here, but we can do you guinea fowl with chips."

"That sounds great.  Guinea fowl and chips it is then!" and I take a seat.

The man who has been talking turns to the other and I overhear him whispering, "Is there any guinea fowl?"  Africans will often give you an answer which will make you happy in the short-term, even if it means disappointing you in the long-term; a peculiarity which has caused many Western visitors considerable stress.  Tonight I'm too tired to be stressed and would be happy to eat almost anything.  As expected, my man comes over to the table:

"I'm sorry, we do not have any guinea fowl, but we can do you some fish."

"Hmmm…I'm not a big fish fan.  Is there anything else?"

"Not really."

Then I have an idea: there are always eggs in Africa, as there are so many chickens.

"Could you make me an omelette?"

"*Oui, bien sûr!*"

"And do you have any cheese?"

"*Fromage, oui!*"

"Okay, I'll have a cheese omelette then."

"*Avec des frites?*"

"Yes, chips too, thanks!"

"*D'accord, Monsieur. Tout de suite!*"

"Oh, and a bottle of *Awooyo* please."

*Awooyo*, is a locally-brewed beer, peculiar to Togo. Unlike most pale, bland, generic beers in Africa, *Awooyo* is dark and tasty – a pleasant change from the norm, and here it's nicely chilled too!

My omelette arrives surprisingly quickly (I know by now that '*tout de suite*' on this continent can mean anything from five minutes to four hours). I tuck in, hungry from another busy day. It's good, but I can't taste – or see – any cheese yet. I'm just about halfway through my meal when the waiter returns with a small saucer of grated cheese and a teaspoon. Without a word, he proceeds to carefully sprinkle a spoonful onto what remains of my omelette, then a second spoonful, then a third. Finally, he ceremonially scrapes the rest of the saucer's contents onto the omelette, which is scarcely visible by now. At least I now know what happened to the cheese – and he's probably just been halfway across town on a moped to find it!

At the end of the meal, the waiter skulks up to my table once more and places a packet of toothpicks before me. I'm not sure which part of my omelette and fries would be likely to get stuck between my teeth, but it's a nice thought all the same.

"Can I pay for my meal and room now?" I ask, knowing I'll be off bright and early in the morning.

"*Bien sûr!*"

The bill arrives a few minutes later – 13,500 CFA, or about £15; not bad at all for dinner and a bed for the night. I hand him two 10,000 notes and he disappears back through his door, but returns almost immediately.

"Do you have any change, Monsieur?"

Uh oh! It's the age-old West African problem – there is frequently a lack of change almost anywhere you go.

"No I don't. Can you get some from somewhere?"

"We will try."

About twenty minutes later, my cheese-sprinkling friend returns with 6,500 francs. Hooray! Time for bed now, before yet another epic journey of goat-dodging, lorry-overtaking and pothole-avoiding. Let's hope *The Beast* behaves itself this time!

A few weeks after the Bassar workshop, I spoke to an older missionary lady who had not been in town during my visit. Thora had nevertheless listened to my recordings and told me:

"I was not altogether happy with the quality of some of those songs."

Well, I couldn't disagree. We did the best we could with the time and resources available. The musicians themselves were great and did a wonderful job given the circumstances. However, with double the number of songs needed and only two thirds of the time I'd expected, it was a tall order to expect every song to be perfect. As my mother-in-law always used to say: "You can't make a silk purse out of a sow's ear!"

Bassar drummers, including the 'talking drum' (right).

# Chapter Six

# Kick-Drums and Chaos

*The Ifè and Idaasha People of Central Togo and Benin*

BEEP BEEP BEEP BEEP BEEP!

"Urgh!  Morning so soon?"

I reach under my mosquito net and glance at the alarm clock beside my queen-sized waterbed.

"5:00am.  Better get up and ready," I think to myself, and dive under a cold shower, trying to mentally prepare myself for another culturally-enriching adventure.

I'm off to Dassa today, a mere three hours or so north of here. Hence the early start so that we can begin the workshop this very morning.  Remember Dorothé, the limping chap who called me 'sporty'?  Well, that's where we're headed today.  But this workshop will be different from all the rest in at least three ways:

Firstly, it's a dual ethnic — and dual nationality — workshop, combining two related people groups: the Idaasha from in and around Dassa (Benin) and the Ifè from just over the border in Togo, more or less due west of there. You see, many of the ethnic similarities run east-west in this part of the world, crossing political boundaries put in place during colonial times. The colonizers all wanted their own bit of coast, of course, and so the countries of West Africa all tend to run from there inland, Togo and Benin being two of the most stark cases in point.

The second reason why this workshop will be different is that it will be held on 'neutral ground' for everyone. Most workshops are held in or near a village where the participants actually live; this one will be at Dorothé's centre, and even the Idaasha present do not live there. And so everybody is travelling in for this gig, myself included of course.

5:15am – time for a quick breakfast: my taxi will be here any minute!

The third reason it will be different is that – for the first time ever – I'll be mixing 'business with pleasure'. My sister-in-law, Barbara Forest, her husband, Harry, and their three teenage daughters Sarah, Nathalie and Bernadette are all coming along to stay on the centre. They're here in Benin to visit us and to have a holiday. Given the chance of a few days near Dassa, and to see a workshop in action, they snapped up the opportunity. The rest of my family will also be coming along. Just as well Dorothé's place has the three nice rooms he showed me last time, as well as the house just over the road, which we'll be needing.

5:30am and the doorbell rings. That will be my taxi. Sure enough, I open my solid wooden front gate to reveal an old-looking yellow Toyota Tercel and its smiling driver.

*"Bonjour, Monsieur!"*

*"Bonjour. On y va!"*

And off we go! Not all of the in-law family are coming along with me today, but my brother-in-law, Harry and the two elder daughters, Sarah and Nathalie, are joining me, along with my daughter of ceiling fan fame, Ruth. They're staying at a house just around the corner, so we pick them up and head off out of town.

Our taxi is far from perfect, but better than some I've travelled in. The windscreen has a large crack across it, the passenger seatbelt does not work and the gears make a loud crunching sound every time they are changed. It also frequently falls out of fifth gear and back into neutral for no apparent reason – a tad disconcerting when you're dodging goats at sixty miles per hour! We all squeeze on board: Harry and the three girls on the back seat, me in the seatbelt-less front one.

Now, you're probably wondering why we're taking a taxi rather than using *The Beast* as normal. Well, as it happens, *The Beast* broke down about a week ago. Ironically, in Dassa itself and – rather obligingly – literally right outside my favourite *auberge*. The whole family was on its way back from a conference up in Kara when suddenly, after a short break in the journey, the car refused to move at all. The engine started fine, but somehow was not making any wheels go round. The only thing to do was for the rest of the family to catch a taxi home from there, whilst I booked into a room at the *auberge* and called Freddie the French mechanic to come and bail me out. Freddie sent up a couple of guys the following day to tow me back to Cotonou – about a five hour ordeal.

Now, when I first bought *The Beast*, Freddie was happy for me: "*Mais, c'est une voiture de luxe, Robert!*" he proudly told me. Since that day, I've paid so many visits to his garage that I usually bypass his secretary and go straight into the inner sanctum of his office. "*Robert, entre!*" he shouts (too many noisy vehicles seem to have turned him slightly deaf in his middle age). The office is small but air-conditioned with venetian blinds on the windows and a large desk bedecked with piles of paper, a few disused car parts, a computer and an ash tray. On the walls are pictures of various off-roading exploits, more car parts and a curious photo of a Citroën 2CV with wings.

"My brother converted his *Deuche* into an aeroplane!" he proudly told me one time. Other notable features in this Aladdin's Cave for *Top Gear* fans include a full-sized wooden aeroplane propeller, an enormous slobbering dog and a fridge stocked full of small bottles of *Flag* and *Castel* (local beers, which he often shares with his regular customers).

After five hours of being towed by a jeep from Dassa, and I was greeted by Freddie's dulcet tones:

"*Zut alors, Robert! Zut! Zut! Cette bagnole-là me casse les pieds!*" which basically means, 'Shame you're having such a bad time with this wonderful vehicle'.

Now, I'm by no means an expert on car parts, but it turned out that the shaft which runs from the engine to the gearbox was broken – every one of the 'teeth' on one end had gradually snapped off until none remained and so the car could not be driven.  Unfortunately, the part needed was not available in Benin and would even be tricky to find in Nigeria without buying an entire second-hand engine!  Interestingly, I then called *Amazon 4x4,* a great company in eastern England (and no relation to the book people).  After e-mailing photos to the guy in charge there, he found the part brand new for £125.  Then to have it DHL-ed out here would cost £175 – more than the part itself!  That said, it still worked out a whole lot cheaper – and better – than going the Nigeria route!

Although Freddie now has the parts he needs, he is still working on *The Beast* this morning, hence the taxi.  We all doze during the journey north; it's nice for once to have someone else to navigate the goats, motorbikes and potholes, I must say.  We make it to Dassa just before 9:00am and are greeted by Dorothé.

"Can we get into our rooms now, to unload a bit?"  I ask him.

"Well…Monsieur…there's a problem.  Not all three rooms are available."

"But you promised them all to me just a few weeks ago."

"You can only have two of the three rooms, Monsieur."

"But why?  I made a booking and I have family coming to stay here and everything. We must have those three rooms."

I've been up since five and have just endured a three-hour long bumpy journey – I'm not in the best of moods to say the least.  I continue my rant:

"This is not good!  *Ce n'est pas bon*! You assured me that we could have these three rooms."

"Monsieur, one of the rooms is already taken."

"Then get the person out!  We had the booking first!"

I know I'm losing my rag way too much here, but when family from the UK are involved and when I'd gone to the trouble of visiting especially to make sure everything would be just right for them, I don't expect this!  Suddenly, the door of the middle room opens and a young American lady appears.

"This room is taken because *I'm* staying here," she says, forcefully but politely. This disarms us all somewhat.

"I…I'm sorry," I mumble. "It's not your fault.  He'd told us *we* could have the room."

"I've been staying here for the past five weeks," the young *Peace Corps* volunteer tells us.  Dorothé is clearly 'out of order' here, as he'd had ample time to let us know of this arrangement.  However, as is often the case, folk are fearful that you may cancel your booking if you know the truth so – once again – go for pleasing you in the short-term rather than the long-term. This is truly a case in point. And the worst is yet to come: the house just across the road which Dorothé had promised for Harry's family is also not available.

"I do not have the keys to open the door," he tells me.

"Then *find* the keys! We need that house for my family, and you promised me…"

"Impossible, Monsieur. The person with the key has travelled."

Arrrgghhh!  It is very hard for a Western mind to understand this kind of thing – can he not see that he has let us down in a big way?

"Monsieur, it's not a problem. There is a hotel just down the road. Your family can stay there and I can take you in my car."

Not an ideal set up and 'just down the road' turns out to be almost a mile away!  Thankfully, we'll manage with the two remaining rooms here tonight, as there are only five of us.

Amidst of all this hubbub, the Ifè and Idaasha musicians are gathering in a small meeting room not far away.  I really hope they haven't heard much of our little discussion; it would not be a great way to begin proceedings for the day.  As it is, I'm already feeling pretty fed up after all that hullabaloo, combined with a very early start and a tiring journey here.

The meeting room is more or less hexagonal, with a tin roof and open sides blocked in by diagonal wooden slats which allow for plenty of airflow whilst keeping out some of the heat. There are exactly fifteen Ifè and fifteen Idaasha as planned, which should work nicely. We start off, as ever, by looking at the song styles. It is interesting to see how many common genres the two ethnic groups share, in spite of their different locations. Although there are some differences, the following genres are found amongst the Ifè and the Idaasha:

*Agbaja* - for rejoicing

*Gèlèdé* - for rejoicing

*Akpokpo* - for hunting

*Gudugbá* - for celebrations/rejoicing

*Ajikpò* (or *Shikpò* in Idaasha) - for rejoicing

*Owó-Otsùkpá* (or *Owó-kpikpa* in Idaasha) - for dancing in the moonlight


As I've mentioned before, at least some of the genres listed as 'for rejoicing' would probably have been linked to more specific events or ceremonies in the past. Nevertheless, we can certainly work with this list. Interestingly, the Idaasha come up with half a dozen extra genres which the Ifè do not seem to have (or be aware of).

For a change, we kick off with parables: three old favourites at that – The Sower, The Good Samaritan and The Prodigal Son. After the usual teaching, they get into six groups – three Ifè, three Idaasha and then off they go to get cracking with their compositions.

Almost immediately, three Idaasha guys approach me:

"We're going back to the village."

"Oh. Why is that?" I reply, perplexed.

"To compose our song with friends there."

They have clearly got the wrong idea about what a workshop entails!

"Normally, you would stay here and compose so that everyone can share their ideas and results."

"No, we're going to the village. We'll be back when our song is finished."

And off they wander, just like that. There's very little I can do to actually stop them; at the end of the day, if they come back with a good song, we'll all be happy!

Shortly after this, there are other problems, particularly in the 'Good Samaritan' group. Instead of 'Levite' they have used the term *'maître catéchiste'*, which means 'catechism teacher' – not entirely the same thing, particularly for the Protestants who are likely to hear this song. I point this out to them and they endeavour to find an alternative term.

Then the 'Parable of the Sower' group encounters an intriguing problem: the only word for 'to sow' in the local language actually means 'to plant with the heel', as this is how it is done in the culture. And so, the whole parable would not make sense, as someone planting with their heel would not throw the seed onto the rocks or path! Tricky one. We try and find a way of explaining the sowing process in Palestine in Jesus' time, especially the fact that throwing seed out with the hand has to be included.

Whilst they are busy working on their songs, I take my brother-in-law, Harry, and the girls off for a short tour of the grounds. At the edge of the compound, large rocks about fifteen feet high rise up out of the earth for no apparent reason. As we approach these curved outcrops, we can see children sliding down the sides on huge teak leaves – a fascinating variation on sledging. It's just too tempting, and some of us grab a teak leaf and join in the fun for a couple of minutes!

"Weeeeee!"

You can only use the same leaf once or twice, as the rough rock quickly makes holes in it, but there are plenty more where this one came from! These kids are clearly very poor and probably don't even go to school. But they at least have one thing we do not: the opportunity to go 'sledging' all year round, and in warm weather!

Next to the rocks, a slim but muscular man is hitting smaller rocks with a mallet and chisel. He has a greying beard and is wearing an old pair of shortish trousers and no top. He greets us with a warm smile as we approach. As a tourist, Harry is particularly interested to learn all he can about African culture during his short visit and asks the man many questions about his work (mostly through me as interpreter). It turns out that the chap has been doing this job pretty much every day for the past two years, making gravel for use in building or road construction. Once smashed small enough, he puts the stones into a sizeable plastic bowl. For each bowlful of gravel he makes about thirteen pence and in one day can fill around twelve bowls – a daily wage of just £1.56. That's a lot of work for not much money! Harry also insists on having a go, and the man is happy for a short respite from his labours. As Harry whacks away at the rock, our man can't help but laugh; whether it's Harry's technique which he finds funny, or the sheer incongruity of a white man perched there doing this job, I don't know!

Back on the compound and the songs are taking shape. The 'Good Samaritan' group has a further problem, which I have to point out to them. Their song concludes with the phrase:

"If you do as the Samaritan, you're sure to go to Heaven."

Now, I can see entirely where they got this from, as Jesus even says: "Do this and you will live." However, their song seems to suggest that merely helping someone in need could somehow 'earn' us eternal life. Of course, Jesus was using the parable to show the need to 'love the Lord your God with all your heart, soul, mind and strength *and* your neighbour as yourself', not to say that helping someone in need could – per se – earn someone a place in Heaven. I ask them to think about the meaning and to try and re-word their concluding lyrics accordingly. This is becoming like hard work!

During the morning's composition session, Harry is doing the things newcomers to Africa always do: taking photos of the lizards, greeting folk awkwardly and sweating profusely. He's also photographing the children and watching the delight on their faces as they see themselves – maybe for the first time in their lives – on the tiny camera screen.

"*C'est vous!*" he says in anglicised French, pointing excitedly at the screen. "Ça, c'est vous!"

The children laugh excitedly, pushing each other out of the way to get a better look.

The Africans, meanwhile, are doing all the things *they* tend to do when a newcomer arrives: asking Harry for his address and phone number so they can 'be his friend', having their photo taken with him, and trying to teach him the local greetings, which he repeats obligingly several times. So far, he seems to be having a better time with them than me!

As each group's song takes shape, I visit them to make a short recording, just for the record and in case anyone forgets the song. It is then that I notice that my headphones are not working properly! I'm not sure what has happened but the cable must have got damaged somewhere along the line. Thankfully, my niece, Sarah, has a pair of *in-the-ear* phones which she obligingly lends me. As soon as I get chance, I call Lois, who is not travelling up here until tomorrow, and ask her to bring more headphones with her.

Lunchtime and it's yam chips with fish and more of the ubiquitous tomato, onion and chilli sauce. Unfortunately, the fish is almost stone cold, maybe due to the fact that lunch was served an hour later than scheduled. You may remember, I'm not a big fish fan, but when it's cold (and still has its head attached), then I'm even less keen!

After lunch, we perform the songs together and suggest improvements, then they're back into their groups. Another guy approaches me:

"I want to marry your daughter!"

"What?!"

I realize this is just one of the many African 'jokes' you often hear (though not necessarily without a hint of truth). When I first came to Benin, it would outrage me until I realized it was not necessarily a serious proposition. Even now, I find it quite disconcerting to say the least. It's very hard for a Western father to take such a 'joke' lightly, and I've just about run out of good cheer this morning!

"She's only nine years old – much too young for you. Please don't say this to me again," I respond, as calmly as I can.

By the end of the day, the first set of songs is more or less done, so we make a start on the second lot. These are some verses from Hebrews, chosen by the Ifè (not sure why, but there you go). They are:

Hebrews 9:11-14
Hebrews 10:9-10
Hebrews 10:19-22


We close for the day and Dorothé takes me, Harry and the girls to the hotel down the road for dinner. The *Auberge du Soleil* is a single-storey, concrete building, which has definitely seen better days: the gravel driveway is now part mud, paintwork is peeling and some of the air-conditioning units look like they could fall off the wall at any moment. However, the gardens are nicely stocked with tropical plants, and the restaurant – although somewhat dingy – has a nice long table and their rice and sauce is good. Harry and I sit and chat over a beer as the telly blares away at one end of the room.

"It's not normally like this," I tell Harry. "Usually, it's so much more positive and they are more focused."

Harry has enjoyed the day regardless; many of the 'stresses' have affected me more directly and, after all, he's on holiday whilst I'm working! He also has no other workshops to compare this one with, and so any sight and sound of African music is going to be exciting and interesting for him. But for me, I feel exhausted and discouraged. The songs were not bad, but there were so many problems and hassles I could have done without. If I were on my own, I would happily brush these off and get on with the work. But as I have relatives – newly-arrived relatives with little experience of Africa – then I am all the more aware of being 'on show' and also of needing to make sure their needs are met.

Back to the compound and we take our two rooms either side of *Peace Corps lady*'s room. Unfortunately, there is no running water in our rooms at the moment (here we go again), but I'm so tired I just hit the sack and am out like a light, Ruth too.


Morning again, and I wish I could say my bad day yesterday was compensated by a good night's sleep. Unfortunately, I cannot. The pillow – for want of a *lesser* word – is filled with straw and was so hard that I woke up with head and neck ache. The straw is packed solid: it may as well have been filled with gravel! It was also a decidedly chilly night, and yet no blankets – or even a sheet – were provided. To top it all, the shower doesn't work! It's not a water-cut, because there is water in the sink tap. So the shower has clearly not been maintained, and certainly not checked before our arrival. This is turning into a saga!

On cue, Dorothé arrives.

"Did you sleep well?"

"Not really," I reply grumpily. "The pillow was too hard and I was too cold."

"Sorry, Monsieur."

"And the shower does not work! Did you not check the shower before we arrived to make sure everything was in order? And also, did it not occur to you that we might at least need a sheet to keep us warm at night?? *Je ne suis pas content!*"

"*Désolé, Monsieur,*" he responds, apologetically.

The trouble is, almost everything has gone wrong at this place so far, and we're certainly not getting the deal we were promised.

"Okay. Where is breakfast served?"

"Breakfast? There is no breakfast."

"No breakfast?!"

"No. There's just African *bouilli*, if you'd like some of that."

Not especially, I must say. *Bouilli* is a kind of watery white porridge. The locals love it, but it's really not my cup of tea. Talking of which, a cup of tea would be nice right now!

"Did you not think that your guests might like tea or coffee and some bread for breakfast?? What kind of a place *is* this? No breakfast! That's outrageous!!"

"*Monsieur, calmez-vous!* There is breakfast at the hotel down the road. I can take you there."

"No time for that: I have to start the workshop in half an hour."

One of the pastors has heard the noise and approaches to try and help.

"What's the problem?" he asks.

Embarrassed, I explain all the shortcomings of this place so far.

"…And to top it all, he hasn't even provided me with a suitable break-fast!" It's enough to test the patience of a saint, and I'm feeling anything but saintly this morning!

Harry and the girls are taken down the road for a 'proper' breakfast (the usual: Nescafé, powdered milk, bread, butter, jam), whilst I get ready for what day two may have in store.

We begin by singing through all the songs, Ifè and Idaasha, and they're sounding pretty decent. The Ifè have brought an instrument which looks like a giant mushroom from a distance. It's yet another gourd – this time a whole one, about eighteen inches across, but narrowing down to six inches at the neck. In many cases, this instrument is played with the opening uppermost, and a cloth or flip-flop is beaten over the hole to make a loud echoing sound. However, the Ifè have it turned the other way up and the musician hits the large rounded end of the gourd with his hands or fists, to create a low, resonant thudding sound.

Besides the usual array of drums, bells and shakers, there is another fasci-nating instrument which I have not seen before: a square drum which also doubles up as a stool! Which came first? Who can tell – but thinking of chickens and eggs just makes me miss my breakfast all the more! Anyway, the 'stool drum' is placed on the floor sideways, so that the square skin is perpendicular to the ground. The player then sits on the wooden rim with the drum skin in front of him, either side of his legs. He plays the drum with both hands, also kicking it with his heel for extra percussion. So that's *two* new uses for the heel I've come across on this workshop! As you may remember, the Tem in Sokodé had square drums too, but this one differs from theirs in almost every way besides the actual shape.

As they continue to practise their songs, Dorothé rushes up with a large white kitchen pan. It has rather attractive red and blue stripes around the sides.

"Monsieur Baker. *Votre petit déjeuner!*"

He's brought me some breakfast – bless him.  I take the pan and thank him.  Sitting down away from the musicians, I remove the lid: fried chicken and chips!  Unusual for breakfast, but as least he's made an effort.  I honestly think that he was so delighted to have this huge booking at his centre that he really didn't think through the implications.  Who knows – maybe this is the most people he's ever had staying here.

It's already ten past ten, but one of the Idaasha musicians is not here yet.  I ask after him.

"He's composing two songs in the village but should be here soon," I'm told.

After my chicken and chips, I wander round the compound, looking for a good recording location.  As usual, I clap my hands in lots of places to see what the acoustics are like.  As I pass by the kitchen area, the cook joins in clapping with me, as if to encourage me in my rhythmic exercises!  There's no ideal recording location here, but I make a compromise under a couple of trees between the main meeting room and our accommodation.

Sometime this morning, my wife, Lois, will be joining us, along with my other two children and the rest of Harry's family.  As if this is not enough company, there will also be three French friends coming along to watch.  Olivier, a French Mennonite, has been in Cotonou for a few months now.  He's very young, but a lovely chap, and bursting with enthusiasm and *joie de vivre*.  Now, Olivier also has a couple of visitors from France and they happen to be travelling through Dassa (as anyone travelling north or south through Benin has to).  I mentioned the workshop to them and they seemed interested.  So, at some point there will be a total of *twelve* visitors come to observe the workshop – which is really great, if I were not so busy with the work to actually spend any decent time with them!

I decide to get the recording equipment set up before lunch, so that we can make a prompt start afterwards.  As I'm doing so, one of the Idaasha musicians approaches me with curiosity.

"Is this the recording equipment?"

"Yes it is."

"Afterwards, you will give me this microphone!"

"Sorry, I can't do that."

It's always worth asking, just in case, eh?!  I then notice that one of the Ifè guys has his own cassette recorder with him and is already trying it out.  I'm not very happy at this – if I've come all this way to make decent recordings of their songs, why would anyone want to use an old tape recorder to make poor quality ones?  To top it all, yesterday one guy asked me to give him some blank tapes!  I don't even have any with me.  Today they've clearly found some, though the tape in their recorder this morning says 'South Shore Baptist Church' on it (wherever that is).

The Ifè have some amazing drones – something you don't hear very much in this part of the world.  A drone, like on the bagpipes or hurdy-gurdy, is a single, sustained note, generally low in pitch, which accompanies the rest of the music and is held on throughout the piece.  The Ifè's drone is a sung one and occurs particularly in the genre called *gudugbá*.  It gives a haunting but appealing tone to these songs and I like it!

One of the pastors, Jean-Claude, tells me: "In the past, everything was calm – we just sang [in church].  Then, gradually, more and more churches started playing the drums."  This all began about thirty years ago; around the time when the same thing started happening in many African countries, as local Christians realized the value of *their* music in worship and evangelism.

Throughout the morning, I am once again torn between the joy of hearing such beautiful music and the constant frustrations of both the poor service on the compound and the *what-can-you-give-me* attitude of some of the participants.  Another comes up to me:

"I have a headache.  Can you give me some tablets for it?"

As if I'm his chemist!  "No, I cannot.  What do you normally do if you have a headache?"

"I go to the shop and buy some tablets."

Lois and the others arrive by late morning.  It's great to see them.  Thankfully, lunch is a slight improvement on yesterday – only half an hour late and almost warm!  We had been promised Cokes and other fizzy drinks with our meals. However, when I ask, I'm told there's only water or beer left. Oh dear! Not much fun for the kids.

Recording begins after lunch. Once the first Ifè song is done, we get set up for the second one. Only then does their pastor tell me: "We have to redo the first song: they missed some details out."

"Well, as we're all set up for the second song now, let's do that and come back to your first one later," I suggest.

He seems to accept this option without too much difficulty. Three songs down and some more 'alien' sounds are coming into my headphones. What's this? It turns out the batteries for my 'phantom power' are low, so I change them and we re-record the track. All the time, *tape recorder man* is standing there, shamelessly making his own recording on the 'South Shore Baptist' cassette, using nothing but the built-in microphone. At one point, he even asks me to wait before recording, so he can rewind his tape a bit!

Halfway through the recording session it begins to rain; not heavily, but enough to put a stop to the proceedings. We quickly move everything into the straw-roofed *paillote* and continue there. However, from an acoustic point of view, it is virtually impossible to have all the drums in the *paillote* too, as they are much too loud. And so the poor drummers have to sit outside, under a mango tree at least, so as to miss most of the rain.

Due to this afternoon's technical problems, we only manage to get five of the twelve songs recorded. Once we add the last set of six songs tomorrow, that will make thirteen more to record, as well as actually composing the last lot. Could be a busy day! The participants are given the final set of verses to start work on this evening. They are:

2 Corinthians 5:17

Colossians 2:6–7

Galatians 5:22–26

I could do with a bit of Galatians 5 myself at the moment! Today has been a bit better than yesterday, but not much.

Tonight we're all staying at the *Auberge du Soleil* together, so I ask Dorothé if I can leave the microphone stands in my old bedroom at his centre, to save carting them down the road and back (a situation for which he was – after all – responsible). "No problem," he replies. "You can leave the equipment in that room."

It's a fun evening at the *Auberge du Soleil* and our three French friends are staying the night here too. After dinner, we play the insanely fast-moving card game of 'Dutch Blitz' with Olivier and company before turning in.

Day Three and it's pancakes for breakfast! Nice. Dorothé arrives to pick us up in his car by 8:30. As there are lots of us, some choose to walk the mile or so down the red dirt road. We also say goodbye to our three French friends and their Dutch Blitz cards; they're heading off for more travels today.

The musicians are all busy composing their last set of songs when we arrive, and they're sounding pretty decent already – a good variety of genres, instruments and sounds. By eleven o'clock we are ready to start recording. It's raining again, though, so we have to settle for the *paillote* option once more. On one song, we have to do *four* retakes, both frustrating and time-consuming, but it happens (and sometimes even more than four times!) The Ifè have decided to precede each song with a short reading; this also takes up time I had not accounted for, but it's a nice touch for their cassette. In between songs, one participant comes up to me and I'm already expecting the worst.

"Can I have my photo taken with you? My pastor will want to see what you look like."

I really haven't the time for this, there's still so much to do.

"Can't you just tell him how good-looking I am?!" I respond, trying to add some humour to an otherwise frustrating situation.

He insists and I have to sit there, headphones around my neck, and smile at his camera before we crack on with the next song.

By lunchtime, we've recorded three more songs. That's eight altogether (and ten still to go). However – surprise, surprise – lunch is not ready for

1:00pm. In fact, it doesn't arrive until after 2:30pm, so we soldier on till then and manage to get a couple more songs in the can before eating.

Now it's three o'clock and I find myself in yet another tricky situation: I had planned to leave at five o'clock today and have already booked a taxi. Lois, my kids and most of Harry's family have already headed off to the *Auberge de Dassa* itself, leaving just me, Harry and his eldest daughter, Sarah. So, the idea was that we would join them by 5:30pm, once it was all over. However, we still have *eight* songs to record in two hours! This is almost unheard-of, and will necessitate unprecedented swiftness on the part of all concerned! I'm already pretty exhausted when the next group set up to record. I call out to the rest, who are practising further away: "Please be ready as soon as this group is done! We have no time to waste – you must come *tout de suite*!" They nod obligingly. Even though I know that urgency is not a strong point in Africa, and that *tout de suite* doesn't always have the same significance here, I nevertheless really hope they will be quick this afternoon!

Three thirty and we're onto the second of the eight remaining songs. One of the leading participants comes up to me:

"We'd like to discuss something with you at the end of today."

I'm tired, I'm impatient and I really don't want any *issues* before I leave.

"If it's about money, I really don't want to hear it!" I snap back at him, and we continue recording. By four o'clock, things start slowing down, as the participants and I get more and more tired. More mistakes are made and more retakes needed. At five o'clock, my taxi arrives and I have to ask him to wait for a while – we still have three songs to record! At 5:25pm precisely, we start recording the final track. However, this turns out to be the longest song of the entire workshop – six minutes in duration! Thankfully, my taxi is in no hurry (the plus side of African laid-backness).

Totally exhausted, sweating onto my notebook so much that my pen won't work, and longing for a nice cool shower, we round up the afternoon by all meeting together in the main room again. It's all I can do to muster up the energy to thank them. They are thankful too and – all things considered – the final recordings are pretty decent, with a good variety of styles and instrumentation. Then it happens: one of them pipes up with, "It was good, but we wish the workshop had been better organized!"

I'm defensive: "Better organized? What do you mean?"

"Well, so that we would receive some money from you."

Money? They want *money* from me! This is a never-ending issue for the expatriate working in Africa: all too often, the issue of money rears its ugly head! To be fair, it does vary depending on location; the Bogo over in Sassanou never asked me for a penny and – in fact – gave *me* several gifts as a token of their appreciation! My theory is that the closer to the coast and/or to a big city you get, the worse it becomes.

"Money! What for?"

"For participating in the workshop!"

I pause for a moment, then continue:

"Let me ask you some questions. Firstly, Ifè participants, did you pay for your transport here?"

"No, it was free," they reply.

"And, everybody, how much have you had to pay for your accommodation during this workshop?"

"Nothing."

"Right. And your meals?"

"They were provided free of charge."

"And what about the hours of technical work I've put in to record your songs? Do I get paid for that? And *my* travel from Cotonou – it cost me 40,000 CFA. Nobody is paying me for that! Furthermore, I will go home from here and spend several days editing all your songs and making the cassettes so that you can benefit from them. You will then each receive a cassette of your songs, also free of charge. And *still* you ask me for money?"

The issue of *per diems* as they are called is still a contentious one. You see, I just spoke as a Westerner, from a Western viewpoint (and a particularly worn-out, fed up Westerner at that!) Now, the African viewpoint is very different: they've given up time to come and take part in this workshop, so should be 'rewarded' for this. They'll also have lost several days' income, which is not going to appear out of thin air, and they need to feed their families somehow. Finally, in Africa, if you have a friend who is richer than you, then it would be completely normal for the rich friend to give some money to the poorer friend. In the West, we try not to mix friendship with money, in case it spoils it; in Africa, friendship and exchange of cash often go hand in hand, almost as a way of cementing a friendship.

"That's all I have to say on the matter." I add. And we end the workshop. Just like that. I'm way too exhausted to continue debating this with them. I quickly pay Dorothé's bill, climb into the taxi with Harry and Sarah and we head off.

"We could tell it didn't end very well, even though we don't understand much French," says Sarah as we bounce along the dirt road back to Dassa town.

"I honestly thought you weren't going to get all the songs recorded in time," Harry adds.

"It was *crazy*," I reply.

Dinner at my favourite *Auberge de Dassa* is delicious as ever: steak, peas and boiled potatoes – just the job! It's good to be back somewhere relatively comfortable, especially for all the family. As we sit there chatting after dinner, I take a look at Dorothé's bill, which I paid in such a rush I didn't have time even to look at it. I carefully read through each item.

"I don't believe it!" I say out loud.

"What?" they all ask.

"Dorothé has charged me for the night I left the microphone stands in the room!"

"Really?!"

"Oh, and he's also charged us 1,000 francs for *every* time he took us to the *Auberge du Soleil* in his car!" The nerve of the man! I guess he's just trying to make a living, but it seems outrageous to my Western mind.

Time for bed now, and the *Auberge de Dassa* has welcome air-conditioning, which makes for a decent night's sleep (finally). Tomorrow, we shall attempt to intercept a passing bus so that we can all travel back to Cotonou.

"Here's one, here's one!" the children all call out excitedly, pointing forwards and jumping up and down. We're standing by the main roundabout in Dassa, just in front of the *auberge* itself. The blue and white 'Comfort Lines' bus approaches, but fails to stop for us, in spite of frantic waving on our part. Must be full, I think to myself.

Then, out of nowhere, an eight-seater Peugeot taxi appears, a tad rusty and with half a dozen sacks of charcoal on the roof.

*"Monsieur. Vous-allez à Cotonou?"*

*"Oui."*

"I can take you."

"No thank you. We're waiting for a bus."

"I can take you for the same price."

"Really? How much?"

"27,000 CFA."

Now, the bus would cost us 2,500 each, totalling 25,000. However, the taxi will take us to our doorstep, which has to be worth the extra money.

"Okay, we'll take it."

I know it's only an eight-seater, but we pile four in the very back, and another four on the 'normal' back seat, then two in the front passenger seat. As we're all piling in, the taxi driver takes my son, Micah, and sits him on *his* lap in front of the steering wheel.

"No, no, no!" I cry. "He cannot sit there – much too dangerous!"

*"C'est bon, c'est bon!"* the driver insists.

"No, he can sit on my lap in the passenger's seat."

"You see, Monsieur, my friend here needs a ride too, so we must fit him on the passenger seat with you." He points at his tall and – thankfully – skinny friend, standing beside the car. I think for a second.

"No, I'm not having that. It's too many people and we've booked the taxi for us. If he gets in, we're all getting out!"

The driver concedes and I get in the passenger seat and take my six year old son from the driver and we move off. Almost immediately, the taxi driver reaches into the glove box for a couple of white tablets and promptly takes them.

"Paracetamol," he tells me.

"Do you have a headache then?"

"No, I always take paracetamol when I'm driving; two in the morning and two in the afternoon.  It helps me concentrate and keeps me awake."

Well, I've never heard of paracetamol having those properties, but far be it for me to contradict him!  I glance round at the eight people squashed in the back and smile.  It's then that I notice something strange out of the back window of the car: a man is standing on the rear bumper!  It's the skinny man I refused to let travel in the car – instead he's hitching a lift on the back.  Talk about resourcefulness!  He stays there for about an hour, balancing precariously on the bumper and holding onto the charcoal sacks.  Then, as we slow down in the next town, he jumps off and we don't see him again.

Another curiosity: I cannot help noticing that this taxi driver also has a leather whip on his front dashboard.

"What's *that* for?" I enquire.

"In case someone jumps in front of the taxi to try and cause an accident to get money.  If they do, I am ready to whip them to show them this is wrong."

Eek!  I hope we don't have to witness that and, thankfully, we don't.

Before dropping us at home, the driver stops off on the outskirts of Cotonou to unload his sacks of charcoal from the roof.  This makes our journey half an hour longer and I begin to wonder whether the bus wouldn't have been a preferable option after all.  The important thing is, we're back in Cotonou at last, and in one piece!

Half an hour after arriving, my phone rings.  It's Freddie.

"*Robert, ta sacrée espèce de casserole est prête enfin!*" he shouts down the phone, which basically means: 'I'm pleased to inform you that your car has once again been mended'.  Good news indeed!

Thinking back, was I too harsh on the Ifè and Idaasha people? Maybe. I could certainly have been more civil at times, but the circumstances brought out the worst in me. The lack of my own vehicle, the inadequate accommodation, the constant demands for money and favours, the delayed and poor meals, the 'bootleg' tape recordings, the rain, the poor sleeping conditions and the fact that nobody (but Dorothé) was 'at home' there, all made it so much harder than other workshops. Add to this the exhaustion, the time pressures, and the desire on my part to make everything 'just right' for my visiting family and it all adds up to a major overload of stress.

Now, if you've never lived outside of your Western culture, you may have been cheering me on in this chapter. "Well said, Rob! They were well out of order and you were right to tell them so." And if you've lived in Africa for any length of time, the chances are you'll have been in similarly stressful situations yourself and will understand how easy it is to let your environment get the better of you. Culture is a massive thing, and cultural differences – or misunderstandings – are at the heart of most friction and stress for an expatriate overseas. I've seen perfectly lovely people (Germans, Americans, French and – I have to add – Brits) *losing their rag* with Africans, because things didn't happen 'just so'. We are conditioned to seeking perfection, creating a world where everything is clear cut and runs according to certain rules (and woe betide you, should you veer from those!) Africa is not like that. Sure, there are rules, but things are often more fluid, negotiable, adaptable; and this is not a bad thing, it's just *how things are done here*.

I've lost count of how many times I've been *queue-jumped* in Africa – a misdemeanour close to a cardinal sin in England! But not in Africa. And seeing how things are done here and adapting to it is – in many ways – what I'm trying to do with music and dance in my workshops. You only really feel at home in your mother culture, and that's what my work is all about.

Christians are called to rely on God in times of stress; I guess I was so distracted on this workshop that I didn't do that enough. A bit more love, joy, peace, patience, kindness, goodness, humility and self-control and I'd have behaved quite differently, I'm sure.  Sorry for giving you a hard time, Ifè and Idaasha people – you did really well and your music was some of the best I've experienced.

The Beast needs a tow home.  Outside my favourite auberge in Dassa.

# Chapter Seven

# Deforestation and Drenching

*The Ditammari People of North-Western Benin*

Natitingou: a nice sounding name for a nice town. Natitingou is a clean, organized, vibrant settlement nestled in the Atakora Mountains of northern Benin. It was the birthplace of Mathieu Kérékou, the former president, doubtless one reason so much money has been thrown at it in recent times. The streets are wide, straight and well-tarmacked, with nicely painted buildings, pleasant hotels and a surprisingly small amount of litter for this part of the world. I like Natitingou. In fact, I try and stay here whenever I can – which is not very often.

Today I'm only planning to pass through Natitingou on my way to Boukoumbé, a smaller, more remote town where the Ditammari, or Somba people live in curious houses. The seven hour drive here has been good so far, and *The Beast* is running nicely. Well, besides the catch on the bonnet coming loose, making it rise up a couple of inches at regular intervals!

When I stopped off in Dassa for lunch, I met a most interesting Belgian chap: sixty-four years old, having spent most of his life in Africa. Some great stories and experiences – I want to be like him when I grow up! I also narrowly missed killing a goat this time, which came out into the road from nowhere. I quite literally screeched to a halt, stopping inches before its startled, slot-shaped pupils. From Dassa to Nattitingou is about four hour's drive, making an entire journey time of around seven. As it's September, there's been lots of rain and many of the rivers and streams of Benin are overflowing onto roads, villages and fields.  In fact, in several neighbouring countries (including Togo), there has been more serious flooding, with whole bridges collapsing in some cases.

Heading northwards in Benin, you notice more and more round mud huts in the villages (rather than the square, brick-built ones seen in the south). Also, more mosques and fewer churches. The vegetation changes too; as the climate becomes less humid, the lush thickly-wooded south gives way to open grassland, ronier palms and majestic baobabs.  It eventually becomes a tad hillier too, as the Atakora mountain range looms to the west.

It's only a few more miles to Natitingou now, which is just as well, as it's around 6:00pm already and the sun will be setting soon.  I should be able to make it to Boukoumbé by nightfall though.

There have been way too many potholes in the last hour or so and, whilst I've managed to swerve and avoid most of them, hitting some is almost inevitable – and I have.  One was particularly harsh, with a loud 'crash' as my wheel struck the broken edge of tarmac at great speed.

The entrance to Natitingou is marked by a pretty roundabout with a monument in the centre – a common sight in many African towns and cities (though I've never quite worked out why).  As I approach this one, three things happen almost simultaneously. Firstly, my mp3 player, which has been entertaining me with an eclectic selection of Louis Armstrong, Abdullah Ibrahim, Steve Reich, Vivaldi, Bill Evans, Eva Cassidy, Steve Green and Jacques Loussier, suddenly stops playing. The single 'AAA' battery has done well to last this long!  The second thing which then happens (and is linked to the first) is that I hear a continuous grinding noise coming from the front nearside wheel.  Oh dear – sounds like one of those potholes has got the better of my wheel bearings. The third thing which happens is that I spot a mechanic's workshop, just off to the right, so turn off and drive up a muddy slope to the garage.

"*Bonsoir, Monsieur!*" The *garagiste* greets me and I explain the problem.

"I think it's your wheel bearings, Monsieur. We're unlikely to find any replacements here in Nati, but probably over in Kara."

Kara! That's in Togo! But, come to think of it, it's only a couple of hours away from here. Still, there's no hope of my continuing to Boukoumbé tonight with the wheel in this state, so I take the mechanic's phone number and hail a taxi to a hotel. I've had a long, tiring day, which has not ended quite the way I had hoped or expected, so I think I'll spoil myself and stay in one of Nati's best: the *Tata Somba Hotel*.

The hotel is a large pink building set in pleasant, leafy grounds with a sizeable pool in its central courtyard. Some young *Peace Corps* volunteers are having a swim at the moment – I'm guessing they're not hotel residents, though, on their income. *Tata Somba* is the name given to the curious houses in which the Ditammari people live, and this hotel, to an extent, has been built to resemble one of these: a perimeter wall joining together smaller towers in a vaguely circular formation. I've never been to a real *tata Somba*, but hope to get the opportunity during this workshop (if I ever make it there!) Talking of which, as soon as I get my room sorted, I return to reception to ask about a taxi for my thirty-five mile journey through the mountains to Boukoumbé tomorrow.

"What time do you have to leave, Monsieur?" the receptionist asks me.

"Around seven o'clock in the morning."

"That would be much too early for a taxi, as they have to fill up with passengers first."

"Oh dear. I must leave early. Is there any other way?"

"You could always travel there by *zemidjan*, Monsieur. One of those could come any time."

Hmmm. A *zemidjan*, or motorbike taxi, would be interesting at least, but what about all my recording equipment? As there's clearly no other way to get there on time, I accept and he immediately calls a *zem* driver he knows, asking him to come at 7:00am. I'll just have to keep my equipment to a bare minimum. My microphone stands are still in the back of *The Beast* anyway, so I'll leave those and figure something out when I get there; you can almost always improvise with sticks as microphone stands – I've even hung them from tree branches before now and it can work quite nicely!

Dinner is steak and chips – one of the standards in 'posher' places. The restaurant itself is nicely turned out, though a bit dated in décor. On the walls are touristy posters advertising the attractions of northern Benin. One poster says "*Bénin: Splendeurs du Nord.*" It also contains an attempted translation into English, which reads "Benin: The North Splendours." Oh well, nice try! It would only have cost them about fifty pence to translate four words, but there you go – we get the gist!

One of the greatest 'splendours of the north' in this country is the Pendjari National Park, a real hidden treasure in a little known African country. It's the place where Freddie the French mechanic flew his hang-glider at low range to scare the elephants ("*C'est vachement cool, Robert, tu ne peux pas imaginer!*"). Here, you can see a huge variety of wild African game, almost unparalleled in West Africa. Now, it's nothing like Kenyan parks or the Kruger in South Africa, but still has a respectable range of animals, most of which you stand a reasonable chance of actually seeing. As well as elephants, there are also lions, hippos, monkeys, buffalo, crocodiles, baboons, antelope, hyenas – even a cheetah if you're very lucky! Oh, and lots of pretty birds of different exotic colours too. The road through the park is almost incessantly 'washboard' or at least bumpy dirt track, but the two to three hours' drive to the hotel near the Burkina Faso border is well worth it.

I've been to the Pendjari twice, but the first time we only saw a couple of elephants in the distance. The second time, though, we saw more than a dozen, some at very close range. In fact, one at almost *too* close range: I was sitting on the roof of *The Beast* whilst my wife drove. We came upon some elephants just beside the track. As I took out my camera to film a young elephant, it turned, stared straight at me and began to run in our direction, trumpeting loudly all the way! I've scarcely been more terrified in my whole life and jumped down into the car shouting, "Drive! Drive! Drive!" with all my might, ripping a massive hole in my shorts in the process. Things you can't do in England…

Back at the Tata Somba Hotel, and after my steak and chips, it's back to my rather nice hotel room. It has *three* sections: a smaller, walk through room on the way in, which contains a single bed, then a main room with an enormous bed – bigger than king size (whatever that would be called), a telly and air conditioning. Finally, there's a bathroom, which even has hot running water! At least, it would have, were there not a water cut at present, but I'm kind of used to that by now, as you know. The air-con seems only to have two settings: 'maximum' and 'off'. That said, I'll keep it on for now, once again in an attempt to ward off the mosquitoes in the absence of a net over my bed. At 3:30am, I wake and turn off the air-con; I'm freezing cold! It's almost as cool outside by now, so I open the screened windows and settle back to sleep. Tonight, I seem to be blessed with a lack of mosquitoes in my room, which is a welcome turn up for the books!

My moto-taxi arrives promptly at seven the next morning, just as I'm paying the bill at reception. However, the hotel does not have the correct change for me, so this takes longer than it ought. Breakfast was good, with nice coffee and very yummy bread, and I was even able to have a hot shower this morning. I have two bags to take with me to Boukoumbé: one with my clothes and stuff in, the other with most of the recording equipment (mixing desk, microphones, leads etc).

My driver is a jovial chap, wearing a thick, green jacket, a baseball cap and sunglasses with white, plastic frames. It's a cloudy day and the sun has scarcely risen, so I'm not sure why he feels the need for 'shades' today! His vehicle is more of a scooter than a motorbike, and has no rear luggage rack. How is he ever going to carry my two bags? He opts to carry them both at the front of the bike, the first wedged down in the gap between the handlebars and the seat; the second perched literally on the handlebars themselves.

The journey from Natitingou to Boukoumbé is one of the most pretty and breathtaking in Benin. It begins with a big climb out of the town to the top of a ridge. On the way up, I notice a large, white house on the hilltop above us and am curious.

"What is that building up there?" I ask my driver.

"It belongs to a former government minister."

"Does he still live there?"

"No."

"I could buy it and move to Natitingou!" I add.  He seems to find this quite amusing.

Once over the ridge, the red dirt road continues along a relatively straight and flat section bordered by tall grass, eucalyptus trees, maize fields, baobabs and random dark bushes. Very little else, besides the odd isolated dwelling. Further on, the red dirt road gives way to a lighter brown surface and impressive, beige-coloured cliffs loom in the distance.  Cloaked in the morning mist and partly covered in rich dark green vegetation, these cliffs form part of the Atakora mountain range, which runs southwest to northeast through Togo and Benin.  They are some of the only decent mountains in Benin, although Togo has plenty.

It's pretty chilly up here, and my ears and nose are slowly starting to go numb with the cold; we're at quite a high altitude for Benin.  To pass the time, I wave at passers-by, who are, as usual, carrying various items on their heads.  They almost always wave back and then my driver responds to their wave by sounding his horn at them.  This happens over and over again throughout the journey:

Wave…wave back…honk, wave…wave back…honk. An interesting little diversion, which keeps everybody happy!

To document the journey, I take out my camera and carefully hold it far enough out so as to get both of us in the frame.  My driver obligingly looks to the left as I snap.

"I'm a photographer," he tells me "but my camera is broken."

Is this true, I wonder, or just a hint so that I might feel moved to give him mine?

"Does it take a small film or a large film?" he continues.

"Neither.  It's a digital camera."

No reply.  I'm guessing he hasn't heard of such modern technology.  It's 2007 and digital photography is still a relatively new kid on the block, especially in this part of the world.

We descend from the plateau, past the impressive cliffs and down towards Boukoumbé. The vegetation on either side is now very green grass – almost as green as green can get; that kind of luminous yellow-green, like those towelling socks we used to wear in the Eighties. Very nice. There are also a number of teak trees, with their oversized leaves, and more and more maize fields, suggesting civilization cannot be far away now.

As we pass the sign at the entrance to Boukoumbé, I take out my phone to try and text Lois. No signal. Well, why would there be, come to think of it? We're rather out in the sticks here, after all!


Boukoumbé is something of an elongated town, which looks more like a very long village, but with a population of around 60,000. Thankfully, I've arrived in time for the workshop and find my contact, Rigobert, waiting outside the town hall as planned.

"*Bonjour, Monsieur Robert*! Welcome to Boukoumbé! We must greet the people in the town hall now."

This is clearly a step on from the old tradition of greeting the village chief; now they have a town hall and a mayor to greet instead! The town hall has narrow corridors, matt grey doors (again!) and turquoise walls (which make a change from the more common mint green ones), though these are – as usual – covered in brown stains everywhere.

"The mayor is not here today," Rigobert tells me, "but we will greet the vice-mayor."

"Okay. How do I say 'hello' in Ditammari?" I ask, always eager to learn the local greetings as soon as possible.

"In the morning we say: '*A yɛn taa?*'"

"And how do I reply?"

"By saying '*Da na ti*' – everything is fine."

Greetings over and we head for the workshop location, a youth centre on the main street. It's a large circular hall with a high, corrugated tin roof. Inside are approximately 130 red metal chairs, all joined together in groups of four (so make that 132!) At the front is a concrete, semi-circular stage. This is way bigger than we need, but it will certainly do the job! As yet, there are only half a dozen or so people here. One man is wearing a spiky headdress, made of animal hair, which rather looks like a *Mohican* haircut. He's also wearing a red and white tee-shirt with the word 'Nokia' emblazoned on the front in capital letters. Another man is wearing a yellow baseball cap which reads, in pale blue lettering, 'Stop Polio' – a good plan if ever I heard one!

"Where are all the others?" I ask Rigobert.

"Some have gone off to have their *bouilli* for breakfast. But the people from Manta are not here yet."

"Manta. Where's that?"

"Twenty kilometres away. Some will be coming on bicycles."

At 10:15, after a considerable amount of sitting around, chatting and generally waiting, my flipchart arrives: it's good to know I'll have something to write on when the workshop finally gets going.

To pass the time, I ask about the maize plantations I saw on the way into town.

"Ah, maize is a very new crop here in Boukoumbé," one man tells me.

"Really?"

"*Oui, Monsieur.* About ten years ago, some young American volunteers came and showed us how to plant and grow it. Now we have much maize for the village."

Good old Peace Corps, eh? Where would we be without them? I often wish the UK had something nearly as large-scale and effective; the whole thing is such a win–win situation for both sides, it has to be worth doing. I've met – and become good friends with – many Peace Corps people over the years and they've always been friendly, down-to-earth folk with a genuine willingness to make their placement count.

I'm quite tired after my long journey yesterday and my early start this morning, so I take the opportunity to lie down on the big concrete stage for a wee nap. When I rouse just before eleven, there are more people here – enough to begin the workshop, in fact. I turn to Rigobert:

"I think we can start now.  Is there a pen for the flipchart?"

"There aren't any here.  I'll go and get you one, Monsieur."

Twenty minutes later and Rigobert returns with a couple of felt markers and we finally make a start, with sixteen participants.  What is interesting this time is the mix of Christians and non-Christians, particularly those who practise African traditional religion (referred to as *animism* by some). An interesting array of people, to say the least.  The first one stands up and introduces himself – it's the chap with the cool headgear:

"My name is Koffi, I am a farmer and a Christian.  I work in literacy."

"You are very welcome, Koffi," I respond. "And next to you…"

"My name is Ngame.  I am a farmer and a composer.  I follow traditional religion and work in literacy."

Each member continues, one after the other, to introduce themselves, always standing ceremoniously to address the rest of the group.

"My name is Ishaak.  I am married.  I have just come along to watch.  I used to be a Catholic, but now I follow traditional religion."

"Hello!  My name is Marc.  I am a farmer.  I follow traditional religion and I play the flute."

"Good morning, Monsieur.  My name is Jean.  I am a school teacher. I used to be into traditional religion, but I am now a Christian.  I have composed many, many songs."

"My name is Francis.  I am a farmer.  I follow *la religion traditionnelle* and I like to dance."

"Bonjour.  My name is Jeannette." (A lady at last!)  "I sing in the choir at my church."

"Hello. My name is also Jeannette.  I am a dancer and I follow traditional religion."

Now, some of you will be thinking 'how can such a mixed and motley crew ever work together to produce meaningful Bible songs?' That is a very good question, but this is Africa and people generally get along and have a great sense of community.  You see, in this instance, it would be difficult to create decent songs without having both religions present: the African traditional religion people know the Ditammari music and dance so much better than the Christians who, for historical reasons, have not always used this in their church services. Meanwhile, we need the Christians there to make sure the Biblical truths are adhered to, or the songs are pointless. And so, in a very real way, there will be some serious *synergy* going on this time. I like that!

The list of song genres is not dissimilar to that of other ethnic groups I've worked with. One interesting genre is *musetie,* which is only sung in November and December (i.e. at harvest time), and where singers mock the harvesters, calling them 'lazy' to encourage them to work harder next time! Then there's *tifiewèènti,* another dance-in-the-moonlight genre, but this one almost resembles Russian *Cossack* dancing, with the performers crouching down kicking out each leg alternately. Most curious! Finally, it is interesting to note that, amongst the Ditammari, there is no circumcision; a practice common in many of the neighbouring ethnicities.

That's about all there is time for before lunchtime. After a tasty meal of rice, fish and a spicy sauce, I wander into town. I always like to get away from the proceedings for a while when I can, and to check out the immediate environment. Towards the town centre (such as it is) I see a phone booth. Like most in this part of the world, this is a manned booth, where you make a call and then pay the attendant, depending on how many units you have used. I make a quick call home and then decide to call the garage in Natitingou to see how the work on *The Beast* is coming along.

"*Allô!*"

"*Bonjour Monsieur.* It's the *yovo* with the Land Rover. How is the work coming along?"

"Ah, *bonjour Monsieur*! Your car is finished! We found the bearings in Nati itself and I have just finished fitting them. You can come and collect it *tout de suite.*"

"Well, I'd like to, but I'm in Boukoumbé. I'll try and come this evening."

As it is ready so soon, it makes sense that I go and fetch it later today. After all, the microphone stands are in the boot and they will be very useful, come recording day.

"*D'accord. A ce soir Monsieur.*"

Walking back from the town, I bump into a couple of our workshop participants, out for a walk themselves and wearing some seriously bizarre footwear, the likes of which I have never seen before (or since!)  From far off, they almost look like *Peter Pan* shoes, with long, curled toes at the front. However, upon closer examination, I can see that they are actually made from recycled car tyres!  All they have done is taken a section of tyre about eighteen inches long and removed the sides to leave only the part which would touch the road. They have then added a band of fabric halfway along, which goes over the top of the foot. Finally, as with flip-flops, a small band of leather runs from the fabric between the big toe and the one next to it. The result is a quirky looking sandal which is likely to last and last, given what it is made from!

The Ditammari are fortunate in that they already have the whole Bible in their language, whereas the majority of Benin's 52 languages only have some Bible or none at all.  As the afternoon session gets started, I realize what an amazing evangelistic opportunity this is; at least half the participants are not Christian.  And yet, we are composing songs with words from John 3:16-18, Romans 6:23 and 1 John 1:8-10, all of which contain the Gospel message in a nutshell!  And, of course, as we're putting them into local song styles in the local language, *everybody* will understand them clearly.  Awesome indeed!

As in Sassanou, I have another long-winded interpreter, who definitely seems to be adding his own commentary to what I say.  At one point, I merely say the word 'patience' and he speaks for almost a minute (leaving me to put the word to immediate use!)

By 2:45pm, they are composing in groups in the customary way. They have a couple of *gitarres traditionnelles* and some metal 'clickers', or *castagnettes* as they call them.  However, I am intrigued – and surprised – by the lack of drums! This is Africa: there must be drums!! Well, it's only the first day, so I decide to wait and see what other instruments turn up tomorrow.

Evening comes fast and I am eager to find a taxi sooner rather than later, so that I can get back to Natitingou to pick up *The Beast* from the mechanic. I'll then stay the night in Nati again (a pleasant by-product of a less than ideal situation), before driving back to Boukoumbé in the morning to continue the workshop. A lady at the town hall has offered to find me a taxi. Whilst she makes some calls, I notice a group of men playing *pétanque* (French bowls) on a sandy piece of ground just in front of the town hall – a remnant of colonial times if ever there were one; whilst we were teaching India to play cricket, the French were in Benin showing them their *boules*. They notice my fascination and invite me to join in. I've got a few minutes to spare, so happily oblige, launching the heavy metal balls into the air in the hope of their landing somewhere near the small wooden ball, or *cochonnet*. I don't do terribly well, but they're all happy to see a *yovo* joining in.

Just then, *town hall lady* comes out.

"Monsieur, we cannot find you a taxi to Natitingou."

Here we go again! Rigobert is there, and offers to find me a motorbike taxi once more. Well, at least I'm used to this form of travel, so it should be no problem. Within seconds, he's flagged a chap down, who is riding a shiny, royal blue bike.

"Can you take my friend here to Nati, please?"

"*Ben oui*! How much will you pay?"

"I know the price," I add, cautious of being overcharged on grounds of race.

"Well say it then!" The driver adds.

Now, I paid 3,500 CFA coming, but I'd still be happier if he tells me this!

 "No, you say your price!"

"Okay, I'll take 2,000 francs, Monsieur."

So I didn't know the price after all! Or, more likely, I paid 'hotel prices' coming here and am paying local rates to go back. Nevertheless, this chap's offer seems more than reasonable and I happily accept. Amazingly, he is even wearing a crash helmet – a rare sight indeed in these parts (though he doesn't have one for me!)

As usual, I wave at the numerous passers-by as we whizz on out of town. And, as usual too, they wave back to us, big smiles across their tired faces. However, rather than honking back to them, this driver takes one hand off the handlebars and waves back to them. This I find somewhat disconcerting, especially with so many potholes on the road, so decide – for safety reasons – to refrain from waving.

We're up on top of the mountains now and it's getting pretty cold, and in the distance, thick, dark clouds are looming! I'm hoping we shall miss them, or at least their contents, on this journey. A minute later, my hopes are dashed as the first drops of rain fall on us. Only a small amount though and, ever the optimist, I'm thinking this may be as bad as it gets. Lightning strikes on the horizon – bright flashes, illuminating the whole sky before us, followed by loud rumbles of thunder. The closer to it we travel, the heavier the rain becomes. I have no waterproof clothing, neither does my driver!

The rain is so heavy now, it is beating into my hands and face with some force. I feel like I'm being sand-blasted, but in a very wet way! As best I can, I curl my upper body into a ball behind my driver, in a vain attempt to escape this precipitational onslaught. If my driver didn't have a crash helmet on, I'm pretty sure he wouldn't be able to keep going. The thunder roars, torrential rain continues to pound us, and the tiny motorbike splashes through the ever-deepening, muddy puddles. Then, suddenly, we turn off to the right and pull up outside a house – an entirely random house, it would seem. We hurriedly dismount and rush under a small terrace with a corrugated metal roof. Phew!

I quickly notice that we are not the only passing travellers to have taken refuge at this place; a couple of others, looking as much like drowned rats as ourselves, are sheltering here too. The owner of the house doesn't seem remotely phased by this. Almost everything is communal in Africa, so invading a stranger's house in the rain would not be seen as an imposition.

We greet him and the others with a wet handshake and stand there watching the rest of the downpour, which is punctuated with bright flashes and almost deafening claps of thunder.

I see that three large metal bowls have been placed on the ground just beneath the end of the sloping tin roof, to get some free water and doubtless save his wife a walk to the well in the morning. Across the flooded courtyard are two round huts and, beyond that, a solitary coconut palm is swaying frantically in the storm.

I'm drenched from head to toe and the lower half of my trousers is caked in dirt. Thankfully, I'm wearing a pair of those 'convertible' trousers where you can zip off the lower sections to make them into shorts. I decide this is the best course of action; at least then I can ring them out and zip them back on before leaving. I then feel inside my pocket – my money, including several 10,000 CFA notes, is totally saturated too! In a quiet area at the back of the house, I carefully peel the notes from one another and lay them out on a dry piece of wall, keeping a watchful eye upon my funds as they slowly begin to dry out.

After about twenty minutes, the rain stops so we thank the owner and continue our epic journey (not before I have retrieved my soggy money). However, the storm has moved off to the east and that's precisely where we're heading! No word of a lie, we drive right back into the very same storm within a few minutes. My teeth are chattering with the cold now and it's getting beyond a joke.

On the horizon, I see a large radio mast. This means we cannot be far from Natitingou now – hooray! The mast is on the brow of the hill and from here it's all downhill to Nati. As if on cue, the motorbike engine cuts out at that very instant and refuses to start again (I couldn't make this story up if I tried, honestly!) So, we free-wheel the last mile or so, down and down into Natitingou. It's dark now and, as we enter Nati, the road levels out and my driver can go no further. But the nearest hotel is at least half a mile further down the road and I don't especially want to lug my drenched belongings that far on foot! Thankfully, another motorbike taxi is passing and we quickly hail it down. This one has an engine which works, but a driver who speaks no French. He mutters away to me in some local language and I notice he has a surprisingly high-pitched voice for an African man. Thankfully, he knows the names of the hotels in town and is able to take me. I bid my waving friend and his damp, blue motorbike farewell and hop on the new one, stating my desired destination:

"*L'Hôtel Bourgogne, s'il vous plaît*"

"*Hein?!*"

"*Hôtel Bourgogne!  BOUR-GO-GNE!!*"

"*Ah ! Hotébugon.  Oui oui!*" he squeaks back at me. Hoorah! We're off! Now, the Tata Somba was a lovely place to stay (and was that really only last night?!)  However, it's a tad on the pricey side for Africa and besides, for the sake of variety, I like to try out different hotels to see what they're like. The *Bourgogne* seems like a decent choice; in fact, according to the Lonely Planet Guide, "This two-storey hotel, on the main road […] is a good, cheap alternative to the Hôtel Tata Somba."[9]  So there you have it! It's also not terribly far from the mechanic's shop. I had hoped to pick up *The Beast* tonight, but tomorrow morning will have to do now.

The hotel's sizeable reception area is a welcoming, busy-looking place, with a long wooden counter to the left and comfortable seating throughout. This also doubles up as the restaurant. It has a significantly more 'run down' feel to it than the other place: the cushions are worn, the furnishings are looking old, but it feels very welcoming too. I walk up to a man at the reception desk.

"*Bonsoir. Avez-vous une chambre de libre?*"

"*Mais bien sûr Monsieur.  Suivez-moi.*"

I follow the hotel receptionist through a small metal door at the back of the reception and out into a concrete courtyard.

"Would you like a room with air-conditioning, Monsieur?"

"Er, no thank you. That will not be necessary."

It's twenty degrees Celsius and windy; I can't see the need for extra cooling tonight. I'm already shivering with cold as it is!

"Are you sure, Monsieur? Air conditioning is good. *La clime, c'est bon!*"

Upon my second refusal, he is convinced. Rather bizarrely, the rooms here are numbered 100, 105, 110, 115 and so on, with the upper floor beginning at 200. Mine is close to reception on the ground floor and is like so many others I've stayed in: double bed, table and chair, ceiling fan, mosquito net and en suite shower and loo. The bathroom is curious – it's a long, thin room with the door at one end. However, the toilet has been placed directly opposite the sink, so to get through to the shower at the far end, one has to either step over the entire toilet, or sit on it briefly whilst sliding through. Time to get out of these wet clothes before dinner. I ring out my trousers, my shirt, even my underwear – they are all full of muddy brown water!

Steak and sautéed potatoes for dinner, so no surprises there. Makes a pleasant change from rice and sauce, mind. Tomorrow will be another interesting day, I'm sure.

Over breakfast next morning, I try calling the mechanic. No reply. I decide to just turn up at the garage hoping for the best, and so get there by 8:40am. At first, the place seems completely deserted, but *The Beast* is there, which is consoling. Then a young chap appears.

"*Bonjour.* I've come to pick up my car."

"Ah, the *patron* is not here yet."

"Can I take the car all the same?" I ask, aware of my tight schedule today, and that his boss may be quite some time.

"Well, he has the keys and he is still at home."

"When will he get here?"

"At nine o'clock, Monsieur."

And, bang on time, he turns up twenty minutes later. I pay him, thank him and happily climb up into the Land Rover. The 2.5 litre turbo diesel engine roars into action and I'm on my way.

At the top end of the town, just before the left turn for Boukoumbé, there is a police check. The policeman beckons me to pull over. Great! That's all I need.

"*Bonjour*, Monsieur."

"*Bonjour*," I reply, warily.

"There is no problem, but would you please give this lady a lift to Boukoumbé?"

I glance over to one side and see an African lady sitting on a small, rickety wooden bench. I think. I consider. All in a split second. I *never* take passengers in Africa: it's a self-protection thing. You just never know when someone may be trying to scam you.

"I'm sorry, officer. I do not take passengers."

"Monsieur, I would understand if it were a man, but this is a lady."

"Sorry, I cannot help you."

Call me heartless if you like, but I have a job to do and a short timescale in which to do it. Taking passengers is not only risky on this continent, but it could also end up slowing me down and preventing me from accomplishing what I came to do. Therefore, and for my own sanity too, I *never* take passengers I do not know.

My journey back to Boukoumbé seems about ten times quicker by car! I slow down at the house where we sheltered yesterday evening. Sure enough, the man is still there, and wearing the same shirt too! I wind down my window and shout a greeting, waving wildly at him. He waves back with a warm smile, though I'm not sure whether he actually recognizes me, dry and in a car!

I arrive back at the youth centre by 9:30am and most of the participants are there, as well as some newcomers, which is encouraging.

"*A yɛn* taa?" I ask, enthusiastically.

"*Da na ti!*" comes a chorus of replies.

Three of the participants have turned up today wearing the intriguing 'Mohican-style' headgear, which one chap had yesterday. They immediately notice my fascination with their curious apparel.

"Mine is horsehair," one of them tells me, "this one is goat, and he's got chimpanzee." In addition, they are all wearing fake leather glasses and holding small axes, all part – I am assured – of the traditional Ditammari costume.

The participants have been working on some of the usual verses for the second lot of songs: 2 Corinthians 5:17, Colossians 2:6-7 and Galatians 5:22-26. We begin by singing through these. Each group has chosen a different genre and these work well. Still no drums, mind, but I find it hard to believe that there could be a *drumless people group* anywhere on the African continent.

Before lunch, I teach them about the last three songs: parables again. As I'm going through the Parable of the Sower, I notice something interesting: just outside the back door of the building (and close to where I am standing) is a field of maize. To this side of the field is a dirt path, on which people are passing by. And in front of the path, guess what? Weeds are growing! This really helps bring my telling of this parable to life – all I'm missing is a bit of rocky ground, but they'll just have to imagine that!

Halfway through the morning, an incredibly tall chap with dreadlocks turns up. "My name is Loubongo," he booms in a deep voice. It turns out he is a musician and singer and even has his own little group. He is also a Christian.

"You are welcome, Monsieur Loubongo."

After a hearty lunch of *fonio* (a local cereal, vaguely resembling couscous) with goat and oily sauce, I am finally shown my room for the night! It seems strange that I've been here so long and done so much, but have not yet spent a night in Boukoumbé! It's a basic room, only a short walk from the centre, but on the other side of the road. The usual basics, though no running water or sink; just a loo outside at the end of a small veranda and a large bucket of water. It has metal doors and windows, which are quite common here and are usually painted a rusty red colour — more for protection than aesthetics, I'm sure. I hang up my still wet clothing and take a short nap.

When I awake and go outside, I can't help but notice that one of my car tyres is quite deflated. Not wanting this to get worse, I drive into town and find a 'tyre-man' close to the main crossroads. These useful chaps are to be found across West Africa, their rudimentary workshops usually marked by a tower of several tyres close to the roadside. Besides a couple of crowbars, a jack, a cross-shaped wrench, a bowl of water and – of course – a pump, his shop contains very little else. Old tyres and inner tubes are strewn everywhere, along with various nuts and bolts. To inflate a tyre, a small engine has to be started to run the compressor; this is done by pulling a cord. As soon as the necessary pumping is done, the little generator is turned off again.

I pull in and greet the owner:

"*A yɛn* taa?"

"*Da na ti*! But, Monsieur, I'm not Ditammari, I am *Fɔn*."

"Ah! Then, *nɛ a fɔn gbɔn?*" I respond, asking him how he woke this morning.

"*Gangi gangi!*" he replies in the language of Cotonou, with which I am very familiar, telling me he woke up well.

"*Xɔntɔnce, peneuce gblé kpédi. A na wazɔ́ɔ̀ nu mi à?*"

("My friend, my tyre is a bit broken. Can you work on it for me?") I'm enjoying this! I can communicate in an African language I know once more. And he's loving it.

"*Eeeen! Enyɔ dín! A na lɛkɔ gan tɛnwɛ ɛgbe gbadanù.*"

He'll do it and I'm to come back at seven this evening.

Back at the centre, all three groups are busy at work on their parable songs. These always take longer than other kinds, as there is so much information which has to be included. I take a mid-afternoon stroll and leave them to it, feeling the need for a bit of a break after three eventful but exhausting days. Besides, I have noticed something just up the road which intrigues me: a sign saying '*Tata Touristique*' and I'm keen to go and see it.

Now, in Ditammari, '*tata*' means 'house' and '*Somba*' is another name for the people. And so, *tata Somba* just means 'Ditammari house'. If ever you get chance to visit one, they are indeed fascinating buildings, the likes of which I have never come across elsewhere. Imagine a typical round, African mud hut, straw roof, the lot. Are you there? Okay, now imagine about six of them arranged roughly in a circle, but they are all two storeys high (so already look more like small towers than mud huts). Oh, and there's one 'tower' in the middle of the circle too. Next, build high boundary walls between your six external towers and put a flat roof on top of the whole thing, a few feet beneath the tops of the towers. This is a *tata Somba*, and – in some ways – resembles a simple, scaled-down version of a medieval castle.

This *tata touristique* is a special, and somewhat sanitized, example of such a house, designed for tourists to visit and stay in. For a small fee, the manager is happy to show me round. The main entrance, located in the widest tower, leads to the 'kitchen' – or at least the area where cooking would be done. As this is a 'posh' *tata*, it even has a fridge-freezer, a somewhat incongruous sight in such a building. There are also concrete floors, electric lighting, and painted magnolia walls inside – all of which would not normally be the case!

The entrance-cum-kitchen leads into the main section of the building, where a narrow circular corridor runs all the way around a large central room (part of your central tower, remember?). Sturdy, dark, horizontal beams hold the roof up and these, in turn, are supported by Y-shaped vertical beams, some quite curved, but very solid. At one point, the corridor is so narrow I can only just squeeze between two beams to get through – maybe I should have gone easy on the goat at lunchtime!

On the outside of the corridor are the remaining rooms; five in total, all of them circular. Between each room, there are windows on the outer wall, providing a lot of natural light to the inside. In this version of the house, the rooms are mostly bedrooms for tourists, but in the seventh and final one is a staircase up to the roof. I use the term 'staircase' very loosely, as this is an African-style one, made of another thick branch with notches cut out of it at regular intervals. Does just the job, but a tad disconcerting to the unaccustomed Westerner, I'm sure.

The view from the roof is most pleasant: pale green fields with tiny beige footpaths running in various directions. Darker green trees, like sticks of broccoli, punctuate the landscape as far as the eye can see. Close by, there is a line of bushy trees with yellow blossom. The landscape is lightly undulating, but in the distance are some pointy, jagged hills. Something about this view reminds me of Mid Wales, though it's hard to say what exactly.

From up here, I can also clearly see the tops of each tower of the tata – seven in total, in case you've not been counting!  Four of them have the classic conical thatch on them; the other three have flat roofs.  But each of these upper floor rooms has a purpose, and every bit of space is utilized. Going round clockwise from the staircase tower, the next one is traditionally used for storing the wife's goods she has bought at the market, followed by a large flat-roofed room (directly above the kitchen), which would be the children's room.  Next is the husband's storage barn, then an open, raised lookout platform (presumably to keep an eye on any potential enemies). After this, there is a room where goods are stored to be taken *to* the market, and finally, right in the centre, is the mother's room.  So now you know!

Back at the 'ranch,' a thin, older, white lady with straight grey hair and glasses is sitting in the hall enjoying the music.  I immediately recognize her as Freda Black, a missionary and colleague.  An incredible woman and decidedly spritely for her age, she started life in Africa decades ago as a Peace Corps volunteer.  Now, many missionaries I've met here speak average French, sometimes not even that.  Freda speaks excellent French and – especially commendable for an American – *sans accent*.  To top it all, she speaks fluent German too, so we often enjoy a good chat *auf Deutsch* for variety's sake.  I'm glad she's come along: it will be even more fun now!

"These songs are great, Rob!" she exclaims with joviality and feeling.

"Thanks Freda.  Good to see you.  *Herzlich Willkommen!*"

"*Danke.  Gleichfalls!*"

The songs are just about done and we do one final sing-through before rounding up for the day.  Tomorrow, they will polish and rehearse their songs before we record them.

This evening, Rigobert has invited Freda and me to his house for dinner, and we are delighted to accept his kind offer.  He lives on the other side of town, but as I've now got my car back from the Fɔn-speaking tyre man, we can drive there easily enough.  We are welcomed into his gravel courtyard, which has a large satellite dish in one corner and a cooking area in another. We sit down around a low, wooden table and chat in the moonlight as we wait to be served.

"Would you like a drink?  There is beer!" Rigobert exclaims.

"You bet!"

And it's not just any old beer: it's the tasty, dark, *Awooyo* – one of Togo's best, and so much more interesting than the rest.  I put it down to the former colonizers of Togo: the Germans.  (*Danke für das Bier, Deutschland!*)

Dinner begins with a nice salad (boy, this chap knows what Westerners like to eat), followed by chicken, spaghetti and *Fulani* cheese: a delicious, locally produced cheese, which is disk-shaped and usually red on the outside.  Best used in cooking, as it doesn't taste too good raw.  As we tuck in, Rigobert's dog sits there and stares eagerly at me, drooling away.

"What is his name?" I ask.

"He doesn't have a name."

Silly question on my part: why would an African (or anyone, come to think of it) give a name to an animal?  A decidedly Western trait – such anthropomorphic practices are virtually unheard of on this continent: animals here are either meat yet to be slaughtered or useful workhorses.  This would have been the case in Europe a century or two ago (and in some ways still is – if you're a farmer, for example).

"He has no name?"

"Well, we call him *Tam* sometimes," Rigobert adds, sensing my shock at the prospect of an anonymous canine.  I'm guessing that 'tam' merely means 'dog' in the local language, but the conversation has moved on by now and we're discussing meanings of other words.  It emerges that, in the Ditammari language, the word for 'bicycle' literally means 'iron horse'.  This is far from uncommon in African languages.  Rigobert tells us that the word for 'car' is 'iron house' and 'aeroplane' is 'flying iron house'.  Fascinating indeed! I share one of my own favourites: the word for 'train' in Fon is *'pín-pàn'*, which is just onomatopoeia for the sound its horn makes.  Freda trumps us all though, with the word for 'aeroplane' in another local language: *'boeing'*.

Next morning and Freda takes me to a rustic local place for breakfast. This will actually be my first breakfast in Boukoumbé – a bamboozling thought, given how long I seem to have been here. It also turns out to be the *best* breakfast I've had on the trip: no bread or coffee, but instead a delicious and varied meal, served by a big lady with lots of pots and pans. There's a hard-boiled egg, some spicy couscous, diced boiled potato, lots of tasty beans and a salad of tomatoes, onion and lettuce. Almost as good – and nutritious – as a full English breakfast; and all for the equivalent of thirty British pence!

Once the musicians are gathered and practising their final set of songs on parables ('Son', 'Sower' and 'Samaritan'), I decide it's time to track down some drums. There *must* be drums somewhere, surely! Rigobert kindly offers to travel with me in *The Beast* to a couple of places he thinks may have some.

"Let's go and see the Catholic Priest," he suggests. "Those Catholics like drums!" After a short drive through town, we arrive at the Padre's house. Unfortunately, he has no drums whatsoever, but suggests we call *chez les soeurs religieuses*, just down the road. The nuns have very little in the way of membranophones either, but manage to muster up one very small drum and also a large hemispherical gourd-shaker, covered with cowrie shells.

"I've got another idea," says Rigobert. "Let's try the Assemblies of God. They use drums, I think."

We pull into the house of the *pasteur*, to be greeted by the words: "*Il est sorti!*" – he's out! No joy here either. "Try the *diacre*," we are told, and so continue our 'wild drum chase' to the house of one of the church deacons. He's out too, and I'm beginning to lose hope of finding any drums before we begin recording! We pass by a clinic.

"Wait a minute! That looks like the *pasteur*'s motorbike."

There must be twenty-five motorbikes parked up in front of the clinic; how can he possibly know?

"Are you sure it is his?"

"I think so."

Rigobert goes into the clinic and quickly returns.

"It is not his."

We return to the workshop virtually empty-handed. We've just spent a good hour looking for drums and finding practically nothing. How can this be? Everyone has drums in Africa, surely!

The parable songs, meanwhile, are ready and each group is rehearsing all of its three songs, ready to record them. We have found a decent recording location: a fairly large school campus near the edge of town. To the rear is a large, open space but with – you guessed it – several mango trees! Just the job! I get there mid-morning to set up the equipment. There is electricity in the school and the mango trees are close enough for us to run a cable from there for power. However, it's school holidays and the buildings are all locked up! Another wild goose chase ensues; thankfully one in which I am not embroiled this time. Rigobert goes to the headteacher's house and returns:

"The *directeur* is not at home. I'll try the bursar's house."

No joy there either, nor at a third option. It is 10:45am and I'm all set up ready, but with no power. Meanwhile, the musicians are all turning up too, but we cannot start until we have electricity. Now, I've recorded in plenty of powerless villages, but was not prepared for that here; had I known, I would have charged up lots more batteries. I have just about enough, but mains electricity – when available – is still preferable (barring power cuts).

Eventually, a school key turns up from somewhere and we can get cracking, but it's midday already. In spite of the lack of drums, there is a complex array of other instruments involved in this session, and this presents something of a challenge for my five microphone set up. As well as the choir and soloist, we have some small metal *castanets*, held by the thumb and middle finger of the right hand and clicked together percussively. A pair of 'traditional guitars' also make an appearance – not dissimilar to the one played in Bassar, but with a slightly curved neck, creating a larger gap between the strings and fingerboard. Interestingly, one of these has *three* strings, rather than two, which is more common. Also, the player of the two-stringed version is using a small stick of bamboo as a sort of hand held capo to bar the strings (a bit like the 'bottleneck' used in some blues guitar playing in the West).

And not only do they have *chordophones*; there are also some *aerophones* in the form of a couple of the typical three-holed flutes (as seen in Gando). Vaguely cone-shaped, with two laterally opposed holes near the top and one at the very bottom. Played by blowing across an opening at the top and placing fingers and thumbs on the three holes (or not), to create a high-pitched melody of limited range. Finally, there are the leg-shakers made from woven palm leaves, like we saw with the millet beer-swilling Nawdm people.

Recording goes reasonably well, but there will be some editing for me to do back home. At one point, there is a particularly loud entry from a soloist. And in the same song, the singer somehow manages to hit the microphone, creating a large 'boom!' sound. In another song, three men are singing, playing metal castanets *and* moving their feet to activate their leg-shakers! For this, I manage to make do with two microphones: an omnidirectional one for their voices, which I point upwards to maximize efficiency. Then a unidirectional one pointing downwards, positioned *below* the castanets to pick up the sound of the leg-shakers. The metal castanets themselves have a loud enough sound to be picked up by the upper omnidirectional mic, but without hindering the sound of the voices. Oh, I so love making field recordings!

All nine songs – 43 minutes and 10 seconds in total – are in the can by late afternoon. As we are finishing the last song, the sky darkens as thick clouds appear in the distance. Literally five minutes after we end, the heavens open once again, not before we have quickly managed to load all the gear into the back of the Land Rover.

That evening, and once the rain has subsided, Freda Black says:

"Rob, I have an old friend I'd like to visit just over in Togo. Would you mind driving me there?"

I gladly accept – there's not much else to do here of an evening after all! Boukoumbé is only a couple of miles from the Togolese border, so we take a small dirt road, now littered with muddy puddles, to get there. The border may as well be non-existent. There is no sign, no guard, no customs – just a feeling of *we're in Togo now.* And we are! On both sides of the border, the countryside is littered with *tata Somba* houses – more than I've ever seen before, and very pleasing to the eye. Some of them are derelict, but many are still very much lived-in. I'm so grateful for this opportunity to see a culture still relatively unscathed by outside influences; in many ways these people are still living how they have done for centuries. And it works!

Day four, and my job is not over: we have seven local musicians (most of whom have been at the workshop) who have some of their own songs they would like me to record. Some are Christian songs; others are for development or education. All good stuff, so I've agreed to spend an extra day helping them in this way. Now, doing a bit of mathematics, each artist has three songs, so that's twenty-one altogether. Given that I usually record no more than four songs an hour, then this could end up being a pretty long day. The only good thing is that each artist has their own 'backing group' and so five groups can be rehearsing elsewhere whilst one group records and another waits in line. This will save a lot of time, I hope.

I arrive at 7:50am, eager to get going early. By 8:20am, we have begun recording. Several musicians have come with their 'hairy headdresses' again, as well as the fake glasses and traditional carved wooden axes. Most intriguing!

There are some great songs, whose titles speak volumes about the culture and its priorities. They include:

> *Deforestation and Bush Fires*
> *A Prayer for Unity*
> *Going to School*
> *Yayi Boni (Benin's new President)*
> *The Trafficking of Girls is Bad*
> *The Ten Commandments*
> *Credit and Borrowing*
> *Fear God Alone*

*Learn to Read and Write*
*The Building of a Country*

Amazingly, these are all done by 1:15pm!  That's almost the five hours I'd counted on, mind, and I have worked solidly from 8:20am until now without a single break!  They want me to stay for lunch but, as usual, I'm eager to commence my long journey home, also to shorten tomorrow's driving load and to arrive back sooner!

So, back over the mountains, through Natitingou and down to Djougou – on a level with Kara, but in Benin.  Here, I stop off at the *Auberge du Lac,* just south of the town, for a decidedly late lunch (or perhaps an early dinner).  My rear wheel on the right is making a strange grinding noise – probably the brakes binding, or more trouble with bearings – but I decide to continue regardless, making it to Savalou just before dark.  Savalou is a small town, an hour or so north of Dassa.  Its *auberge* is, in fact, the 'little brother' of the Dassa one – same owner and even the same pale green doors and windows!  Nice steak and rice for dinner and a there are a few other charity workers scattered around the dining room, all on their way to or from their work, making a difference in this country.

My room is decent, and nicer than most I've stayed in.  However, some of my clothes are still damp from my dousing a couple of days ago, so I hang a couple of pairs of pants and a shirt from my ceiling fan and switch it on.  I don't recommend you try this at home, but it does work rather well actually.  And besides, I've suffered enough traumas from ceiling fans already – it's about time they gave me something back!

Thinking back over the workshop, I realize one key fact: the one drum the Ditammari had was not only very small, but was also hardly used at all today.  Meanwhile, they had a plethora of other interesting instruments they were only too happy to play.  And as the only drum they used was found by me at a church, and was played sparingly, I can't help wondering if they did so merely 'to please the white man'.  Is it possible that the

Ditammari are, in fact, the only drumless people group I have ever come across in Africa?  Intriguing indeed – wish I'd had more time with them to research this in detail!

The summit of the infamous Aledjo Pass in northern Togo.

# Chapter Eight

# Dedication Songs and Dust
*The Moba People of Northernmost Togo*

Dapaong: the final frontier.  Both in Togo and in this book!  You can't get any further north than Dapaong without ending up in Burkina Faso. This reasonably sized town is miles from anywhere and has a name which, to me at least, sounds more Chinese than African!  To get there, I first have to travel through Kara, which will be nice, as I haven't been there for some time (since Chapter Two, in fact!)  I'll be running a special song-writing workshop there, ready for the dedication of the Moba New Testament later this year.  Two older ladies, Thelma and Kitty, have been in Dapaong working on it for the past thirty-five years and the fruit of their labour is finally finished!

Thelma is a *Geordie* which, for non-Brits, means she comes from Newcastle and talks 'funny'.  Geordies are generally cheery people who like a chat, and Thelma is no exception.  She is a bubbly, enthusiastic lady with a sense of fun and adventure.  Interestingly, she is also a big fan of *Bollywood* movies, but that's another story.

Kitty is Australian and a little more calm and composed than her colleague. A lovely couple of ladies who have sacrificed 'normal' life in the West to give the majority of their working lives over to providing God's Word for the Moba people – amazing indeed!

Today's journey northwards has been all the easier as Jane, an American colleague, has shared the driving.  She needed to come to Kara for meetings and so it made sense that we help each other out in this way. Mind you, she's been a little dubious about some of the less mainstream tracks on my iPod, but there you go! ("Why, what in the world is that, Rob?! That's kinda weird!")

The infamous *Aledjo Pass* south of Kara was as treacherous as ever: at one point, a couple of big lorries were passing dangerously close to the ravine. One of them was so near the edge I honestly thought it was going to topple down the side! Thankfully, it didn't.

So, we arrived in Kara about an hour or so ago and I'm just rousing from a wee snooze when, who should turn up at the door but my old pal, Evan Davidson.

"Welcome back to Kara, Mr. Baker!"

"Evan! Great to see you again, mate!"

I'm delighted to catch up with my piano-playing, culturally-aware, linguistic friend: it's been a while. Evan has just about finished his PhD which, incidentally, he is writing entirely in *French!* Awesome! (Some people have just too many brain cells, eh?)

"I've brought you a *petit cadeau,* Evan!"

Evan looks intrigued as I pull out of my bag no fewer than five jars of 'Marmite'. I was back in the UK last month, to see the supervisors for *my* thesis, and, knowing how much Evan loves the brown stuff (not just beer!), I made the most of the opportunity to do a bit of shopping!

"Marmite! Wonderful! Thanks Rob!" he exclaims, with plenty more vocalized Cornish Rs. Personally, I loathe the stuff, but I'm happy for him! Just then, my mobile phone rings.

"Rob, how was ya jorney?"

It's Thelma, the Geordie translator–lady, calling from Dapaong.

"So far, so good, Thelma."

"I wos joost ringin to saay, bring a sweata if ya have wun, pet. It's gettin' reet cooold up hyar now, speshly at nayt."

"Okay, thanks. Good idea!"

Did you catch all of that?

Before thinking of sleep, a celebratory bowl of millet beer with Evan is the order of the day. We head to a village just down the road where the stuff is being served. Same procedure as usual – we're each served a half gourd full of the bubbling, magnolia-coloured brew for the equivalent of three pence! This time, though, I manage to throw the dregs away in the *right direction*, to the delight of my onlookers. One dentally-challenged old lady utters something to Evan in Kabiyé, whilst gesticulating in my direction. He laughs and replies to her in the local language.

"What did she say?" I ask with great curiosity.

"She says she wants to be your wife!"

Well, she must be almost twice my age and, as it happens, I'm already taken. "*Ah, non, non, non!*" I say to her, shaking my head violently and trying not to laugh. I explain that I'm already married: "*Pas possible, Madame! J'ai déjà une femme!!*" Not that this would stop many African men, some of whom have up to *seven* wives!

Next morning and frivolities over, it's time to continue my journey to Dapaong. I leave Kara at 7:00am, without having had breakfast. There will surely be somewhere I can stop for a bite to eat on the way. It's a total of three hours from here, heading north past Bago (Nawdm country), then past the turning for Gando (with its incredible baobab-shaking lady). From there, it's two hours' drive through virtual desolation – nothing to be seen but a flat, straight road continuing ever northwards  and surrounded by yellowing vegetation. The only town I pass through is called *Mango*, which I've always liked the sound of! The skies are cloaked with the dry, dusty Harmattan, which blows across this part of Africa from December to February. Today it is particularly thick, affecting long-distance visibility and blocking out the light of the sun. I'm getting decidedly peckish by Mango, but find no place to eat.

At one point, I pass a square container lorry crammed full of people: long, thick branches have been slotted into gaps across the open top of the large metal box and people are sitting on these. Many also have one leg over the side or back, perched precariously on the very edge and – maybe – holding on with one hand. The vehicle is not going terribly fast, but were it to crash, brake suddenly, or even swerve, it could spell instant disaster for many of its passengers.

I finally make it to the outskirts of Dapaong. Parched and hungry, I decide to stop at the first available opportunity: the *Hôtel Lafia* – a nice name for a hotel (as it means 'peace' in Moba and several other local languages). I'm especially grateful for the peace which ensues once I turn off the roaring engine of *The Beast*. I step into the sizeable hotel reception area, with its usual large wooden desk, and ask about breakfast.

"Do you serve coffee?" I ask, knowing that nothing is to be assumed in such a place.

"Oui, Monsieur. Coffee: 150 francs; coffee with milk: 200 francs; coffee, milk and bread: 300 francs; coffee, milk, bread and butter: 350 francs."

Wow! He's got his prices all sussed out! And, as they are all very reasonable, I go for option four and take a seat at one of the several square tables, each bedecked with a red and white checked table cloth. Nice touch! The place is deserted and – as always – the television is immediately switched on to keep me company. It's a channel I don't recognize – maybe from Burkina Faso, just up the road. No news, debates, or wild dancers today. Instead, an African stand-up comedian is making jokes about diarrhoea! Seriously! ("It never happens when you're at home, eh?! It always comes when you're out somewhere.") I'm so hungry by now; even this doesn't hinder my appetite in any way. I tuck into my two slices of semi-stale bread (hey, what can you expect for ten pence?) and pour the Nescafé sachet into my chipped, grey mug. Then a thought occurs to me:

"*Excusez-moi, Monsieur.* Do you sell bottled water? *Eau minérale?*"

"*Non, Monsieur.* But the shop across the road sells it for 400 francs."

That's not a bad price, but I cannot help but ponder the irony that a litre and a half of water is going to cost me more than my entire breakfast.

"Okay, thank you."

"We can fetch the water for you, if you like, Monsieur."

"That would be helpful. Thank you.  I'll take four bottles."

It always pays to stock up on decent water here – you never know what you're going to get, and the stuff from wells or taps can often make us foreigners sick very quickly (and I'd rather not be the subject of an African stand-up comic's routine, if that's okay!)

Breakfast all eaten and I'm ready to pay the bill.  I'm shocked that it comes to 800 francs more than I had calculated and question the receptionist.  He replies:

"This is correct, Monsieur.  350 francs for breakfast and 2,400 for your water."

"You said the water was 400 francs and I had four bottles, so that should be 1,600."

"If you buy it here at the hotel, the water costs 600 francs, Monsieur.  It's 400 francs at the shop over the road."

Arggghh!  WAWA!  West Africa Wins Again!!  So, I've just paid a guy 200 francs per bottle for carrying my water 20 yards.  Good job breakfast was so cheap!


"Welcome to Dapaong, pet!"

"G'day Rob.  Welcome!"

I've made it to the Bible translation compound and am duly greeted by Thelma, Kitty, two dogs, and a cat.

"Woould ya layk a coop of tea, pet?"

"Why aye – that would be dead canny, like!" I respond, unable to resist the temptation to mimic her Geordie brogue.

"All reet then!"  She responds, humouring me.

The compound is made up of four main buildings, arranged roughly in a rectangular formation.  On two sides, facing one another, are a couple of meeting rooms, or classrooms – one of which I will be using for the workshop.  On a third side are the Bible translation offices and opposite those, on the fourth side, is Thelma and Kitty's house itself. A pleasant compound indeed, though smaller than many I've been to.

Over tea, we discuss the logistics of the workshop. The main aim is to get some special songs composed for the forthcoming Bible dedication ceremony. These will be based upon Bible verses which underline the importance of the Word of God for everyone. The songs are also likely to contain quite a bit of thanksgiving, too. We'll base them on three key references which talk specifically about God's Word, namely: 2 Timothy 3:16-17, Hebrews 4:12 and Romans 15:4.

"Rob, would ya layk to witness a historic event?" Thelma suddenly asks me.

"Sure! What is it?"

"Well, the Moba New Testaments have just arrived, so we're going to open the first box to take a look."

"Wow! Excellent! I'd love to. Can I take some photos of this auspicious event, too?"

They think for a moment.

"Our hair looks awful," says Kitty.

"That's true," Thelma continues. "Maybe we should wait and open them tomorrow."

"Yis, let's do that."

And so we do (or rather, we don't!)

As we continue chatting and sipping tea, I discover that the word for 'God' in Moba is 'Yendu'. A nice sounding word, I think to myself. Remembering the much uglier Nawdm equivalent, I say to Thelma:

"In Nawdm, the word for God is '*Sangband.*'"

"Yes, I know," she replies with a smile, "and the funny thing is that '*sangband*' means 'dog' in Moba."

"Really? How curious!"

"Aye, it does! And so the Moba often mock the Nawdm saying 'Your God is a dog!'"

Uncanny indeed! Fancy that! Who would have imagined such a coincidence could exist anywhere in the world?! Reminds me of the dyslexic, agnostic insomniac, who lies awake at night wondering whether *dog* exists or not!

That evening – and after a significant siesta – I sit down to dinner with the two ladies, watching telly at the same time. The climate here is so dry that they keep their bread in sealed plastic bags, even during mealtimes. I also notice that their television remote is in a plastic bag, to protect it from all the Harmattan dust, which gets literally everywhere at this time of year. Amazingly, they have satellite TV rigged up so that they can watch CNN news and keep up-to-date with what's happening in the world – a good idea when you live so far from anywhere else. Besides the television, their lounge-diner is a well-established, cosy place – in spite of the usual concrete floor. There's a large bookshelf at one end, a coffee table covered with various magazines and newspapers, a basic three-piece suite, a sturdy wooden sideboard, and yet more brightly coloured curtains.

After dinner, I retire to my room with a copy of 'National Geographic' from the coffee table. It's a special 'Africa' issue of the magazine, which gives some fascinating statistics about the continent. For example:

*It contains 20% of the world's landmass.*

*Its population is 900 million, or 14% of the world.*

*71% of Africans are under the age of 25.*

*It has 358 million Muslims and 410 million Christians.*

*Democratic governments (in 2005): 19 out of 53.*

*Richest nation: Mauritius.*

*Poorest nations: Burundi, Malawi, Sierra Leone and Somalia.*

*Life expectancy in North Africa: 67 years.*

*Life expectancy in sub-Saharan Africa: 46 years.*

*Percentage of its population dependent upon agriculture for living: 66%.*

*Most populous city: Lagos, Nigeria (16.9 million).*

*Percentage of literacy (aged 15 and over): 60%.*

*Of the 38 most heavily indebted countries in the world (as defined by the IMF), 32 are in Africa.*[10]

On that sobering note, I hit the sack, probably dreaming about eradicating world poverty, ridding the continent of corruption, and putting an end to Western exploitation of the developing world. Sadly, this is only a dream.


It was a chilly night, especially compared to sticky, hot Cotonou. Down there, it's usually between 28 and 34 Celsius and at least 70% humidity. Here today, it's 10% humidity with temperatures between 22 and 27 – not hot at all for Africa, and the dryness makes it seem even cooler! To top it all, there is only a cold shower, but I brave the icy stream all the same and emerge shivering and wide awake, even before coffee!

After a fairly early breakfast, Thelma suggests:

"Well, why dooon't we open the Bibles this mornin' before tha workshop gets goin'?"

We all agree that there's no point delaying such a momentous event, and so once their Togolese translation colleague, Jules, has arrived, we head over to the office, where several parcels are waiting in a large pile. Jules picks up one of the packages and places it on the central wooden table. The packet is light brown, measuring about thirty inches by fifteen, and around ten inches deep. On the side is written 'MOBA NT' in large black letters. Jules takes out a small Stanley knife and makes a cut from one of the top corners across the length to another, Thelma and Kitty looking on with great excitement and expectation. He pulls back the cardboard lid to reveal a set of handsome-looking books with darkish green covers. On the front in golden lettering is written the words: '*Yendu Kadapaaɔnŋ*' and lower down in small letters is written: '*Le Nouveau Testament en Moba (Ben), Togo.*' They each take a copy to examine. The delight on their faces is a picture indeed, and the excitement of this moment is so tangible you could almost cut it with a knife (or even a two-edged sword).

"May I have a look at one, too?" I ask, eagerly.

"Of course, Rob. Here you go!" They hand me one and I carefully open the silky, green plastic cover. The pages are so smooth, white and… well…new-looking. Lovely typeface and all very nicely done! I always enjoy looking at the contents page of Bibles in other languages, to see how similar (or different) the names of the books are. In Moba, the four gospels are called: *Matieog, Mark, Luk* and *San.* This tells me there is probably no 'J' sound in Moba. Also, that words can end in a consonant in this language (which is not the case in many other West African languages I know). Most of the other books are recognizable, although Acts is called *Yiesu Sundi Tuona.* Then Hebrews is *Ebro-nba,* James is *Sak* (a variation on the French 'Jacques') and – finally – Revelation has the somewhat bizarre name of *Dɔgdu,* which I'm sure means something nice in Moba!

Perusing the pages further, I'm a little disappointed at the choice of artwork in this New Testament. It's great they have put pictures in and some are even in colour. However, they all seem quite 'Western' to me, with little or no attention to making them culturally appropriate or un-derstandable to the Moba people. I once had a mildly heated debate with a missionary in Nigeria about this. He said that the illustrations in a Bible are there to provide information only, and so should be completely 'neutral'. I beg to differ: firstly, there is no such thing as 'neutral art' – any work of art (like music) is loaded with cultural references, whether we realize it or not. The colours used, the way people are standing, the use of perspective and the general composition of the picture itself could all aid or hinder understanding within a given culture. Now, I'm not necessarily saying we should have paintings of a black Jesus in African Bibles, but we could – at the very least – have African artists paint pictures how *they* interpret the stories. That said, throughout the world, you can find works of art depict-ing the life of Christ and, in virtually every case I've come across, He has the same face as a person from that country, be it Chinese, Latin American, Indian, or Russian. Does this shock you? Well, we do the same, believe it or not: most of our European or American depictions of Christ make him look anything but Jewish and decidedly more Anglo-Saxon. Even in Holman Hunt's famous 'Light of the World' painting ('behold I stand at the door and knock…'), Jesus has fair skin, light-coloured wavy hair and fine-ly-shaped thin eyebrows. It's a wonderful work of art, which has touched many people over the years – even helped bring some to faith.  However, this picture would not necessarily move someone from another culture to the same extent. We've come a long way in contextualizing music in the church in many parts of the world. Visual art, however, is still a few steps behind, I feel.

Participants for the workshop have been trickling in since 8:30 and now, almost an hour later, we have thirteen people – enough to make a start! Interestingly, everyone speaks French, so for almost the first time ever, I'll be working without an interpreter. This should speed things up, if nothing else!  Almost as soon as I mention traditional song genres, a list is reeled out of the usual range to be found.  There's nothing particularly different from other groups I've worked with, but many have names which sound interesting – even amusing – to the Anglophone ear.  Here are just a few:

*Binbaad* – sung by women for rejoicing
*Caapuod* – used during a ceremony for old ladies
*Jabaapiebd* – for divining
*Kpanjam* – for storytelling
*Saab* – for the initiation of a boy
*Sɔgi* – for flattening out the earth
*Wam* – for initiation

As is often the case, all of the above – and more – have already been adopted by the Catholic church. 'Second place' goes to the Assemblies of God, who use roughly 40% of the genres gathered, closely followed by the Lutherans.

Struggling to remove thoughts of comfortable Swedish cars and 80s pop groups from my head, I ask them to perform as many of the above as possible. They do a marvellous job, the infectious energy of African music as vibrant and inspiring as ever. There's really nothing quite like it!

An interesting discussion ensues on *dance:* some churches represented do not dance and some participants do not like the idea of men and women dancing together in church.  The latter objection can easily enough be remedied and this is often how it is done anyway. But dance done well, and with a sincere heart of worship, is a wonderful thing indeed and a part of cultural heritage worth preserving. Now, I know why some of these churches don't dance and it's got nothing to do with being African. Presuming you have read this far (and have not merely randomly opened the book at this page), then hopefully you'll know why, too: Early Western missionaries, whilst doing a great job of spreading the Gospel in Africa, often did little to respect or preserve African cultural traditions. This includes dance which, in many cases, would have been forbidden in church and even deemed 'sinful'. So today, several decades later, the same attitudes are still ingrained in many African believers. They may well dance for hours at a village festival, but still not in church, even though King David himself danced for the Lord!

After a considerable amount of singing and dancing, we move on to discussing the instruments in Moba culture, which also have somewhat curious names. Have a look:

*Biɛɔg* – the ubiquitous two-stringed guitar

*Bimba yogdi* – a pair of small woven shakers, one held in each hand and played by women

*Gbegli* – metal shakers on a triangular frame, worn around the lower leg

*Gumi* – a pair of long, thin metal drums, narrowing off towards the bottom. Free-standing on a metal frame and open at the low end (almost identical to those played by the Nawdm lady in Chapter Two)

*Najun* – a percussive belt, worn around the waist and covered in cowrie shells

*Yeli* – the three-holed flute again


"Do we have any *yeli* players here?" I ask, remembering Gando.

"No, Monsieur. You will have to pay to hire a *yeli* player."

"Really? But maybe someone will come along and play for free."

"That is unlikely. There are very few *yeli* players these days."

"And why is that? Why are there not more people playing it?"

"Well," one participant continues, "it makes your teeth fall out."

"What?!"

"Yes, Monsieur, it's true!" another interjects. "I know several people who have played the *yeli* flute and they end up losing all their teeth as a result of tensing the jaw muscles so much."

Well, I've heard of oboe players getting piles, but this is a new one on me, I have to say!

"Then there's the association with leprosy."

What? The plot is indeed thickening! What can this be?! He continues:

"I knew two *yeli* players who were both lepers. When they died, another man started playing one of their flutes, but everyone thought he was a leper too, so he didn't want to continue playing."

Wow! Issues one could never imagine existing are coming up here. This is why preliminary research is so important for ethnomusicologists.

At lunchtime, a Russian meal is served for Kitty, Thelma and me. Interesting, and yesterday we had Chinese! Most curious, given our location, miles from anywhere, but decidedly delicious!

When Kitty and Thelma first arrived in Dapaong back in the Seventies, there was little else but tomatoes and okra to be had in the way of veg, and their living conditions were decidedly basic. Things have come a long way, seeing as they now have mains electricity, running water, satellite television and Chinese food!

Like most missionaries and ex-pats in general, Thelma and Kitty have a cook. This may sound like a huge luxury to the outsider, but to expect someone to do a day job as well as shopping at the market and cooking meals is simply unreasonable in this climate. And things take so much longer here, not to mention the lack of a dishwasher or even running hot water in many cases. It is also providing a stable job and income to a local person. These two ladies have certainly done well in teaching their cook to make dishes from various parts of the globe – all very tasty too!

Tonight, CNN news is talking about the forthcoming elections in the United States.

"Have ya huurd about this chappie, Barack Obama, Rob?"

"No, who's he?" I reply, showing my utter ignorance of current affairs, even if in February 2008 he's relatively new on the scene.

"Well, he's one of the candidates fo' President. He seems to be doin' reet well so far."


It's Day Three and I'm so chilly I can't face another cold shower. Instead, I sacrifice one of my bottles of mineral water, which are several degrees warmer than what's coming out of the tap this morning! Still, 600 francs for a very short shower is a bit steep, don't you think?! The guys at the *Hotel Lafia* would laugh if they knew…

Back to work, and we have over twenty participants today, which is great. We begin composing and, without my initiation, they are using some novel techniques I've rarely encountered: in one group, each member is separately writing out their own words, then they reconvene to pool all their ideas. In another group (if you can call it that), each member has gone off to compose an entire song by themselves; they will then gather together later to choose the 'best' one.

The resulting songs are good, with catchy refrains and decent words. Literacy levels are relatively high for this group and so everything is written down, rather like the Tem composers in Sokodé. However, there are several cases of 'recycled' melodies: rather than creating an entirely new tune, existing ones are being used with the new words. This is always a tricky one, as a given genre may only have one kind of tune, so to ask them to make up a new one would – by definition – mean being unfaithful to the chosen genre. A Western example of this would be the *blues,* where tunes are often similar and always follow a certain scale.

The Bible dedication songs sound great and I can't wait until the actual day, when they are sung in front of hundreds of people. One of the most memorable songs has a refrain which goes:

> *T tien man yendu balg!*
> *T tien man yendu balg!*

*U kadaaɔg nba ku diɛn n po.*
*T tien man yendu balg!*

This means:

> We give thanks to God!
> We give thanks to God!
> For his book which he has written to us.
> We give thanks to God!

So, that's the dedication songs all done and dusted! But, rather than leave it at that, I thought we may as well make the most of our time together and do a bit more composing. So before the end of the day, we move onto parable songs. I was planning to do my three favourites, but it turns out that songs already exist in Moba for 'The Good Samaritan' and 'The Prodigal Son.' Rather than repeat these, we decide to change them for 'The Unforgiving Servant' and 'The Parable of the Talents'.

That evening before dinner, I take a stroll. I've scarcely left the compound since arriving, and always like to get a feel for a new place, as you'll know by now. Outside the large metal gates, the landscape is verging on desolate, with yellow grass, dry fields, hard ground, and dust everywhere. Electricity cables hang from tree branches and half-built, concrete houses punctuate the horizon at various points. The empty fields are also littered with black plastic bags, the bane of West Africa if ever there were one.

I make it to the main road and head towards town. Almost immediately, a strange-looking man appears.

"Chief, chief! Make an effort for me! Make an effort! For me!"

This is his way of asking for money. He grabs me by the arm, but I pull away and keep on walking, trying to ignore him. He follows me, still calling out all the time. In one hand he is holding a bowl made from half a gourd, which could be misconstrued as being a begging bowl. However, I instantly recognize it as a bowl for drinking *chouk* or millet beer. Eventually, my blokey drops back, leaving me in peace. A few yards ahead, a couple of guys are looking at me and smiling – they've clearly witnessed the whole event.

"Is he a madman?" I ask them, knowing how often I seem to encounter these on my travels.

"No!" comes the reply.

"Too much *chouk* ?" I continue.

"He's a bit *malade*," they tell me. "It's not the *chouk*; that clears out of your head after a few hours. This man used to be a school teacher before he went like that. If he had the right medication, he could become normal again."

Tragic. I so wish there was more help available for the mentally ill in Africa. All too often, local religion merely puts it down to an evil spirit or a curse, rather than attempting to actually care for the person. I walk on a bit further, then decide to find my way back to the compound through the fields; both for variety's sake and for crazy guy avoidance tactics!

When I get back, Thelma and Kitty's bathroom sink is blocked and no water is going down.

"I can unblock it for you now if you like."

Kitty is not sure – she realizes that if I break anything it could be days before they can find a replacement part. Thelma, however, being of a similarly spontaneous nature to myself, is keen for me to have a go. Kitty can't watch, in case I end up making a big mess of things. However, I have unblocked a few u-bends in my time, so it should be fairly routine. I unscrew the plastic fitting and remove a load of thick, dark, rancid gunge. Sorted!

At dinner, Thelma asks me a question:

"Rob, what's the 'Face Book'? Someone just sent me an e-mail invitation, but I've no idea what it is!"

Well, she was able to fill me in on Obama and I'm more than happy to return the favour now, explaining the ins and outs of friending people, poking or tagging them, status updates, walls, photos, liking something and creating events. It must sound pretty strange when explained purely theoretically though…

A missionary friend once told me he believed that if you worship in spirit and in truth, then this supersedes all musical, cultural and ethno-musicological boundaries.   Sounds like a nice idea, but it could scarcely be further from the truth.  Let me explain why.  Take, for example, a *sitar* player from India, a *kora* player from Senegal, an *urhu* player from China, a *balalaika* player from Russia and finally a *charango* player from Peru.  Put them all in a room together and say: "Make music!"  What will happen? There will be something close to chaos, much misunderstanding and they will be unlikely to find anything which they can all play and make musical 'sense' of together.  And these are all stringed instruments with many structural and technical similarities.  If we were to add wind or percussion to the mix, the complications would only escalate!

So, why is this?  It's because, just as each culture speaks a different language, so their 'musical language' differs. The choice of scale, the rhythmic patterns used, the shape of the melody, the way a piece starts and ends, dynamics, tempo and articulation all differ hugely from culture to culture. English grammar is not the same as Chinese grammar; neither is its musical grammar.  And, so, pick even any *two* of these musicians and ask them to work together and it will be impossible without compromise from at least one party.  I've heard some hideous examples where African musicians have been asked to create a concert with some Westerners – the result is often that the music sounds either too Western for the African musicians to genuinely 'feel at home' or that it becomes too African for the Westerners to know what's going on.

Now, banjo player Belà Fleck did a great job travelling through Africa and jamming on his banjo with local musicians in his documentary '*Throw down your Heart*', so what's the difference?  Firstly, Belà is a very talented musician, but secondly – and more significantly – he was consciously trying to imitate the way the local people played, modifying his technique to match theirs.  Finally – as you'll see if you watch the film – the banjo was originally an African instrument, modified and modernized in the USA. And so, his starting point is something which already has a lot in common with local African musical traditions going back centuries. Even then, there are moments when, I feel, the blend of the two musics doesn't work as well as it might. Furthermore, although the end results on his album are very pleasing to the average Western ear, this doesn't mean that every African involved would necessarily prefer this to the 'raw' original versions of their music.

I once heard a good definition of culture: 'That's the way we do things around here.' Practices *do* cross cultures, but it can take generations before these are actually seen as 'belonging' to them. Four of the main defining aspects of any culture are:

The way people dress
The food people eat
The language spoken
Its music/dance/arts

Now, I love going out for an Indian curry or a Chinese meal, but when I go to my Mum's house, I want meat and two veg, or cheese soufflé, like when I was growing up. Another example: many Africans now dress in Western shirts and trousers, sometimes even with a jacket and tie. However, if you attend an African wedding or funeral – particularly in a village – then you will see people wearing traditional dress, playing their own indigenous music, eating their local food and speaking in their mother tongue. This is culture and it is what defines the very substance of a community.

People often say: "Ah, music! The universal language!" It's a nice thought, but this is a completely false statement. Music is a universal *phenomenon,* but not a universal language. The latter would imply that everyone in the world understands music in the same way, which is not the case. As I hope we've seen in this book, music differs from culture to culture, not only in how it sounds, but also in what is *means* to people. A happy tune in one part of the world could sound like a dirge in another, and a tune of huge local significance may be entirely meaningless elsewhere. Culture is a deep thing, which takes generations to instil. Music communicates so much more than merely sounds – it is loaded with associations, attitudes and the underlying ethos of a society.  So, going back to the original statement, worshipping in spirit and in truth will not transcend these boundaries; moreover, the ensuing musical confusion would be more likely to *hinder* people from being able to truly worship from their heart.  There you go!


At breakfast next morning, I mix hot chocolate with Nescafé to make mocha, just for a change.

"Do ya knooow tha origins of the wurd 'mocha'?"  Thelma asks me.  These translator types are suckers for a bit of etymology first thing in the morning!

"No, I don't.  Pray tell!"

"Well, it's actually pronounced  'mow-ka' and is named after a coffee bean, which gets its name from a port in Yemen where they used to ship them from."

"Really?  Wow, I didn't know that.  I love finding out the origins of words.  Do you have any more?"

"Well, ya know that 'parka', as in the coat, means 'animal skin'?"

"No I didn't!"

"And so does 'berzerk.'  That's Norse for 'bear skin.'"

"Thanks!  Fascinating stuff, Thelma!"

From bearskins, we quickly move on to another form of clothing, as Thelma energetically announces:

"Tha tee-shirts are arrivin' this mornin'!"

"Tee-shirts?"  I enquire.

"For the Dedication. We've 'ad tee-shirts mayd speshly for the occaysion!"

Rather like the Bibles a couple of mornings ago, we now unveil the Moba dedication tee-shirts.  On many such occasions, a special fabric, known locally as a 'pagne' (pronounced: 'pan-yuh') is printed and everyone has costumes made out of it.  However, this time they've gone for tee-shirts instead. These are grey with blue lettering across the front, reading: *'T tien man Yendu balg'* which, like the words of their new song, means: 'We give thanks to God'. On the back of the shirts, it says *'Yendu Kadapaaɔnŋ Jaanm, 15-3-2008,'* meaning: 'New Testament Dedication' and the date.

"These are nice!" I exclaim. "How much are they selling for?"

"You can have one for 1,300 CFA."

That's very reasonable indeed! Just then, a thought occurs to me:

"What if I buy one of these for each of the workshop participants? It would be a nice souvenir for them, and then they'll be able to wear them at the dedication."

"That's a great idea, Rob," says Kitty.

I do a bit of maths and it's really not going to cost me a lot, but will mean so much to these folks. I think back to the Ifẹ and Idaasha workshop, where they were disappointed I hadn't given them anything. Realizing I could (should?) have been more generous with them, I decide to do so this time.

There is more animated singing in the meeting room as I arrive this morning. Their second set of songs is just about ready and they are singing through them with great energy and joy; drums banging, people dancing, expressions of great happiness written across every face. I stand and watch for a few minutes, not wishing to quell their enthusiasm. The sight of Africans truly worshipping God in their own way is an amazing one indeed; why anyone ever thought it would be a good idea to have them standing still in rows holding hymn books is beyond me!

Eventually, their songs finish and I am able to make an announcement.

"Today we are going to record your new songs."

Cheers and applause – they're still on a high from the singing!

"Also, as a small token of thanks for your hard work, each of you will receive one of these," and I pull one of the dedication tee-shirts from a large bag.

More cheers, applause and cries of: *"Merci beaucoup, Monsieur!"* and *"C'est bon!"*

For recording, there are really no decent locations near the compound – everywhere is so exposed and with hardly any sizeable trees. We decide the best option is to record in the compound itself, although it has a few too many walls for my liking. However, there is one corner which has relatively little reverberation, so that's where we'll record. Sometimes, you just have to make a compromise in field-recording. So, after lunch and much rehearsing, we're ready to roll.

For some reason, one of my microphones is constantly buzzing and there's nothing I can do to stop it. I've tried changing the cable, plugging it into a different socket, everything! I have four microphones with me on this trip, but will now have to make do with only three! Far from ideal, but the results will still be okay.

Thankfully, it's a relatively simple set-up this time. Besides the usual soloist and choir, we have a couple of guys playing a pair of long 'conga' drums (or *gumi* in Moba). Although these are made of metal and painted bottle green, they still have a pretty good sound. Their two players are wearing tee-shirts reading 'Chicago Bulls' and '*100% Jeune*' respectively. Then there's an older chap who's playing a medium-sized barrel drum with a single snare across the top. This is played with a curved wooden stick. Finally, there's a man playing metal 'castanets' like the Ditammari used and a lady with the classic gourd shaker covered in cowrie shells. Interestingly, we never did manage to find a flute player (leprous, toothless or otherwise).

Recording goes well without too many hitches. However, one soloist – a great singer – is swaying from side to side with the music as he sings. Unfortunately, this makes the sound of his voice get louder and quieter as he moves towards and then away from the microphone. As was the case in Sassanou, I ask him to stand still for the sake of a good recording! There are also a few dodgy entries from the choir, but nothing I cannot edit out later.

We're all done by mid-afternoon. To conclude the session, there are the usual speeches of thanks and appreciation; they've done so well on this workshop! It would be great if this talent could continue to be used after I'm gone, so in my speech I encourage them to form a group that meets regularly to continue composing new songs. They seem quite taken by this idea, so I really hope it actually happens. There's so much talent here; they could easily create several dozen excellent new songs within the next year or two.

Goodbyes and thanks over and done with, I head back to my room to pack. As I open up my big black hold-all, a couple of dozen mosquitoes fly out into my face! They always tend to gravitate towards dark colours, doubtless for camouflage purposes. They also like humidity and, as it's been closed up since I got here, this bag will still have quite a bit of the southern dampness inside. However, Cotonou has more than enough of its own mozzies, without me taking more stowaways back with me over the border!

I notice the tyres on *The Beast* are looking a little deflated, so I drive down the road to the nearest petrol station to get them pumped up. Whilst this is happening, I check the oil too. Pulling the dipstick out of the engine, I instantly notice a complete lack of any oil – the stick is bone dry! What's happened here? I turn it around and notice there is oil on the other side of the stick, which is strange. This must be why I didn't notice the lack of oil before now. I wipe the stick clean and put it back in and then pull it out again: nothing! This could be serious.

"*Vous avez de l'huile, Monsieur?*"

"*Bien sûr !*"

I buy a litre of oil and pour it into the top of the engine, then try the dipstick again. Still nothing! A second litre and there is a tiny drop of oil on the very end of the stick. This is getting expensive! After the third litre, the oil is just about at the 'maximum' notch on the stick. Wow! I'm amazed – and grateful – that the whole engine didn't seize up on the way here; another few miles and I reckon it would have done so.

After a final delicious-and-international meal with Thelma and Kitty, their guard comes to the door, holding a curious-looking insect in his hand. It's a greyish-black beetle no more than an inch long, with yellow legs and a small yellow spot on each wing. The two ladies recognize it immediately.

"Ooh, coom an' look at this, Rob. It's very exciting!"

"What is it?" I ask. It doesn't look especially exciting to me!

"The Moba call it a '*jiimuu*.' When it gets angry, it shoots fire out of its bottom."

"Really? Wow! Can you make it do it now?"

The guard brings their dog over and puts it right next to the *jiimuu*. Nothing, but the dog looks absolutely terrified!

"So, what does '*jiimuu*' mean in Moba?" I ask.

"It literally means 'excreter of fire'."

Wow!  So this really is a 'flame poo-er' then!"

I've never seen – or heard of – such a creature before or since.  Fireflies are quite common in West Africa, their flashing yellowish bodies often lighting up the night sky, but a creature which can actually produce flames from its rear end (and without a match)?!  That's a new one on me.  Shame this *jiimuu* is not going to perform tonight, though…

Spot the odd one out!  Rob tries on traditional Ditammari dress.

# The final journey of *The Beast*

Freddie the French mechanic has had plenty of money out of me over the past three or four years; replacing so many parts that *The Beast* must be almost half new by now ("*Zut alors, Robert  C'est une voiture chère!*"). However, when it comes to bodywork, I take the Land Rover to Nicholas, a Beninese mechanic.  Now, I wouldn't want to have Nicholas doing anything too mechanical on the car; he's not a bad mechanic – he just doesn't have Freddie's experience, know-how or equipment.  However, for metal and welding, Nicholas is second to none (and also much cheaper than Freddie).

This time – and a few weeks after the Moba trip – the driver's door is not shutting well, and when you open it, it drops an inch or two.  I take *The Beast* to Nicholas and ask if he can weld the sill under the door to make it sturdier.  He says he'll take a look and see what he can do.  He calls me back a bit later:

"*Monsieur Robert*, we have a problem."

"*Qu'est-ce que c'est*, Nicholas?"

"Well, I cannot weld the door sill, as there is nothing to weld it to!  The entire floor is rusted through at the front on both sides."

Another big job, requiring him to remove both the driver and passenger seats in order to replace the entire floor in the front of the car.  This he does ably and at a very reasonable price.  However, (and this is where it all starts, setting off a chain of events I'd rather have avoided), he has also done a bit of mechanical work without asking:

"There was a problem with the clutch, so I replaced the *réservoir, Monsieur Robert.*"

I am, of course, grateful, although he has put in the cheapest, nastiest clutch fluid reservoir I've ever seen. Not to worry. As I leave for my next trip up north tomorrow, it'll have to do.

No question of delaying the trip: I have my first ever ethnomusicology intern, Chris Phoenix, with me – a young, 6'2"Texan; a great singer, pianist/organist and all-round nice bloke. He's come out here for six weeks to find out what it's all about and this trip has been planned with him in mind.

The journey north the next day goes well to begin with. The usual motorbikes, potholes, goats, chickens, trucks – and torrential rain so strong that *The Beast* lurches to the side through a couple of deeper puddles. About two hours north of Dassa, we stop at a toll booth. We're almost at our destination! After paying my 500 CFA to the attendant, I push down the clutch pedal ready to go into first gear. Nothing. The clutch is simply not working. Oh no! Nicholas' dodgy reservoir was even less reliable than I'd expected! So, it's still a good half an hour to our final destination and there's nothing much in between. What shall we do? Only one thing for it: I select third gear and turn the ignition key. *The Beast* lurches awkwardly forwards and, with plenty of revving, begins to move down the road! It takes over an hour to make the relatively short journey, as we can't go particularly fast in third. Chris the intern seems bemused and mildly stunned by the whole event, but takes it all in his stride.

When we finally get there, I make my first mistake. The house where we are staying has a long driveway and I drive all the way down it before parking. Oops! This means I'll have to do the 'start up in gear' thing in *reverse* to get out again. This I do the next day, before taking the Land Rover to a local mechanic in this small town.

The mechanic's workshop is just an open space next to a rubbish dump. For shade, he has erected a shelter made of sturdy branches covered with palm leaves.  He takes a look under the bonnet.

"Ah, your clutch reservoir is not good!  It's made by the *Igbos*.  Look how worn it is."

"But I only had it replaced last week!" I reply.

The 'Igbo' are an ethnic group in southern Nigeria, although many Beninese use it as a general term for the entire nation.  Pretty sure this reservoir wasn't *made* in Nigeria, but it may have been imported from there.

The next morning, I phone the mechanic to see how he's doing.  "We have called in another mechanic from the town and he knows what to do. Your car will be ready tomorrow morning."

Good news indeed – if only it were true!  Next day, the clutch is done and working.  However, when I call, he says:

"We started the engine, revved it up a bit, then it made a strange noise and stopped."

Oh dear!  I'm due to leave tomorrow. This could get 'interesting'!

By 4:30pm that day, the mechanic's progress report is as follows:

"Monsieur, we need to dismantle the engine further to see what the problem will is."

"And how soon will you know?"

"This evening, around seven o'clock."

"And have you any idea already what it could be?"

Now, Africans don't always like giving such information, and this chap is similarly cagey – a bit like many African doctors, who will tell you what to do or take to get well, but do not always explain what is actually wrong with you.  I push mechanic blokey for a response:

"Well…it could be the *segments*."

*Segments*?  What are those in English?  Ah, from his description, I figure this is the piston rings – a big job I'd sooner avoid!

"Well, let me know as soon as you have found something out."

At 6:30 that evening, my phone rings.

"Monsieur, it's your *arbre à cam*. It's broken."

*Arbre à cam…arbre à cam…*what could that be?  Ah – camshaft!  Eek! That's even more serious than the *segments*!  Looking on the bright side, at least I'm improving my French vocabulary of engine parts!

A replacement camshaft would be very hard to find up here and – if the part has to come from Cotonou or Lagos, then the car may as well go there first!  Also, my niece, Sarah Forest, is flying out from England for a visit tomorrow evening.  She's only seventeen, but enjoyed her visit with the whole family last year so much (in spite of the Dassa traumas), that she's saved up and is coming out again to help us pack. Yes, pack!  Another reason the car needs to get home is that we're leaving Benin for good in ten days' time and I've still got to sell *The Beast*.

My jazz guitar-playing Dutch friend, Pieter, has already expressed an interest:

"Is it a good car then, Rob?"

"Well, it's had a lot of parts replaced already."

"But it's okay, yes?"

"It's okay, but it's an old car now.  Things may still go wrong, Pieter."

Undeterred, Pieter is still keen to have the car, but he is – of course – unaware of my current predicament!  I turn to the mechanic.

"Is there anyone here who could tow me back to Cotonou?"

A crazy idea in many ways: that's almost six hours' drive at normal speed!

"I'll enquire for you, Monsieur."

Later I get a call.  It's pouring with rain and the line is bad, but I can just about make out the mechanic's voice:

"I've found someone to tow you home.  It's a minibus and he'll charge 80,000 CFA."

That's almost a hundred British pounds – a bit steep by local standards.

"Ask him if he'll take sixty."

"Okay."

It's bright and early next morning, and I'm hoping to leave today and be back home tonight.  My phone rings.

"Good news, Monsieur.  The man with the minibus says he'll take 160,000."

"What?!?  But you said 80 yesterday!"

"No, I said 180."

The rain and poor line must've meant I misheard him.

"That's way too much!"

I arrange to go and see the chappie, to discuss costs.  It's a decent enough looking minibus – just a few years old, painted white with a somewhat incongruous pink rose emblazoned across one side.  Besides a cracked windscreen and no seatbelts, it seems in good shape!

"So, what's your final price?" I ask him.

"150,000.  Take it or leave it."

That's almost two hundred pounds — an exorbitant amount, so I leave it and return to my host's house for breakfast.  I discuss the problem there and also text Lois for her advice. We all agree that, whilst the price is ludicrously high, time is of the essence and it's much better to have the car home in Cotonou than to leave it here and hope to come back and collect it later. And that would be presuming the mechanic here can get the part and has the know-how to put the engine back together properly!  So I agree to have the minibus tow me home and arrange to meet them at the garage at 9:30am the next day.  Meanwhile, I call Freddie, the French mechanic, so he can be ready to work on *The Beast* when I get back to Cotonou.

"*Allô?*" he bellows down the telephone in his customary manner.

"*Bonjour Freddie, c'est Robert. Je suis près de Djougou et mon* arbre à cam *est cassé.*"

"*Zut, Robert!  Zut! Zut! Zut alors!*"  I give him the serial numbers for the engine and what have you, so that he can be ready to start the work as soon as possible.

The minibus and Land Rover are already lined up and connected by a tow bar when I get to the mechanic's place. When I say 'tow bar,' it's actually a long tree branch, fixed to each vehicle with some blue cord!  Should do the trick though, and much safer than a tow rope. Whilst they're finishing off the linkage, I pay the mechanic's bill, fortunately a mere 7,000 CFA or eight British pounds, which will offset the towing fee a tad!

We're ready to roll. Thankfully, the minibus driver has two accomplices: one will join him in the minibus, and the other will sit in *The Beast* to do the steering and what have you. This means I can sit in the back of the minibus and have a bit of a rest.  Between all this to-ing and fro-ing, I have actually been running another songwriting workshop with field recording at the end!

As we pull away, I glance up at the mechanic's workshop and notice something I find both shocking and amusing: one side of his shelter has been dismantled, and one of the longer branches has been removed!  It takes me only a split second to realize what has happened here – the branch which is towing *The Beast* has come from the roof of his garage!  Well, I'm sure he'll get it back in a day or two…

The journey home is not without its points of interest.  Firstly, the driver is making phone calls and looking in a book as we travel.  Thankfully this stops when we get to a faster section.  He's managing around 50 miles per hour, the Land Rover bouncing merrily along behind us.  Meanwhile, every door and window frame of the minibus is rattling violently on the bumpy road.  Also, the ignition key keeps falling out onto the floor, especially on the big bumps!  Most disconcerting.

After about three hours, the minibus itself breaks down and so both vehicles grind to a halt by the roadside.  The two drivers quickly tilt their front seats forward to reveal the engine.  They seem to know what's wrong already and quickly detach a fuel pipe and the fuel filter.

What happens next astonishes me: they take it in turns to suck petrol into their mouths through the fuel pipe and then blow it out through the fuel filter in order to unblock it! Whilst doing so, they communicate with each other with sounds like "Hmph hmph" and "Mmm mmm."  I guess they know what they're saying!  One of the two crawls underneath the vehicle and begins sucking petrol out from that end too.  I can't imagine how bad it must taste, but I somehow get the feeling it's not the first time they've done this.  In fact, their vehicle breaks down once more two hours further along the road, and they repeat the same process all over again.  It can't be good for their health, now can it?  I'm just grateful neither of them smokes…

Back in Cotonou just before dark, and I'm welcomed by Freddie.

"*Bienvenu, Robert. Tu veux une bière ?  Ah, ce sacré véhicule-là!*"

In spite of the cost, I'm grateful to be home and dry – and in one piece after another journey not without risks.  That said, I'm thankful for this journey and all the others related in this book.  None of my trips have ever gone exactly to plan; every one of them has been an adventure in a variety of ways. Yet, in spite of the setbacks, the dangers, the madmen and the heat, I thank God for His protection and for the privilege of being able to touch so many people's lives with music.  And not just any music, but music which will bring them life everlasting.

Thank  you God!

Visiting a real Tata Somba house in Ditammari country.

# Publications Referred to in this Book

1 Biddlecombe, Peter (1993), *French Lessons in Africa,* Little, Brown and Company, London, UK.

2 *Lonely Planet Guide to West Africa* (2006). Lonely Planet Publications Pty Ltd.

3 Olson, H.S. (1971). African Music in Christian Worship. *African Initiatives in Religion.* Nairobi, Kenya: East African Publishing House.

4 Krabill, J.R. (2008). Chapter 4: Encounters: What Happens to Music when People Meet. *Music in the life of the African Church.* Waco, TX: Baylor University Press.

5 Jans P. (1956). Essai de Musique Religieuse pour Indigènes dans le Vicariat Apostolique de Coquilhatville. *'Aequatoria', No. 1, 1956.*

6 *Lonely Planet Guide to West Africa* (2006). Lonely Planet Publications Pty Ltd.

7 Biddlecombe, Peter (1993), *French Lessons in Africa,* Little, Brown and Company, London, UK.

8 Ukpong Justin (1994). Christology and inculturation: a New Testament Perspective, *Paths of African Theology* (Ed: Rosino Gibellini). Orbis Books, NY.

9 *Lonely Planet Guide to West Africa* (2006). Lonely Planet Publications Pty Ltd.

10 National Geographic Magazine (date unknown – approx. 2007).

It's always good to let the musicians listen back to their recordings,
and to see the joy on their faces as they do so.

# Some Places Where You Can Study Ethnomusicology

**Ethnomusicology in Missions (Ethnodoxology)**

All Nations Christian College, Hertfordshire, UK: http://www.allnations.ac.uk/index.php?pageid=112§ion=Studying

European Training Programme, Wycliffe UK, Buckinghamshire, UK: http://eurotp.org/uk/session.php?sessionid=286

Fuller Theological Seminary, California, USA: http://www.fuller.edu/academics/school-of-intercultural-studies/certificate-programs/certificate-in-global-christian-worship.aspx

The Graduate Institute of Applied Linguistics (GIAL), Dallas, Texas, USA: http://www.gial.edu/academics/world-arts

Liberty University, Virginia, USA: http://www.liberty.edu/academics/arts-sciences/worship/index.cfm?PID=17234

Moody Bible Institute, Chicago, USA: http://www.moody.edu/edu_MainPage.aspx?id=1482

Payap University, Thailand:
http://ic.payap.ac.th/graduate/linguistics/certificate-ethnoarts.php

YWAM School of Missions, Panama:
http://www.ywampanama.org/schools/arts/


## Ethnomusicology (secular)

Brown University, Rhode Island, USA: http://www.brown.edu/Departments/Music/undergraduate/programs.html

University of California, Berkeley, USA: http://music.berkeley.edu/academics/graduate/ethnomusicology/

Cardiff University, Wales:
http://courses.cardiff.ac.uk/postgraduate/1002.html

University of Florida, USA:
http://www.arts.ufl.edu/music/musicology/degree_g.html

Indiana University, Bloomington, USA:
http://www.indiana.edu/~folklore/ethno.shtml

University of Manchester, England: http://www.arts.manchester.ac.uk/subjectareas/music/worldmusic/

Queens University, Belfast, N.Ireland: http://www.qub.ac.uk/schools/SchoolofHistoryandAnthropology/ProspectiveStudents/UndergraduateStudies/Ethnomusicology/

University of Sheffield, England: http://www.shef.ac.uk/music/research/areas/ethnomusicology/courses

SOAS (School of African and Oriental Studies), London: http://www.soas.ac.uk/music/programmes/

UCLA, Los Angeles, USA: http://www.ethnomusic.ucla.edu/index.php?option=com_content&view=article&id=883&Itemid=59

UNISA (University of South Africa): http://www.unisa.ac.za/Default.asp?Cmd=ViewContent&ContentID=10818

Field recording under a mango tree – it's the best place!

Bogo people dancing to their first ever indigenous church songs.